Student Edition

Skills for
RHETORIC

ENCOURAGING THOUGHTFUL CHRISTIANS TO BE WORLD CHANGERS

By James P. Stobaugh

10-Digit ISBN: 0805458980
13-Digit ISBN: 9780805458985

Published by Broadman & Holman Publishers
Nashville, Tennessee

DEWEY: 808
SUBHD: LITERATURE

Unless otherwise noted, scripture text is from The Holy Bible, *Holman Christian Standard Bible* ®, Copyright © 1999, 2000, 2001, 2002, 2003 by Holman Bible Publishers. Other "Credits, Permissions, and Sources" are listed at the back of the book.

Cover and interior design by Paul T. Gant, Art & Design — Nashville, TN

1 2 3 4 5   09 08 07 06 05

This Book is gratefully dedicated to
Karen
and
our four children:
Rachel, Jessica, Timothy, and Peter.

He has given us a ministry of reconciliation . . .
2 Corinthians 5:18

Students, to you 'tis given to scan the heights
Above, to traverse the ethereal space,
And mark the systems of revolving worlds.
Still more, ye sons of science ye receive
The blissful news by messengers from heav'n,
How Jesus blood for your redemption flows . . .

—Phillis Wheatley

ACKNOWLEDGMENTS

From the Broadman and Holman Home Education Division, I wish to thank Sheila Moss, whose editorial assistance and encouragement have been greatly appreciated; Matt Stewart, whose vision and perseverance have made this project possible; and Paul Gant and Mark Grover for their work with graphics and the DVD. Likewise, I thank my four children and my distance learning students who so graciously allowed me to use their essays. Finally, and most of all, I want to thank my best friend and lifelong editor, my wife, Karen. "Come, let us glorify the Lord and praise His name forever . . . ." (Psalm 34:3)

Contents

Preface

INTRODUCTION

Skills for Rhetoric **is a dialectic** or early rhetoric level, middle school or early high school, basic course. It is for the writer who must be equipped with writing skills requisite for high school and college. *Skills for Rhetoric* has three components: an academic and expository writing component, a public speaking component, and a research paper preparation component. In short, *Skills for Rhetoric* prepares you to participate in apologetics. Apologetics is a systematic argumentative discourse in defense of Christianity. In other words, apologetics is the tool you will need to share Christ to an unsaved world.

STUDENT ROLES AND RESPONSIBILITIES:

Focus on the box in the right top corner of the first page of every lesson. It will tell you what goal will be accomplished in this lesson. It will also "look ahead" to next week's lesson.

Discuss the background material with your parent/evaluator. Every lesson highlights a particular academic/expository essay. For example, in Lesson 1, you learn now to write a descriptive essay. Your Final Project (explained below) is due in Lesson 22. Then, in Lesson 23, you will be taken step-by-step through the process of writing a research paper. For example, in Lesson 23, you will choose and narrow your topic. In Lesson 24, you will write your thesis statement.

> You will learn how to write a descriptive essay. Looking Ahead: Eyewitness Account.

Review the Writing Style section. This would be a good time for you to review and to correct manifested grammar deficits. If you are still having difficulty with grammar specifics, your parent/evaluator may give you a worksheet to complete. Grammar review will be in addition to your regular assignments.

Writing Style

Writing style concerns quality and substance, not content. It is, simply, the way students write. Traits of an effective style include six components: Focus, Concreteness, Vitality, Originality, Grace, and Commitment.

Who is the audience? What is the task? How can you bring your reader to a point of enlightenment? Are you trying to entertain? To inform? Both? Answers to these questions, and other stylistic questions, will either focus your paper and move your reader to a desired conclusion or they will move your reader into a place of confusion. Is the focus clearly stated? To what audience is this essay written? Does it focus the reader or confuse the reader? Are your ideas relevant and fully developed? Finally, is your paper logically organized?

Discuss the type of essay highlighted for the lesson with your parent/evaluator. The highlighted essay type is defined in simple language and illustrated by a readable example. If you need more information, access other composition handbooks.

Discuss the public speaking component for the lesson with your parent/evaluator. Then, compose the assigned speech and present it in front of a live audience. Your parent/evaluator can access an Oratory Evaluation template in the Appendices.

Complete all assigned activities, including one essay or other written project. Complete other activities your parent/evaluator may assign.

Complete one warm-up essay every day. The warm-up essay should be one page or less; it should not take more than one-half hour to write. The warm-ups do not need to be edited or rewritten. Every day you should see improvement in your writing as you tend to specific skills.

WARM-UP ESSAYS:

	DAY 1	DAY 2	DAY 3	DAY 4	DAY 5
Descriptive	Describe a moment that changed your life.	Describe your best friend.	Describe the causes of World War I to a four-year old.	Describe the emotion jealousy.	Describe the sunset.

Complete Other Activities:

Complete literary reviews. You will not be assigned particular works to read during this course; however, as time allows, read books from the enclosed list (See Appendix). You should read most of the books on the enclosed supplemental book list before you graduate from high school. After reading a literary work, for this course or for any other reason, you should complete a literary review (See Appendix). Keep these book checkups as a record of your high school reading. The supplemental book list is not meant to be exhaustive but is intended as a guide to good reading. A suggestion is to read 35-50 pages per night (or 100-250 pages per week), which includes reading the books for this course.

Part of the reason for reading so many challenging literary works is for you to increase your functional vocabulary. Your best means of increasing vocabulary is through reading a vast amount of classical, well-written literary works. If you were given 15 new words to learn every week, studies show that most of you would forget those words within 24 hours. While reading these works, you should harvest as many unknown words as you can. *You should use five new words in each essay you write.*

Create 3x5 vocabulary cards.

When you meet a strange word for the first time,
    do your best to figure out the word in context,
    check your guess by looking in the dictionary,
    write a sentence with the word in it.
Use the illustration above to formulate your vocabulary cards of new words.

Then most conspicuous, when great things of small,/Useful of hurtful, rosperous of *adverse*/ We can create . . .

Front

Harmful, Evil Adj., Adversity is Noun The <u>adverse</u> effects of smok- ing are great.

Back

Write in a prayer journal. If you don't have a prayer journal, try using the prayer journal template in the appendix. Make 25-50 copies of this page and put it in a notebook. As often as you can—hopefully daily—file out one of these sheets on a biblical passage. Journal writing is one the best forms of reflection. This prayer journal should be a narrative of your spiritual journey. While these entries should be mechanically correct, the primary purpose is to pique creativity and spiritual formation. In *Skills for Rhetoric*, you are invited to journal through 1 & 2 Kings.

Begin the final project Lessons 1-22. See appendix for more specific instructions.

Your final project should include corrected essays, literary reviews, writing journal, vocabulary cards, pictures from field trips, and other pertinent material.

Begin and complete the research paper Lessons 23-34. You will be prompted as you proceed to complete all requisite components of the research paper.

SUGGESTED WEEKLY IMPLEMENTATION SCHEDULE

If you follow this schedule, you will get all your work done in a timely way.

SUGGESTED
Weekly *Implementation*

DAY 1	DAY 2	DAY 3	DAY 4	DAY 5
Write a Warm-up Essay.	Write a Warm-up Essay.	Write a Warm-up Essay.	Write a Warm-up Essay.	Write a Warm-up Essay.
Read 35-50 pages/day.	Read 35-50 pages/day.	Read 35-50 pages/day.	Read 35-50 pages/day.	Read 35-50 pages/day.
Find five new vocabulary words.	Find five new vocabulary words.	Find five new vocabulary words.	Find five new vocabulary words.	Find five new vocabulary words.
Reflect on the speech assignment for the week.	Compose a first draft of your speech.	Revise your speech and submit to your evaluator/guardian/parent.	Prepare to present your speech tomorrow.	Present your speech to a live audience.
Write your assigned essay or complete your assigned tasks.	Write your assigned essay or complete your assigned tasks.	Write your assigned essay or complete your assigned tasks.	Finish your assigned essay or complete your assigned tasks.	Submit your assignments to your evaluator/guardian/parent.
Make a journal entry.	Make a journal entry.	Make a journal entry.	Make a journal entry.	Submit a copy of your paper to a peer for evaluation.
				Take Lesson Test
				Make a journal entry.

Scope and Sequence
World Literature

LESSON	WRITING SKILL	STYLE (WRITING AND SPEAKING)	PUBLIC SPEAKING SKILL	JOURNAL PASSAGE
1	Overview	Components of Writing and Planning	Overview (A) Types and Purposes of Speeches Outline	1 Kings 1:1-53 The Adonijah Factor
2	Overview	Paragraph (A) Topic Sentence/Thesis	Overview (B) Selecting your Topic Researching your Topic Knowing your Audience	1 Kings 1:41-53 The Solomon Factor
3	Eyewitness Account	Paragraph (B) Introduction	Introduction Converting the Eye-Witness Account to a Speech	1 Kings 3 Solomon Asks for Wisdom
4	Firsthand Experience	Paragraph (C) Main Body	Main Body Converting the Firsthand Experience to a Speech	1 Kings Overview
5	Descriptive Essay	Paragraph (D) Conclusion	Conclusion Converting the Descriptive Essay to a Speech	1 Kings 8: 22-53 1 Kings 10: 1-14
6	Persuasive vs. Coercive Essay	Paragraph (E) Unity and Coherence	Delivery (A) and Converting the Persuasive Essay to a Speech	Queen of Sheba
7	Persuasive Advertisement Essay	Coherence Paragraph (F) Transitional Devices	Delivery (B) and Converting the Persuasive Advertisement Essay to a Speech	1 Kings 11 Foreign Wives
8	Summary Report	Sentences (A) Overview	Overcoming Fear Converting Summary Essay to a Speech	1 Kings 11: 14-24 Solomon's Enemies

9	Précis	Sentences (B) Emphasis	Presentation Aids (A) Converting a Précis Essay to a Speech	1 Kings Themes
10	Character Profile	Sentences (C) Expanding Sentences	Presentation Aids (B) Converting a Character Profile to a Speech	1 Kings 1-17 Life's Lessons
11	General Analysis Essay	Sentences (D) Writing Complete Sentences	Converting the General Analysis Essay to a Speech	1 Kings 16 Evil King Ahab
12	General Synthesis Essay	Sentences (E) Writing Clear Sentences	Converting a General Synthesis Essay into a Speech	1 Kings 18:9 Obadiah
13	Literary Analysis	Sentences (F) Sentence Variety	Converting a Literary Analysis into Speech	1 Kings 18 Elijah
14	Evaluation	Words (A) Using the Dictionary vs. Thesaurus	Converting the Evaluation Essay to a Speech	1 Kings 16-19 The Evil Jezebel
15	Cause/Effect	Words (B) Connotation vs. Denotation	Converting the Cause/Effect Essay into a Speech	1 Kings 19 Down and Out
16	Comparison/Contrast	Words (C) Standard and Sub-standard English	Converting the Comparison/Contrast Essay into a Speech	1Kings 19:10-18 In the Cleft of the Rock
17	Problem/Solution	Words (D) Idioms	Converting the Problem/Solution Essay into a Speech	1 Kings 19:19-21 Call of Elisha
18	Definition	Words (E) Adjectives and Adverbs in Comparative and Superlative Cases	Converting the Definition Essay into a Speech	1 Kings 20 Using Donkeys and Apostates
19	Explanatory	Words (F) Precise Language	Converting the Explanatory Essay into a Speech	1 Kings 20: 35-41
20	Fact, Inference, and Opinion	Usage (A) Pronoun and Subject/Verb Agreement	Converting the Fact, Inference, and Opinion Essay into a Speech	1 Kings 21
21	Historical Profile	Usage (B) Pronoun Usage	Converting the Historical Profile into a Speech	1 Kings Overview
22	Final Project Due	Final Project Due	Final Project Due	Final Project Due

23	Research Paper: Designing a working plan	Usage (C) *Fewer/Less, Good/Well, and Double Negatives*	Effective Listening	1 Kings 21:29
24	Research Paper: Thesis Statement	Usage (D) *Who/Whom*	Oratory	1 Kings 22
25	Research Paper: Preliminary Bibliography and Works Cited Page	Usage (E) *Further/Farther; Than/As.*	Dramatic Readings	1 Kings 22
26	Research Paper: Taking Notes (A)	Usage (F) *There, And/Nor/Or, There/Their*	Speech: Poetry Reading	1 Kings 22
27	Research Paper: Taking Notes and Preliminary Outline	Usage (G) Use of Comparatives and Superlatives	Debate	1 Kings 22
28	Research Paper: Designing a Working Plan	Quotation Marks	Debate	2 Kings 1 Ahaziah's bad choices
29	Research Paper: Introduction	Introductory Words and Phrases	The Spoken Introduction	2 Kings 2 Chariots of Fire
30	Research Paper: Introduction (B)	Using the Right Word: Being Specific	Impromptu Speech	2 Kings 2: 23 Mocking God's authority
31	Research Paper: Body	Avoid Sexist Language	Didactic Speech	2 Kings 3 The Moabite Revolt
32	Research Paper: Body	Avoid Pretentious Language, Evasive language, and Euphemisms; Footnotes and Endnotes	Summary	2 Kings 4 The Shunammite's Son
33	Writing the Research Paper: Conclusion	Mixed Metaphors	Enunciation (A)	2 King 5 Namaan Healed of Leprosy
34	Research Paper: Rewriting and Submission	Summary	Enunciation (B) Summary	2 Kings 6

Audio presentations of most of the readings in the book may be obtained from Blackstoneaudio.com

My prayer for you is

"For this reason I bow my knees before the Father from whom every family in heaven and on earth is named. I pray that He may grant you, according to the riches of His glory, to be strengthened with power through His Spirit in the inner man, and that the Messiah may dwell in your hearts through faith. I pray that you, being rooted and firmly established in love, may be able to comprehend with all the saints what is the length and width, height and depth of God's love, and to know the Messiah's love that surpasses knowledge, so you may be filled with all the fullness of God. Now to Him who is able to do above and beyond all that we ask or think—according to the power that works in you—to Him be glory in the church and in Christ Jesus to all generations, forever and ever. Amen."

(Ephs. 3:14-21)

James Stobaugh

From the Editor

Developing appropriate curricula for a specific audience is a major and intricate endeavor. Doing so for the homeschool and Christian communities is perhaps even more difficult: homeschool approaches, methodology, and content are as diverse as traditional educational trends have ever dared to be. Homeschooling is complex—from unschooling to the Classical approach, there are myriads of opinions of what to teach, when to teach it, and how to teach it to whom at what age and at what level of development. Perhaps you struggle with choices between a *whole-book* approach to literature study or a more traditional and inclusive canon. Perhaps you are still wading through myriads of questions associated with homeschooling teenagers. However, perhaps your decision is final and you merely need a solid literature-and-writing-based English curriculum. Keep reading.

In one-year literature/writing-based courses, including all the quality literature that has ever been published is impossible—there is simply too much good literature and not enough space to include it; neither is there time enough to read it all. Regrettably, many selections of quality literature have not been included in this course—not because they are unworthy, but because they all cannot fit into the designated framework. The author and I have done our best to include whole-book or whole-work selections from the major genres of literature (prose, poetry, and drama). In the *Literary Analysis, Rhetoric,* and *American, British,* and *World Literature* courses in this series, literary selections incorporate many ethnicities from both male and female writers. We believe our selections inform the purpose of the curricula: *Encouraging Thoughtful Christians to be World Changers.*

According to a well-known author, homeschool conference speaker, and long-time homeschooling mom, two of the greatest needs in the homeschool community reside in curricula for high school and for special needs. These English curricula consider those needs; they were conceived in prayer, deliberated through educational experience, and nurtured with inspiration. We are providing unique five-year curricula for required English studies for the multifarious Christian community. Canonical and Classical literature is emphasized; students are meticulously guided through carefully honed steps of *critical thinking, biblical challenge for spiritual growth,* and even additional *enrichment* motivators. A major key to the successful completion of these courses falls in the statements, <u>"Teachers and students will decide on required essays for this lesson, choosing two or three essays. All other essays may be outlined, discussed, or omitted."</u> These statements, repeated in every lesson, allow tremendous flexibility for various levels of student maturity and interests. Since each lesson may offer 10-15 essays, choosing essays each week is vital.

In any literature course offered to Christian audiences there will be differences in opinions regarding acceptable and appropriate content, authors, poets, and playwrights. Some educators may object to specific works or specific authors, poets, or playwrights included in these curricula *even though we have been very conscientious with selections.* For that reason we highly encourage educators and students to confab—choose units according to students' maturity, ability, age, sensitivity, interests, educational intentions, and according to family goals. Educators decide how much they want to shelter their students or to sanction certain works or authors, poets, and playwrights.

On a broader note, our goal in this series is to provide parent educators and Christian schools with educationally sound, rigorous literature courses that equip students

1. to think critically about their world and their participation in it;
2. to write their thoughts, primarily through essays;
3. to articulate their thoughts through small group discussions with peers, families, broader communities, and through occasional formal speeches;
4. to enhance vocabulary through reading and studying quality literature;
5. to converse about the major worldviews of authors of literature, past and present;
6. to develop and refine their own worldviews through participating in biblical application and Christian principles in weekly studies.

Additionally, we provide educators with an instructional CD in the back of each teacher edition. Narrated by the author, the CD is designed to provide extra commentary on the unit studies.

Ideally, students will complete these entire curricula; however, parent educators and teachers are free to choose literary selections that best fit their goals with students. Regardless of the choices, I pray that students come away from studying *Skills for Literary Analysis, Skills for Rhetoric, American Literature, British Literature,* and *World Literature* not only highly educated but also equipped to participate in and contribute to their earthly home while preparing for their heavenly home.

Enjoy!
Sheila Moss

Introduction

I am profoundly enthusiastic about the future. Not only do I trust in our Mighty God, I am greatly encouraged by what I see in this generation. God is doing great things in the midst of students.

There is much need in our physical world. In his seminal work *The Dust of Death* (Downers Grove, Illinois: Intervarsity Press, 1973), social critic Os Guinness prophetically argues that "western culture is marked . . . by a distinct slowing of momentum . . . a decline in purposefulness. . . . Guinness implies that ideals and traditions that have been central to American civilization are losing their compelling cultural authority. In short, there is no corpus of universally accepted morality that Americans follow. As Dallas Willard in *The Divine Conspiracy* (San Francisco: HarperCollins Publishers, 1997) states, ". . . there is no recognized moral knowledge upon which projects of fostering moral development could be based."

In his poem "The Second Coming" William Butler Yeats writes

The best lack all conviction, while the worst
Are full of passionate intensity
Turning and turning in the widening gyre;
The falcon cannot hear the falconer.

In the beginning of the twenty-first century, America is spinning out of control. She is stretching her wings adventurously but is drifting farther away from her God. America is in trouble. How do we know?

You are America's first generation to grow up when wholesale murder is legal; the first generation to access 130 channels and at the same time to access almost nothing of value. In 1993 in their book *The Day America Told the Truth* (NY: Simon & Schuster Publishers, Inc.), James Patterson and Peter Kim warned that 87% of Americans do not believe that the Ten Commandments should be obeyed and 91% of them tell at least one lie a day. Unfortunately, I doubt things are any better today than they were over 10 years ago. The challenge, the bad news, is that this is a time when outrage is dead. Whatever needs to be done, you and your friends are probably going to have to do it.

I think the good news is that we are turning a corner. I believe that in the near future Americans will be looking to places of stability and strength for direction. Besides, by default, those people whose lives are in reasonably good shape, who have some reason to live beyond the next paycheck, will have an almost inexorable appeal. Those who walk in the Light will draw others into the very-same Light. My prayer is that these curricula will help you walk in the Light in a modest way.

I believe that God is raising a mighty generation at the very time that many twenty-first century Americans are searching for truth—at the very time they are hungry for things of the Lord. You will be the culture-creators of the next century. You are a special generation, a special people.

Young people, I strongly believe that you are the generation God has called *for such a time as this* to bring a Spirit-inspired revival. God is stirring the water again at the beginning of this century. He is offering a new beginning for a new nation. I believe you are the personification of that new beginning.

You are part of one of the most critical generations in the history of Western culture. Indeed, only Augustine's generation comes close in importance to your generation. In both cases—today and during the life of Augustine, Bishop of Hippo—civilizations were in decline. Young Augustine lived through the decline of the Roman world; you are living through the decline of American cultural superiority. Even though the barbarians conquered Rome, the Christians conquered the barbarians.

Similar to Anne Bradstreet and other young Puritans who settled in 1630 Boston, you will need to replace this old, reprobate culture with a new God-centered, God-breathed society, or our nation may not survive another century.

While I was a graduate student at Harvard University in the mid-1970s, I attended a chapel service where the presenter self-righteously proclaimed that we Harvard students were the next generation of culture creators. Indeed. Perhaps he was right—look at the moral mess my generation created!

Evangelical scholars Nathan Hatch and George Marsden argue, and I think persuasively, that you young people will be the next generation of elites: important politicians, inspired playwrights, and presidents of Fortune 500 companies.

I profoundly believe and fervently hope that you young people will also be the new elite of culture creators. I define "elitism" as the ability and propensity of an individual or a group to assume leadership and culture-creation in a given society. In his essay "Blessed Are the History-Makers," theologian Walter Bruggemann reminds us that culture is created and history is made by those who are radically committed to obeying God at all costs.

Will you be counted among those who are radically committed—being smart, but above all, loving, worshipping, and being obedient to the Word of God? In your generation and for the first time in 300 years of American cultural history, the marriage of smart minds and born-again hearts is becoming visible. This combination is potent indeed and has revolutionary implications for twenty-first century cultural America. Now, as in the Puritan era, a spirit-filled elite with all its ramifications is exciting to behold.

This book is dedicated to the ambitious goal of preparing you to be a twenty-first century world changer for the Christ whom John Milton in *Paradise Lost* called "the countenance too severe to be beheld." (VI, 825)

James Stobaugh

LESSON 1

OVERVIEW (A)

The heart of *Skills for Rhetoric* is the notion of rhetoric, which is the ability to communicate effectively through the written and spoken word. Written and spoken are the crucial concepts of understanding rhetoric. Rhetoric is a discipline demanding that the writer dutifully follow rules of grammar, logic, and communication to explain, describe, and clarify.

Quality rhetoric is important and necessary. Greek philosophers proffered that a democracy demands a responsible, well-considered rhetoric. It is absolutely necessary that we participate in legitimate conversation about important issues. Rhetoric will help us do that.

Rhetoric demands that we reclaim the use of metaphor. A metaphor is a word picture. It describes one idea, thought, or object with another dissimilar idea, thought, or object. It effective use demands discipline and control. A four-year-old cannot understand predestination, for instance, unless the communicator pulls out experiences and images that are familiar to the four-year-old. To describe predestination from the perspective of a seminary professor may be accurate, but would not be rhetoric to the four-year-old. We can take a picture of a sunset and send it to millions of people via e-mail, but that is not rhetoric either. Rhetoric is the attempt to communicate a sunset by the use of the spoken or written word. Thus, metaphor is at the heart of rhetoric, and rhetoric is at the heart of classical education.

Rhetoric is also at the heart of apologetics, a systematic argumentative discourse in defense of Christianity. It is my prayer that these courses will ultimately prepare your students to think apologetically.

To ignore rhetoric is to invite ourselves on a dangerous search for truth. Our mindless search for relevance and literalness has gotten us pretty lost in the cosmos. When something we seek is easily obtained by

> It is my prayer that this course will prepare you to think apologetically.

Writing Skill: Overview (A)

Style (Writing and Speaking): Overview—Components of Writing and Planning

Public Speaking Skill: Overview (A): Types and Purposes of Speeches and The Outline

Looking Ahead: (Writing) Determining the purpose and planning the Composition; (Speaking) Knowing your Audience, and Researching Your Topic

computer chip or digital photograph, then we lazily refuse to engage ourselves in the discipline of metaphor. For example, love is not easily photographed. Only the metaphor does it justice. Question: if we lose the written metaphor, will we also lose love? How can we understand 1 Corinthians 13 without first understanding metaphor? Metaphor, or comparison between two ostensibly dissimilar phenomena, is absolutely critical to understanding abstract theological concepts, and, for that matter, it is critical to creative problem solving.

The problems of this age demand a kind of thinking that is promoted and encouraged by rhetoric. The problems of this age will "literally" remain unsolved. However, rhetoric, through the power of metaphor, will invite this generation to look for more creative solutions. Immorality, for instance, will not be removed unless we look to the written Word, that is, the Bible, for answers. Nothing in our experience offers a solution. We will not understand the Bible unless we can employ metaphorical thinking. How else will we apply the Savior's ethical teachings spoken 2000 years ago? Metaphor, along with other mysteries, has been victim of twentieth century pretension, pomposity, and obsequious thinking.

Loss of metaphor is only the beginning of the problem. Gertrude Himmelfarb, *On Looking into the Abyss*, laments that great literary works are no longer read—and if they are, there are no rules for interpreting them. In philosophy, indeed in all communication, truth and reality are considered relative. Without rules the rhetorician is invited to come to any kind of conclusion and is on pretty shaky ground. Gordon Conwell's Seminary professor David Wells in *God in the Wastelands* argues that evangelical Christians who believe in a personal relationship with God, as well as non-Christians, have both drunk from the trough of modernity. We have both embraced a sort of existential faith instead of a confessional faith. If it feels good do it and believe it. Unless evangelicals participate in serious apologetics, God will be "weightless."

The rise of relativism has had disastrous results. British historian Philip Johnson laments "the great vacuum" that has been filled with totalitarian regimes and facile thinking. Rhetoric ferrets out truth. If there is no truth, can there be any sense of authority? And can a society survive if there is no authority? Without a legitimate, honest, well-considered rhetoric, will history be reduced to the pleasure principle? Literary Criticism, at least in the area of the written classics, forces us to dance with reality.

In some ways American Evangelical Christianity's loss of rhetorical skills—and I think rhetoric is akin to apologetics—has presaged disaster in many arenas. Without rhetoric we Christians have no tools to engage modern culture. In some ways we have lost mainline denominations to neo-orthodoxy, and we have lost universities to liberals. Where is a modern Jonathan Edwards? A modern C. S. Lewis? Good thinking and good talking may redeem the Church from both the overzealous and the skeptic. Rhetorical skills may help us regain the intellectual and spiritual high ground we so grievously surrendered without a fight (Alister McGrath, *Evangelicalism and the Future of Christianity*). George Marsden in *The Soul of the American University* and Leslie Newbigen in *Foolishness to the Greeks* both conclude that we Christians have conceded much of American culture to modernism by our inability to merge thought and communication in a clear thought and inspiration. We fail to persuade modernist culture. Without the main tool to do battle—rhetoric—evangelicals allow orthodoxy to be sacrificed on the altar of relativism.

In conclusion, the *Encouraging Thoughtful Christians to be World Changers* series is more than an English course: it is an attempt to equip you to participate in apologetics.

STYLE (WRITING AND SPEAKING): OVERVIEW

Writing style concerns quality and substance, not content. Simple stated, style is the way you write. An effec-

---

Three elements of style that you will need to address:
• *focus*: awareness of an audience/task; a clear purpose.
• *content*: ideas are specific, relevant to focus and fully developed.
• *organization*: there is a logical order of ideas.

---

tive style includes six components: Focus, Concreteness, Vitality, Originality, Grace, and Commitment.

Who is the audience? What is the task? How can you bring your reader to a point of enlightenment? Are you trying to entertain? To inform? Both? Answers to these and other stylistic questions will focus your paper and move your reader to a desired conclusion or it will move your reader into a place of confusion. Is the focus clearly stated? To what audience is this essay written? Does it focus the reader or confuse the reader? Are your ideas totally relevant and fully developed? Finally, is your paper logically organized?

The British author, Alexander Pope, in his "Essay on Criticism," wrote:

'Tis hard to say, if greater Want of Skill
Appear in Writing or in Judging ill,
But, of the two, less dang'rous is th' Offence,
To tire our Patience, than mis-lead our Sense:
Some few in that, but Numbers err in this,
Ten Censure wrong for one who Writes amiss;
A Fool might once himself alone expose,
Now One in Verse makes many more in Prose.
(Project Gutenberg:
    http://wsmf.org/texts/emonks/Project GuterbuergDVD/access/gtnletPQ.htm)

Writing is indeed a task that requires skill. "A fool might once himself alone expose,/Now One in Verse makes many more in prose." (Project Gutenberg: http://wsmf.org/texts/emonks/Project GuterbuergDVD /access/gtnletPQ.htm)

The beginning of writing invites readers into action while carefully introducing each person and event. Writers make no presumptions at all—they assume that the reader needs the writer to explain everything.

WRITING TIPS

How do students produce concise, well-written essays?

Every essay includes a *prewriting phase, an outlining phase,* a *writing phase,* a *revision phase,* and for the purposes of this course, *a publishing phase.*

GENERAL STATEMENTS

___ Essays should be written in the context of the other social sciences. This means that essays should be written on all topics: science topics, history topics, social science topics, etc.

___ Some essays should be rewritten, depending on the assignment and the purpose of the writing; definitely, those essays which are to be presented to various readers or a public audience should be rewritten for their best presentation. Parents and other educators should discuss with their students which and how many essays will be rewritten. Generally speaking, I suggest that students rewrite at least one essay/week.

___ Students should write something every day and read something every day. Students will be prompted to read assigned whole books before they are due. It is imperative that students read ahead as they write present essays or they will not be able to read all the material. Remember this too: students tend to write what they read. Poor material—material that is too juvenile—will be echoed in the vocabulary and syntax of student essays.

___ Students should begin writing assignments immediately after they are assigned. A suggested implementation schedule is provided. Generally speaking, students will write about one hour per day to accomplish the writing component of this course.

___ Students should revise their papers as soon as they are evaluated. Follow the implementation schedule at the end of each course.

PRE-WRITING THINKING CHALLENGE

THE THINKING GAME

ISSUE
State problem/issue in five sentences.

State problem/issue in two sentences.

State problem/issue in one sentence.

NAME THREE OR MORE SUBTOPICS OF PROBLEM.

NAME THREE OR MORE SUBTOPICS OF THE SUBTOPICS.

WHAT INFORMATION MUST BE KNOWN TO SOLVE THE PROBLEM OR TO ANSWER THE QUESTION?

STATE THE ANSWER TO THE QUESTION/PROBLEM
—In five sentences.

—In two sentences.

—In one sentence.

STATED IN TERMS OF OUTCOMES, WHAT EVIDENCES DO I SEE THAT CONFIRM THAT I HAVE MADE THE RIGHT DECISION?

ONCE THE PROBLEM/QUESTION IS ANSWERED/SOLVED, WHAT ONE OR TWO NEW PROBLEMS/ANSWERS MAY ARISE?

Once the problem or question is answered or solved, what are one or two new problems or answers that could arise?

ABBREVIATED PRE-WRITING THINKING CHALLENGE

What is the issue?
State problem/issue in five sentences.
State problem/issue in two sentences.
State problem/issue in one sentence.
Name three or more sub-topics of problem.
Name three or more sub-topics of the sub-topics.
What information must be known to solve the problem or to answer the question?
State the answer to the question/problem
—in five sentences —in two sentences —in one sentence.
Stated in terms of outcomes, what evidences do I see that confirm that I have made the right decision?

PRE-WRITING PHASE

Often called the brainstorming phase, the pre-writing phase is the time you decide on exactly what your topic is. What questions must you answer? You should articulate a thesis (a one sentence statement of purpose for why you are writing about this topic. The thesis typically has two to four specific points contained within it). You should decide what sort of essay this is—for instance, a definition, an exposition, a persuasive argument—and then design a strategy. For example, a clearly persuasive essay will demand that you state the issue and give your opinion in the opening paragraph.

Next, after a thesis statement, you will write an outline. *No matter what length the essay may be, 20 pages or one paragraph, you should create an outline.*

SAMPLE OUTLINE WITH TWO MAJOR POINTS

Thesis: In his poem *The Raven*, Edgar Allan Poe uses literary devices to describe such weighty topics as *death* and *unrequited love*, which draw the reader to an insightful and many times emotional moment. (Note that this thesis informs the reader that the author will be exploring *death* and *unrequited love*.)

I. Introduction (Opens to the reader the exploration of the writing and tells the reader what to expect.)

II. Body (This particular essay will include two main points developed in two main paragraphs, one paragraph about death and one paragraph about emotions. The second paragraph will be introduced by means of a transition word or phrase or sentence.)
    A. Imagining Death
    B. Feeling Emotions

III. Conclusions (A paragraph which draws conclusions or solves the problem mentioned in the thesis statement.)

One of the best ways to organize your thoughts is to spend time in concentrated thinking, what some call brainstorming. Thinking through what you want to write is a way to narrow your topic.

SAMPLE OUTLINE:

PERSUASIVE PAPER WITH THREE MAJOR POINTS (ARGUMENTS)

I.   Introduction: <u>Thesis statement</u> includes a listing or a summary of the three supportive arguments and introduces the paper.

II. Body
     A. Argument 1
         Evidence
         (transition words or phrases or sentences to the next topic)
     B. Argument 2
         Evidence
         (transition words or phrases or sentences to the next topic)
     C. Argument 3
         Evidence
         (transition words or phrases or sentences to the conclusion)

III. Conclusion: Restatement of arguments and evidence used throughout the paper (do not use the words *in conclusion*—just conclude).

NOTE: For greater detail and explanation of outlining, refer to a composition handbook. Careful attention should be paid to parallel structure with words or phrases, to correct form with headings and subheadings, to punctuation, and to pairing of information. Correct outline structure will greatly enhance the writing of any paper.

SAMPLE OUTLINE:

EXPOSITORY ESSAY WITH FOUR MAJOR POINTS

I.   Introduction: <u>Thesis statement</u> includes a listing or summary of four examples or supports and introduces the paper.

II. Body
     A. Example 1
         Application
         (transition words or phrases or sentences to the next topic)
     B. Example 2
         Application
         (transition words or phrases or sentences to the next topic)
     C. Example 3
         Application
         (transition words or phrases or sentences to the next topic)
     D. Example 4
         Application
         (transition words or phrases or sentences to the conclusion)

III. Conclusion: Restatement of thesis, drawing from the evidence or applications used in the paper (do not use the words *in conclusion*—just conclude).

NOTE: For greater detail and explanation of outlining, refer to a composition handbook. Careful attention should be paid to parallel structure with words or phrases, to correct form with headings and subheadings, to punctuation, and to pairing of information. Correct outline structure will greatly enhance the writing of any paper.

THE THINKING CHALLENGE

The Following is an example of a Thinking Challenge approach to Mark Twain's *The Adventures of Huckleberry Finn:*

THE PROBLEM OR THE ISSUE OR THE QUESTION:

Should Huck turn in his escaped slave-friend Jim to the authorities?
State problem/issue in five sentences, then in two sentences, and, finally, in one sentence.

Five Sentences:
Huck runs away with Jim. He does so knowing that he is breaking the law. However, the lure of friendship overrides the perfidy he knows he is committing. As he floats down the Mississippi River, he finds it increasingly difficult to hide his friend from the authorities and to hide his feelings of ambivalence. Finally he manages to satisfy both ambiguities.

Two Sentences:
Huck intentionally helps his slave friend Jim escape from servitude. As Huck floats down the Mississippi River, he finds it increasingly difficult to hide his friend from the authorities and at the same time to hide his own feelings of ambivalence.

One Sentence:
After escaping with his slave-friend Jim and floating down the Mississippi River, Huck finds it increasingly difficult to hide his friend from the authorities and at the same time to hide his own feelings of ambivalence.

Name three or more subtopics of problem.
Are there times when we should disobey the law?
What responsibilities does Huck have to his family?
What should Huck do?

Name three or more subtopics of the subtopics.
Are there times when we should disobey the law?
    Who determines what laws are unjust?
    Should the law be disobeyed publicly?
    Who is injured when we disobey the law?
What responsibilities does Huck have to his family?
    Who is his family? Jim? His dad?
    Is allegiance to them secondary to Jim's needs?
    Should his family support his civil disobedience?
What should Huck do?
    Turn in Jim?
    Escape with Jim?
    Both?

What information must be known?
Laws? Jim's character? If he is bad, then should Huck save him?

State the answer to the question/problem in five, two, and one sentence(s)

Five Sentences:
Huck can escape with Jim with profound feelings of guilt. After all, he is helping a slave escape. This is important because it shows that Huck is still a moral, if flawed, character. Jim's freedom does outweigh any other consideration—including the laws of the land and his family's wishes. As the story unfolds the reader sees that Huck is indeed a reluctant criminal, and the reader takes comfort in that fact.

Two Sentences:
     Showing reluctance and ambivalence, Huck embarks on an arduous but moral adventure. Jim's freedom outweighs any other need or consideration.

One Sentence:
     Putting Jim's freedom above all other considerations, Huck, the reluctant criminal, embarks on an arduous but moral adventure.
     Once the Problem or Issue or Question is solved, what are one or two new problems that may arise? What if Huck is wrong? What consequences could Huck face?

WRITING PHASE

Every essay has a beginning (introduction), a middle part (body), and an ending (conclusion). The introduction must draw the reader into the topic and usually presents the thesis to the reader. The body organizes the material and expounds on the thesis (a one sentence statement of purpose) in a cogent and inspiring way. The conclusion generally is a solution to the problem or issue or question or is sometimes a summary. Paragraphs in the body are connected with transitional words or phrases: *furthermore, therefore, in spite of.* Another effective transition technique is to mention in the first sentence of a new paragraph a thought or word that occurs in the last sentence of the previous paragraph. In any event, the body should be intentionally organized to advance the purposes of the paper. A disciplined writer *always* writes a rough draft. Using the well-thought out outline composed during the pre-writing phase is an excellent way to begin the actual writing. The paper has already been processed mentally and only lacks the writing.

WRITING PHASE

The writer must make the first paragraph grab the reader's attention enough that the reader will want to continue reading.

The writer should write naturally, but not colloquially. In other words, the writer should not use clichés and everyday coded language. *The football players blew it* is too colloquial.

The writer should use as much visual imagery and precise detail as possible, should assume nothing, and should explain everything.

REWRITING PHASE

Despite however many rewrites are necessary, when the writer is satisfied that she has effectively communicated her subject, she is ready to write the final copy.

TOP TEN MOST FREQUENT ESSAY PROBLEMS

<u>Agreement between the Subject and Verb</u>: Use singular forms of verbs with singular subjects and use plural forms of verbs with plural subjects.
    WRONG: Everyone finished their homework.
    RIGHT: Everyone finished his homework (*Everyone* is an indefinite singular pronoun.)

<u>Using the Second Person Pronoun</u>—"you," "your" should rarely, if ever, be used in a formal essay.
    WRONG: You know what I mean (Too informal).

<u>Redundancy</u>: Never use "I think"or "It seems to me"
    WRONG: I think that is true.
    RIGHT: That is true (We know you think it, or you would not write it!)

<u>Tense consistency</u>: Use the same tense (usually present) throughout the paper.
    WRONG: I was ready to go, but my friend is tired.
    RIGHT: I am ready to go but my friend is tired.

<u>Misplaced Modifiers</u>: Place the phrase or clause close to its modifier.
    WRONG: The man drove the car with a bright smile into the garage.
    RIGHT: The man with a bright smile drove the car into the garage.

<u>Antecedent Pronoun Problems</u>: Make sure pronouns match (agree) in number and gender with their antecedents.
    WRONG: Mary and Susan both enjoyed her dinner.
    RIGHT: Mary and Susan both enjoyed their dinners.

<u>Parallelism</u>: Make certain that your list/sentence includes similar phrase types.
    WRONG: I like to take a walk and swimming.
    RIGHT: I like walking and swimming

<u>Affect vs. Effect</u>: Affect is a verb; Effect is a noun unless it means to achieve.
    WRONG: His mood effects me negatively.
    RIGHT: His mood affects me negatively.

<u>Dangling Prepositions</u>: Rarely end a sentence with an unmodified preposition.
    WRONG: Who were you speaking to?
    RIGHT: To whom were you speaking?

<u>Transitions</u>: Make certain that paragraphs are connected with transitions (e.g., furthermore, therefore, in spite of).
    RIGHT: Furthermore, Jack London loves to describe animal behavior.

PUBLIC SPEAKING: OVERVIEW (A)

Types and Purposes of Speeches
The Speech Outline
General Types of Speeches:
    Informative (didactic) speech,
    Impromptu (extemporaneous) speech,
    Persuasive speech

Every speech has a beginning, middle, and ending. The beginning is called the introduction, the middle is called the body, and the ending is called the conclusion. The main purpose of the introduction is to capture the reader's attention. The purpose of the body is to fulfill the promise given in the introduction, and the final thoughts in this speech bring a conclusion to the audience. The theme of the essay is reiterated. The body is

normally two-thirds to three-fourths of the entire speech. A speech can include many points, but the speaker usually chooses to make one to three main points. Subordinate points support the main points, which likewise are backed by ample evidence.

In speech writing, as in essay writing, the outline is critical. The introduction normally includes a provocative statement or rhetorical question to begin the speech with supporting statements to propel the listener into the intended direction. As in essay writing, stating the thesis or purpose of the speech in the introduction is a necessity. Next, the body presents the many points with supporting details and argument. Finally, the conclusion restates the arguments, summarizes the points, and brings solution or conclusion.

Sample Speech Introduction:

(The thesis is underlined; the transition to the first body paragraph is also underlined.)

Death and pretense are real entities with which we will all ultimately deal. Jesus really died on the cross. This was not some metaphorical event or pretense or some dramatic hoax. No, He really died. Today, we have as much problem believing that Jesus died as we do that He arose from the grave. Our ever-present media promises us eternal bliss and immortality. Eat your vegetables, drink plenty of water, take these vitamins, exercise daily, and you will live forever. Nowadays, we pretend death will not affect us, but it was not always so.

[This introduction sets the tone, direction, and content for the reader. The reader knows to expect some commentary about death in general, about the death of Jesus, and something about pretense and understandings about death. Next, the body of the speech fulfills the expectations that the introduction has set up. Notice the points from the introduction.]

Sample Speech Body:

(The speech's major points are highlighted in bold. The transitional sentences are underlined.)

Death was something our parents and grandparents had to face with more finality and frequency, perhaps, than we do. The average life span was lower than it is now. **Medical science** was not as successful as it is now in saving human life. Infant mortality was higher. Since there were fewer hospitals and no nursing homes, sick and dying relatives died at home. It was the custom years ago for the "wake" to be held in the family's living room, followed by the burial of the dead in a local church cemetery. When our grandparents went to **church** on Sundays, they were reminded of the reality of death as they passed the marble grave markers of their loved ones. Death was always present in one form or another. There is another death that was significant then, as it is now.

Sample Speech Conclusion:

(The final thoughts in this speech excerpt bring the audience a conclusion. The theme of death, with its surrounding attitudes of pretense or reality, is reiterated).

Jesus Christ died on the cross. He was not pretending. There was no magic trick. He was really dead—really dead. He did not die quietly in bed with all His friends surrounding Him. No, He died a humiliating, messy, public death. In other words, until the women visited the tomb, one thing was certain on this first Easter morning: Jesus bar Joseph was very, very dead. That explains why, at first, the disciples did not believe these women who had been sent to them specifically by Jesus. If you had watched the Lord die on a cross two days previously, would you have believed them? In this tangible world, death and dying are not mere pretense. It is into the world of reality, of death and dying, that the early disciples—and you and I—are invited to enter by the Apostle Paul. . . (James Stobaugh)

Speech Assignment

Compose a one-minute speech on the topic "My Many Virtues" and present it in front of an audience. Entice and earn your audience's interest with your introduction, fulfill the promise that you make in the introduction, and then present your audience with a final conclusion(s).

Your evaluator should complete an oratory evaluation (Appendix). Remember: since a speech is inevitably based on a written manuscript, you will need to organize and write an essay on the topic before you present the speech. Typically, speech writing follows the same patterns as essay writing: pre-writing, writing, re-writing, (and in the case of speech making) cue cards and oral practice—in preparation for the speech presentation. A general guideline is to orally practice the speech until you can present it within its prescribed time limits, with comfortable and appropriate voice inflection, and without excessive use of cue cards.

BOOK LIST

A book list is included in the Appendix. It is not meant to be exhaustive but is intended as a guide to good reading. You should read most of the books on the list before you graduate from high school. After reading a book, complete a novel review (Appendix). Try to select readings from four different genres (i.e., types of literature): a novel, a short story, a play, and a nonfiction piece. Generally, read 35-50 pages per night (or 200 pages per week). At the same time, create 3-by-5 vocabulary cards (an example is in the Appendix). Use five new words in each essay you write.

JOURNAL WRITING

Journal writing is one the best forms of reflection. This prayer journal should be a narrative of your spiritual journey. It is suggested that you use a three-ring notebook exclusively for this task. You may use the Journal Guide Questions (Appendix) to help you. Mechanics of writing is not the major emphasis for these journal entries; the primary purpose is to pique creativity and to transform spiritually. In the next lessons, you are invited to journal through 1 & 2 Kings.

WRITING ASSIGNMENTS

1. Write a one-two page essay of your choice or an essay on the topic "My Many Virtues." Next, underline

the thesis statement, *italicize the introduction*, put in **bold letters the transitions**, and, finally, type/write the CONCLUSION IN CAPITAL LETTERS.

Emphasize the following elements of essays: Starting Point, Purpose, Form, Audience, Voice, and Point of View.

This essay should include an outline with thesis statement, a rough draft, several revisions, a final copy, and five new (circled) vocabulary words. Your essay must pay particular attention to style (focus, content, organization).

Give a copy to a peer/friend to complete a peer evaluation form (Appendix) and to instructor to evaluate.

2. Read a book from the reading list or a book assigned in your literature and/or history elective (or another approved book). Read at least 35/50 pages/day. Make vocabulary cards from words in your reading.

3. Write, practice, and present your speech; have a teacher evaluate it with a speech evaluation form. (Appendix)

4. Concentrate on writing and speaking style this week. Pay particular attention to the way you organize and write your papers.

5. Using the devotional questions as a guide

Using the Dictionary

Many problems in usage result because students use a thesaurus (not the dictionary). A thesaurus invites students to use synonyms whose meaning is not completely understood. A better strategy is to use an unabridged dictionary that illustrates the usage of the unknown word in a sentence.

(Appendix), write at least three journal entries. Reflect on the biblical characters in 1 Kings 1:1-53. Compare the collapse of intellectual and political Israel with the moral and cultural demise of America in the last 150 years. What choices does King David make that may lead the nation into a generation of apostasy? Speculate on what King David is thinking as he chooses Solomon over Adonijah. Write in essay form. This journal is meant to be private, but you are invited to share reflections with others.

6. Complete one warm-up essay every day. The warm-up essay should be one page or less; it should not take more than one-half hour to write. The warm-ups do not need to be edited or rewritten. Every day will build progress with writing ease, and over time you will experience improvement.

Final Project

Correct and rewrite all essays and place them in your Final Portfolio.

Warm-up Essays:

	DAY 1	DAY 2	DAY 3	DAY 4	DAY 5
Elements of Writing	Create a thesis for an essay entitled "My favorite pencil."	Create an introduction for the same essay.	Create a three-point body for the same essay.	Create a conclusion for the same essay.	Rewrite the same essay.

SUGGESTED
Weekly *Implementation*

DAY 1	DAY 2	DAY 3	DAY 4	DAY 5
Write a Warm-up Essay. Read 35-50 pages/day. Find five new vocabulary words. Reflect on the speech assignment for the week. Write an outline and thesis for your essay. Make a journal entry.	Write a Warm-up Essay. Read 35-50 pages/day. Find five new vocabulary words. Outline and compose a first draft of your speech. Work on the first draft for your essay. Make a journal entry.	Write a Warm-up Essay. Read 35-50 pages/day. Find five new vocabulary words. Revise your speech and submit to your evaluator/ parent. Revise the first draft of your essay. Make a journal entry.	Write a Warm-up Essay. Read 35-50 pages/day. Find five new vocabulary words. Prepare to present your speech tomorrow: cue cards and oral practice. Finish the final copy of your essay. Make a journal entry.	Write a Warm-up Essay. Read 35-50 pages/day. Find five new vocabulary words. Present your speech to a live audience. Submit your assignments to your evaluator/ guardian/parent. Submit a copy of your paper to a peer for evaluation. Take Lesson 1 Test Make a journal entry.

LESSON 2

WRITING TASK: OVERVIEW (B)

As you write, it is imperative that you know the purpose of your essay and that you have identified your audience. Why are you writing this essay? Who will read what you write? What expectations do you bring to this paper? What expectations do your readers bring?

The purpose of your essay will probably fall into four categories: Persuasive, expository, descriptive, and narrative. Persuasive essays argue a point. Descriptive essays describe a person, place, or thing. Expository essays give information and explain. Narratives are stories.

When you think about your audience, ask yourself these questions: What prejudices exist in your audience? What is the age range of your audience? Background? Are they friends? Enemies? Who are they? What terms must you define to prevent misunderstanding and to fully inform the audience of what you mean when you use a particular word or set of words? Will you need to write in a formal or informal style?

Often you want to write what others have written, actually what you have read. In fact, you will be influenced by whatever you have read about your topic and may even be writing about what you read, but you need to develop your own writing style; you need to write your own stories. As one scholar explains, "The best writers tend to be people with something on their minds that they want to get off, curious people who want to discover things, or think things through, and tell what they have come up with." You choose, or you are given, a subject—soccer. Then, you choose, or you are given, a topic—defensive tactics. The biggest challenge for most writers is in limiting—not broadening—your topic (see the discussion on The Thinking Game from Lesson 1). The thesis and outline help you limit your topic and organize it into a paper. Finally, you must ask yourself, "What tone do I want to exhibit in this paper?" If you are writing a paper discussing your

Writing Skill: Overview (B).

Style (Writing and Speaking): Paragraph—Topic Sentence/Thesis

Public Speaking Task: Overview (B): Selecting your Topic, Researching Your Topic, and Knowing your Audience

Looking Ahead: Eyewitness Account (Writing), Researching your Speech and Converting the Eyewitness Account to a Speech (Speaking)

Computer Editing

Be attentive and careful when you use spell and grammar check. Since even the best computer editing programs inevitably miss some mistakes, you will still need to edit your paper. Also, it is not uncommon for computer programs to be inaccurate regarding grammar and usage specifics. Check with comprehensive grammar texts.

brother's bedroom, you can afford to be whimsical and humorous. On the other hand, if you are writing a paper on the Holocaust your tone will be somber and serious.

In summary, follow these steps:

1. Choose your subject and topic. Decide on the purpose of your essay.

2. Identify your audience. Adapt your topic to your audience.

3. Read, research, and then create a thesis statement and an outline.

4. Write your essay carefully following your thesis and outline. Every essay has an introduction, a body, and a conclusion.

5. Use transitions between each paragraph.

6. Revise your essay as many times as necessary.

STYLE (WRITING AND SPEAKING): PARAGRAPHS (A) TOPIC SENTENCE/THESIS STATEMENT

Paragraphs are more than a bunch of connected sentences. They are the building blocks of the prose essay. They are the core of the essay. No matter how effective words and sentences may be, they fail to communicate without the effective creation of paragraphs.

You have already heard about the thesis statement, and you will review this concept when you study the research paper later in this course. The thesis is a one-sentence statement of the overall projection of the paper; it is in the introductory paragraph of the essay and is clearly observable. Similar to a map for a traveler, the thesis statement provides direction for your reader.

Paragraphs in a paper are not merely random thoughts of prose; they are integrated units of thought, all of which hover around the thesis statement. They are rockets aimed toward a target. Every paragraph in the paper can be predicted from a carefully planned thesis statement and a well-constructed outline.

Every paragraph has a topic sentence that is related to the thesis statement. In a sense, the topic sentence of each paragraph can be considered the thesis statement of the paragraph. The thesis statement, however, has a more universal application. It is the one-sentence purpose of the much larger prose piece—the essay—whereas the topic sentence is the one sentence purpose of the paragraph.

Some writers prefer to introduce their essays by having the thesis statement occur at the beginning of the paragraph. Others place it at the end of the introductory paragraph where it can also serve as the transition into the first body paragraph.

The thesis statements or topic sentences of the following paragraphs are underlined.

In "The Pardoner's Tale" Chaucer uses personification and irony to make a point about hypocrisy. He subtly but effectively implies that hypocrisy is the gravest sin. His implication is accomplished through the character of the pardoner, who is the personification of the sins he condemns.

Often a writer will begin a paragraph with a rhetorical question—a question whose answer is obvious or a question whose answer is in the question. Some writers also use a "topic question" to introduce the question they will be exploring in the paper.

How does Chaucer discuss hypocrisy in "The Pardoner's Tale?" He subtly but effectively implies that hypocrisy is the gravest sin. His implication is accomplished through the char-

acter of the pardoner, who is the personification of the sins he condemns. In "The Pardoner's Tale" Chaucer uses personification and irony to make a point about hypocrisy.

In any event, every paragraph has a topic sentence and every essay has a thesis statement.

PUBLIC SPEAKING: OVERVIEW (B) SELECTING YOUR TOPIC, RESEARCHING YOUR TOPIC, AND KNOWING YOUR AUDIENCE

How does one write a speech? First you need to select your topic. The topic is usually dictated by the circumstances or demands of the occasion but should also be sufficiently focused to be manageable but sufficiently broad to be comprehensive. You now must decide exactly what you want to accomplish with your speech. But you are not merely giving your speech to an empty room. You must know to what kind of people you will be speaking, how many there will be, and where you will be presenting the speech. Effective speeches are written on a specific topic to a specific audience in a specific place. Next, gather material for your speech. A speech is not an essay but it is a well-constructed, grammatically correct oral presentation based on a written manuscript (unless it is an impromptu/extemporaneous speech). Always begin your speech with an outline. An outline will establish the main points and balance the supporting material for each point. It usually makes writing and then presenting the final speech easier. After your speech is ready, you must practice it aloud. This will also help you to be more confident in your speech delivery.

The following is the body of a speech presented to a group of young people. The speaker is discussing the importance of taking a stand for Christ in a hostile culture:

There are four key issues that must be settled in your mind:

Identity: Who am I?

Responsibility: What will I do with my life?

Priority: What is really most important to me?

Commitment: How much am I willing to commit?

First, as you begin a new phase of your life, make sure you know who you are and who your God is. "By faith Moses, when he had grown up, refused to be called the son of Pharaoh's daughter" (Hebrews 11:24). He refuses and then chooses. You are a special child. Much loved. You live among a people who do not know who they are. A people without hope. A people who do not know they are loved.

We live in a dysfunctional, dying culture. In *The Aeneid*, (http://classics.mit.edu/Virgil/aeneid.html) Virgil describes our world:

O happy men, thrice happy, four times happy,
Who had the luck to die, with their fathers watching
Below the walls of Troy! (lines 94–96)

But they will look to you to lead them. . . .

Sometimes in a great nation, there are riots,
With the rabble out of hand, and firebrands fly
And cobblestones: whatever they lay their hands on
Is a weapon for their fury, but should they see
One man of noble presence, they fall silent. . . .
(Lines 148–156)

The Christian teacher Os Guinness encourages Christians with the fact that Americans in the near future will be looking to places of stability and strength for direction. By default, those people whose lives are in reasonably good shape, who have some reason to live beyond the next paycheck, will have almost an inexorable appeal. Like Aeneas in Virgil's *Aeneid*, people will all, someday after the storm, be thrown on somebody's beach. I hope you will show more discernment than Dido!

Second, Moses accepts responsibility for his life. He "chose to suffer with the people of God rather than to enjoy the short-lived pleasure of sin" (Heb. 11:25). You will be persecuted because you will join the stream of faith that believes Christ is the Way, the Truth, the Life. This is about responsibility. You will have to be responsible for the call that God places in your life. One of the greatest problems in this generation is confusion about individual responsibility.

Third, you will need to decide fairly soon what is important and valuable in your life, or others will do it for you. You need a cause worth dying for (as well as living for). "For he [Moses] considered reproach for the sake of the Messiah to be greater wealth than the treasures of Egypt, since his attention was on the reward" (Heb. 11:26). You must exhibit the faith and courage of the three teenagers in Daniel 3:14-18:

Nebuchadnezzar asked them, "Shadrach, Meshach, and Abednego, is it true that you don't serve my gods or worship the gold statue I have set up? Now if you're ready, when you hear the sound of the horn, flute, zither, lyre, harp, drum, and every kind of music, fall down and worship the statue I made. But if you don't worship it, you will immediately be thrown into a furnace of blazing fire—and who is the god who can rescue you from my power?"

Shadrach, Meshach, and Abednego replied to the king, "Nebuchadnezzar, we don't need to give you an answer to this question. If the God we serve exists, then He can rescue us from the furnace of blazing fire, and He can rescue us from the power of you, the king. But even if He does not rescue us, we want you as king to know that we will not serve your gods or worship the gold statue you set up."

Finally, you must never take your eyes off the goal. "By faith he left Egypt behind, not being afraid of the king's anger, for he persevered, as one who sees Him who is invisible" (Heb. 11:27). How long can you wait? How long can you persevere? The artisans who built the great European cathedrals built them without hope of seeing the completion of the work or, for that matter, without knowing if the work would be completed. However, the artisans were hopeful that technology would be available in the next generation to accomplish the necessary tasks, and that the next generation would have the energy to do the task.

You must have hope. As John Milton in *Paradise Lost* writes:

A mind not to be chang'd by place or time.
The mind is its own place, and in itself
Can make a heaven of hell, a hell of heaven.
(line 253)

Here we may reign secure; and in my choice
To reign is worth ambition, though in hell:
Better to reign in hell than serve in heaven.
(line 261)

How do speech writers accomplish their task of speech writing? Speech writing is very similar to essay writing: select the topic, decide on the purpose, identify the audience, read and research, consider the direction of the speech, outline the points to be made, and conclude the points of the speech. The topic is usually dictated by the circumstances or demands of the occasion; it should be sufficiently focused to be manageable but sufficiently broad to be comprehensive. Decide exactly what is to be accomplished with the speech. Since you are not merely giving your speech to an empty room, you must know what kind of people will be hearing what you say, how many there will be, and where you will be presenting the speech. Effective speeches are written on a specific topic to a specific audience in a specific place.

Next, gather material for your speech through reading and researching. A speech is not an essay, but it is a well-constructed, grammatically correct oral presentation based on a written manuscript (unless it is an impromptu/extemporaneous speech).

The topic will power your search for information. If your speech requires technical information, you will need to consult books, periodicals, and perhaps even internet sources. In some cases, you will need to interview specialists in the field of the topic. Once you find your sources, be very careful to give the source credit in your speech. When you utilize outside sources in your speech, imagine that the authors of these sources are in the audience. Will they know that you are giving them credit? Finally, quoting a source is only half the battle—you must also understand the source. Often speechwriters will present quotes that they really don't understand, thereby giving false impressions or even false information. Be certain that you understand a quote or statement before you present it to an audience; be very careful not to take it out of context and make it mean something that the original author did not mean. If you are confused by what you say you can be certain that your audience will be doubly confused.

Always begin your speech preparation with an outline (Lesson 3). An outline will establish the main points and balance the supporting material for each point. It usually makes writing and then presenting the final speech easier. After your speech is ready, you must practice it aloud, helping you be more confident in the speech delivery.

The following is the outline of a speech presented to a group of young people who are graduating into a new phase of life. The speaker is discussing the importance of taking a stand for Christ in a hostile culture.

Sample Speech Outline:
Thesis: There are four key issues that must be settled in a Christian's mind: identity, responsibility, priority, and commitment.

I. Identity: Discerning self
   A. New phase
   B. Dying culture
   C. Near future

II. Responsibility: Deciding life
   A. Example of Moses
   B. Expectation of persecution
   C. Response from decision

III. Priority: Declaring essentials
   A. A cause
   B. Faith and courage

IV. Commitment: Proclaiming intention
   A. Constancy
   B. Consistency
   C. Hope

Sample Speech:
As you begin a new phase of your life, make sure you know who you are and who your God is. "By faith Moses, when he had grown up, refused to be called the son of Pharaoh's daughter" (Hebrews 11:24). He refuses and then chooses. You are a special child. Much loved. You live among a people who do not know who they are—a people without hope. A people who do not know they are loved.

We live in a dysfunctional, dying culture. In *The Aeneid*, Virgil describes our world:

O happy men, thrice happy, four times happy,
Who had the luck to die, with their fathers watching
Below the walls of Troy! (lines 94–96)

But they will look to you to lead them. . . .

Sometimes in a great nation, there are riots,
With the rabble out of hand, and firebrands fly
And cobblestones: whatever they lay their hands on

Is a weapon for their fury, but should they see
One man of noble presence, they fall silent. . . .
(Lines 148–156)

The Christian teacher Os Guinness encourages Christians with the fact that Americans in the near future will be looking to places of stability and strength for direction. By default, those people whose lives are in reasonably good shape, who have some reason to live beyond the next paycheck, will have almost an inexorable appeal. Like Aeneas in Virgil's *Aeneid*, people will all, someday after the storm, be thrown on somebody's beach. I hope this culture's young people will show more discernment than Dido!

Accepting responsibility for life is a second tenant for the Christian life. Moses provides a good example of responsibility: He "chose to suffer with the people of God rather than to enjoy the short-lived pleasure of sin" (Heb. 11:25). You will be persecuted because you will join the stream of faith that believes Christ is the Way, the Truth, the Life. Responsibility hovers around this knowledge. You will choose whether or not you will be responsible for the call that God places in your life. One of the greatest challenges in this generation is confusion about individual responsibility.

A third challenge comes with the need to decide what is important and valuable in your life. When you do not decide, others decide for you. You need a cause worth living and dying for. "For he [Moses] considered reproach for the sake of the Messiah to be greater wealth than the treasures of Egypt, since his attention was on the reward" (Heb. 11:26). Consider the faith and courage of the three teenagers in Daniel 3:14-18:

Nebuchadnezzar asked them, "Shadrach, Meshach, and Abednego, is it true that you don't serve my gods or worship the gold statue I have set up? Now if you're ready, when you hear the sound of the horn, flute, zither, lyre, harp, drum, and every kind of music, fall down and worship the statue I made. But if you don't worship it, you will immediately be thrown into a furnace of blazing fire—and who is the god who can rescue you from my power?"

Shadrach, Meshach, and Abednego replied to the king, "Nebuchadnezzar, we don't need to give you an answer to this question. If the God we serve exists, then He can rescue us from the furnace of blazing fire, and He can rescue us from the power of you, the king. But even if He

does not rescue us, we want you as king to know that we will not serve your gods or worship the gold statue you set up."

Finally, the goal must be constantly and consistently before you. "By faith he left Egypt behind, not being afraid of the king's anger, for he persevered, as one who sees Him who is invisible" (Heb. 11:27). How long can you wait? How long can you persevere? The artisans who built the great European cathedrals built them without hope of seeing the completion of the work or, for that matter, without knowing if the work would be completed. However, the artisans were hopeful that technology would be available in the next generation to accomplish the necessary tasks, and that the next generation would have the energy to do the task.

Hope is an integral part of commitment. As John Milton in *Paradise Lost* writes:

A mind not to be chang'd by place or time.
The mind is its own place, and in itself
Can make a heaven of hell, a hell of heaven.
(line 253)

Here we may reign secure; and in my choice
To reign is worth ambition, though in hell:
Better to reign in hell than serve in heaven.
(line 261)

Young people are challenged in many directions from many people. Opportunities for decision-making and choices abound. Tending to issues of identity, responsibility, priority, and commitment can help the transition from being a dependant teen-ager to a Christ-centered young adult capable of being world changers.

SPEECH ASSIGNMENT

Prepare and then present one speech for two audiences on the topic, "the importance of finishing my chores before I go to soccer/ballet/practice." The first speech is presented to your team. The second speech is presented to your parents. Speech preparation includes an outline with thesis, rough draft, final copy containing five new (circled) vocabulary words, and cue cards (index cards), oral practice for speech delivery. Give a copy to a peer/friend to complete a peer evaluation form (Appendix) and to your instructor to evaluate.

WRITING ASSIGNMENTS

1. Write two 75-word essays on the topic, "the importance of finishing my chores before I go to soccer/ballet/practice." The first essay is written for your team. The second essay is written for your parents. Write as precisely as possible. This essay should include an outline with thesis, rough draft, final copy containing five new (circled) vocabulary words, and cue cards (index cards). Give a copy to a peer/friend to complete a peer evaluation form (Appendix) and to your instructor to evaluate.

2. Read a book from the reading list or a book assigned in your literature and/or history elective (or another approved book). Read at least 35/50 pages/day. Make vocabulary cards from words in your reading.

3. Present your speech and have a teacher evaluate it with a speech evaluation form (Appendix).

4. Consider writing and speech style this week. Be sure to create a precise but inspiring thesis statement.

5. Using the devotional questions as a guide (Appendix), write at least three journal entries. Reflect on 1 Kings 1:41-53. Relate the incident first from the viewpoint of Solomon and then from Adonijah. Again, record your reflections in essay form. This journal is meant to be private although you are invited to share your reflections with others.

6. Complete one warm-up essay every day. The warm-up essay should be one page or less; it should not take more than one-half hour to write. The warm-ups do not need to be edited or rewritten. With time you will see a difference with your writing comfort and improvement in your writing.

FINAL PROJECT

Correct and rewrite all essays and place them in your Final Portfolio.

WARM-UP ESSAYS:

	DAY 1	DAY 2	DAY 3	DAY 4	DAY 5
Speaking/ Writing to an Audience	Write an essay defending the Atkins Diet. Audience: Wheat Growers Association.	Write an essay defending the Atkins Diet. Audience: Atkins Diet Support Group.	Write an essay arguing for a vegetarian diet. Audience: National Beef Growers Association.	Write an essay arguing for a vegetarian diet. Audience: Vegetarian Diet Support Group.	Write an essay arguing for classical music. Audience: Rolling Stone Magazine Board of Directors.

SUGGESTED
Weekly *Implementation*

DAY 1	DAY 2	DAY 3	DAY 4	DAY 5
Write a Warm-up Essay.	Write a Warm-up Essay.	Write a Warm-up Essay.	Write a Warm-up Essay.	Write a Warm-up Essay.
Read 35-50 pages/day.	Read 35-50 pages/day.	Read 35-50 pages/day.	Read 35-50 pages/day.	Read 35-50 pages/day.
Find five new vocabulary words.	Find five new vocabulary words.	Find five new vocabulary words.	Find five new vocabulary words.	Find five new vocabulary words.
Reflect on the speech assignment for the week.	Compose a first draft of your speech.	Revise your speech and submit to your evaluator/ parent.	Prepare to present your speech tomorrow.	Present your speech to a live audience.
Write an outline and thesis for your essay.	Complete the first draft for your essay.	Revise the first draft of your essay.	Finish the final copy of your essay.	Submit your assignments to your evaluator/ parent.
Make a journal entry.	Make a journal entry.	Make a journal entry.	Make a journal entry.	Submit a copy of your paper to a peer for evaluation.
				Make a journal entry.
				Take Lesson 2 Test

LESSON 3

WRITING TASK: EYEWITNESS ACCOUNT

An eyewitness account is an essay that attempts to recreate an event as it actually happened. Using powerful imagery and precise language, the eyewitness account recreates an event in precise language. The reader vicariously experiences the described event. The following is an eyewitness account.

6:30 A.M. I stepped into our back yard. It felt like home. The hardy St. Augustine grass irritated my innocent feet too long the captive of black Converse tennis shoes. I quickly jumped to an interloper crab grass patch. Ironically, my toes preferred the less pretentious, uninvited crab grass. Our yard man, Aubrey, either missed the crab grass patch or was sympathetic to an antediluvian ant hill rising out of the crab grass. Neither I nor the crab grass belonged here this morning.

> In most eyewitness accounts 80% is description and 20% or less is narration.

Monday through Friday Aubrey rode his bicycle to our property to care for my grandmother's grass and my mother's flower garden. A southern garden was both afflicted and blessed by a ten month growing season. It was constantly battling Johnson grass and rodents. While northern flowers sported vivid colors and vigorous stems vitalized by cool summer evenings and short growing seasons, southern Arkansas begonias and roses had to endure endlessly long, hot summer days. Their pale colors were the result of too much sun, not too little. I was fifteen years old, and I had embarrassingly small feet. Russell had size ten and Ricky had size eleven D's! I only sported 8 or maybe an 8 1/2 if I could stuff paper at the end. It was another of those things that made me different.

As I stepped into our yard, I quietly moved toward my dad's kennel. Dad's prize-winning bird dogs, Sandy and Jim (my namesake), were delighted to see me. They supposed that I was a harbinger of better things—like a bird hunting expedition. I was forced to apologize and merely scratched their prickly ears. This futile appeasement accomplished nothing. With disappointed presentiment unavoidably present, Sandy and her friend Jim rudely snubbed the offspring of their master by turning their backs and growling. They were my father's bird dogs; I was merely his son. They were acutely aware of the differences of our station and pushed it to their advantage at every occasion. They knew full well that no little league game could compete with a potential bird hunting excursion.

As I crossed the yard, I heard a biplane crop duster dropping DDT on old man Henley's cotton field nearby. Small sticky droplets accumulated on my arm.

The robust lawn had an artificial look to it. It was too green, too healthy. We were told never to walk on the lawn. Our yard was the final remnant of my grandmother's legacy to my father. She had given our mansion to my father, her youngest son, as a wedding present. The house was hard enough to give up; her sacrosanct yard was impossible. In fact, my grandmother often strolled beside the magnolia tree lusting for the hybrid St. Augustine that was no longer hers.

My father maintained loyal deference to his mother by guarding that yard.

(James P. Stobaugh)

STYLE (WRITING AND SPEAKING SKILL): PARAGRAPHS (B) INTRODUCTION

Every paragraph has a beginning, middle, and ending. Every essay has a beginning (or introductory) paragraph, one or more middle (or main body) paragraphs, and an ending (or conclusion) paragraph. Later in this series, the research paper will be discussed and the introductory paragraph will be discussed in greater depth. However, at this point, suffice it to say that every essay must have an effective introduction. An effective introduction is crucial to the paper. Your reader will read with eagerness a paper introduced with an inspiring introduction and will read with despair a paper with a boring or missing introduction.

The primary goal of the introductory paragraph is to introduce readers to the purpose of the paper. The introduction is one paragraph in the essay. You have one chance to pique your readers' interests. Without actually using the word "purpose" you will give in specific detail the purpose of the paper and then inform readers about what the rest of the paper will reveal or argue. This step is critical to the writing style of your prose creation. The following is an introduction to an essay on themes used in *Anne of Green Gables* by Lucy Maud Montgomery:

SAMPLE INTRODUCTORY PARAGRAPH:

The storyline of Anne of Green Gables *is the perfect backdrop for its author, Lucy Maud Montgomery, to develop her theme of patient love. In this delightful story of Anne, an orphaned girl who is unexpectedly placed in the care of the elderly Matthew and Marilla Cuthburt, readers live with them on their beautiful Prince Edward Island farm, Green Gables. At first, they are horrified to see that they have a girl instead of the requested boy, but, later, as Anne charms them with her poise and winsome personality, they grow to love her dearly.*

This introductory paragraph is full of information. Readers meet the protagonist and other main characters. They understand the basic storyline, the setting, and even one of the themes. This introductory paragraph introduces readers to all the main points of the essay. In fact the introduction makes sure that readers have no unexpected topics as they read the rest of the paper. Later in the essay the points will be expanded, illustrated, and supported more thoroughly, but in the introduction readers know what they will be reading about.

In an interesting way, the introduction sets the stage for the rest of the essay. The props are set on the stage; the characters are introduced; the story is launched. Now, the writing begins . . .

PUBLIC SPEAKING: THE ENGAGING-STORY APPROACH AND THE EYEWITNESS SPEECH

By necessity the speech has to both secure the listener's attention and inform the listener—in some ways mutually exclusive operations. The topic must quickly interest the audience, but it cannot distract the hearer from the main point of the speech.

An engaging, true story is an effective way to earn the listener's attention, but it is only the beginning. You must be sure to move to the next step, stating the points you will make in your speech and lobbying for their significance.

The following is the *Engaging-Story Approach* to beginning a speech that discusses the way God sometimes allows us to be broken so that we will be more useful for His work:

SAMPLE SPEECH: THE ENGAGING-STORY APPROACH

A father smiles when he hears that one son will soon graduate from Harvard Business School; another son is busily pursuing a successful career in education; and a final son will soon enter Princeton Theological Seminary. His life in Christ is adequate, but he still feels empty, so this budding saint prays that God will turn his life around.

Later, we see this same 49-year-old husband/father lying in a modern hospital. For four years, he has fought the inhuman ravages of cancer. As the doctors frantically practice their incantations and magic formulas, this broken, gentle man looks up from among the tubes, bandages, and IV bottles, and whispers, "I am not enjoying this, to be sure." A chuckle breaks from his lips. "In fact, this is a horrible way to die. But, you know, in spite of all the pain, I would not change a thing. Oh, I do not want to die. But if I was healed, and it meant that I lost all that I've learned about the Lord, well . . . I would rather die just the way I am now." "Everything", he said with quiet power, "everything I've experienced is worth what I have gained in the knowledge and love in Jesus Christ!" He died two hours later. This unpretentious, unlikely hero was my father, who died one cloudy, miserable Sunday afternoon — on Father's Day, 1983.

SAMPLE SPEECH: THE INTRODUCTION PROPER TO THE SPEECH PRESENTED ABOVE

There is a lesson all Christians will learn at one time or another: inevitably, we must be *broken* before we will be *blessed*. We must be broken before we can *grow*. Have you ever tried to hug a stiff kid? Impossible! It is relatively easy to hug a muddy kid or a sticky kid, but a stiff, wooden, rebellious child is the hardest child to love. God is in the business of breaking us so that we can really love Him and so that He can really bless us. It is easier to love a limp, broken saint than to struggle with a stiff one. Without brokenness, we are ill-prepared to face the violence we see around us.

The final statement "Without brokenness, we are ill-prepared to face the violence we see around us" would be the thesis of the speech.

SPEECH ASSIGNMENT

In front of an audience, present a 3-5 minute eyewitness account of how your family eats dinner. The eyewitness speech, like the eyewitness account/essay, requires that you give the reader generous metaphors and imagery to describe your person, place, or event. For this assignment you don't actually have to be present to be an eyewitness, but you must write as if you were.

There is no argument to defend; there is no story to write. You are merely an eyewitness — a neutral, dispassionate observer of a human event. That does not mean that you cannot search for metaphors or compare to other scenes what is happening in your scene so that your audience can understand what you are observing.

SAMPLE CLIMAX: CONTINUING THE SPEECH PRESENTED ABOVE

"I have seen God face to face." Genesis 32:30. This is one of the most intense sections of Scripture in the Old Testament. Imagine! Enveloped in eerie darkness, humankind is fighting desperately with Almighty God. There is something of fury, something of evil, in the intense struggling. All of Jacob's ample trickery, all of his pseudo-spirituality, is struggling with the Perfect God. The wrestlers groan, gasp for breath, and cry as each pushes to even greater efforts. Silhouetted against the rising moon, at times the two figures seem to lose all temporal location. For a moment, generations upon generations of Christians are standing on that hill, struggling, for all they are worth, with Almighty God. Paul, the Pharisee, is struggling along-side Jacob. He snickers as Stephen screams in mortal pain. Peter is pushing against God, even as he denies Him three times. The fire into which he peers cannot warm his heart, cannot dry the tears that grow out of his betrayal. We see anxious Martin Luther, tired Martin Luther; who has struggled with God all night. We see Luther courageously nail his 95 theses on the Wittenberg Door. We see Wesley preaching to the prison inmates of 18th-century England; there is brokenness etched on his face. And we take our place on that hill, for we have struggled — we are struggling — we will struggle — with God. The night is not over.

At the most emotional moment of the speech, the speaker is inviting the audience to become eyewitnesses themselves of this life-changing moment. The accomplishment of this feat may be the greatest compliment to an eyewitness account.

WRITING ASSIGNMENTS

1. Write a one-page eyewitness account of "How My Family Eats Dinner." Using vivid imagery and precise language, recreate this event in your essay. This essay should include an outline with thesis statement, rough draft, several revisions, and a final copy with five new (circled) vocabulary words. Give a copy to a peer/friend to complete a peer evaluation form (Appendix) and to your instructor to evaluate.

2. Read a book from the reading list or a book assigned in your literature and/or history elective (or another book approved by his parents). Read at least 35/50 pages/day. Make vocabulary cards from words in your reading.

3. Present your speech and have a teacher evaluate it with a speech evaluation form (Appendix).

4. Pay particular attention to the introduction that you write for your essay and speech.

5. Using the devotional questions as a guide, write

at least three journal entries. This week reflect on 1 Kings 3, where Solomon asks for wisdom. Answer this question: How does Solomon change between chapters 3 and 11? By chapter 11 Solomon has married foreign wives and led Israel into apostasy. Record your reflections in essay form.

6. Complete one warm-up essay every day. The warm-up essay should be one page or less; it should not take more than one-half hour to write. The warm-ups do not need to be edited or rewritten. Over time you will experience greater comfort with writing and will see improvement in your writing if you are attentive to the evaluations and revisions.

FINAL PROJECT

Correct and rewrite all essays and place them in your Final Portfolio.

WARM-UP ESSAYS:

	DAY 1	DAY 2	DAY 3	DAY 4	DAY 5
Eyewitness	Imagine that you are a dog, sleeping in the rain.	Imagine that you have one hour to share Jesus Christ with 19-year-old Adolf Hitler.	Imagine that you were never born.	Imagine that no one came to your birthday party.	Imagine that you were adopted by someone of another race.

SUGGESTED
Weekly *Implementation*

DAY 1	DAY 2	DAY 3	DAY 4	DAY 5
Write a Warm-up Essay.	Write a Warm-up Essay.	Write a Warm-up Essay.	Write a Warm-up Essay.	Write a Warm-up Essay.
Read 35-50 pages/day.	Read 35-50 pages/day.	Read 35-50 pages/day.	Read 35-50 pages/day.	Read 35-50 pages/day.
Find five new vocabulary words.	Find five new vocabulary words.	Find five new vocabulary words.	Find five new vocabulary words.	Find five new vocabulary words.
Reflect on the speech assignment for the week.	Outline and compose a first draft of your speech.	Revise your speech and submit to your evaluator/ parent.	Prepare to present your speech tomorrow.	Present your speech to a live audience.
Write an outline and thesis for your eyewitness account.	Work on the first draft for your eyewitness account.	Revise and finish the first draft of your eyewitness account.	Finish the final copy of your eyewitness account.	Submit your assignments to your evaluator/ parent.
Make a journal entry.	Make a journal entry.	Make a journal entry.	Make a journal entry.	Submit a copy of your paper to a peer for evaluation.
				Make a journal entry.
				Take Lesson 3 Test

LESSON 4

WRITING SKILL: FIRSTHAND EXPERIENCE

A firsthand experience is a detailed description and analysis of a significant event. Unlike the Eyewitness Account, the Firsthand Experience is not merely observation. The opening of the essay must establish the *setting* of the event. In the rest of the paper the author presents a detailed description of the actual event. The more imagery offered to the reader, the better. The following is a firsthand experience essay:

SAMPLE ESSAY: FIRSTHAND EXPERIENCE

I was too late. Forrest Lewis had died twenty minutes earlier. Like wrinkled drapes on a huge bay window, hospital bed sheets lay in an obscene fashion on the shiny tile floor next to an empty hospital bed. Obviously my congregant, Lewis, was not there, but I looked anyway.

Forrest was gone. His sheets were still warm from his body heat, and I could smell his aftershave. But where was Forrest?

My eyes focused on something else in the room—a crumbled piece of paper and cellophane wrap lying next to the trash can like two ominous signals. The cellophane wrap offered no evidence of its genesis, but the paper read: "Turn the corpse over and fold the arms behind its back" Then I knew. Forrest was dead. This was the packaging that held a shroud.

Forrest Lewis had been a member of my church for most of his life. He was a good man. A very good man. Quiet, unpretentious, hard working, he was every pastor's dream parishioner! But now he was dead. . . .

It is finished. . . .

Two weeks earlier I had traveled to his small but very impressive urban home to give him communion.

"This is my body that is broken for Students. . . ."

"How many times, my old friend, have Students heard these words?" I thought.

"Take, eat. This is my body that is broken for Students. . . ."

"What right do I have to serve Students communion?" I silently mused. "What do I know about life?

About remembering? About death? Teach me, Forrest Lewis, teach me."

With his pallid hands Forrest steadied my shaking. "Do this in remembrance of me. . . ."

It is finished. . . .

I thought of the future and I shuddered to think how long it would be before it arrived. Forrest thought of the present and shuddered to think how soon it would be over. . . .

It is finished. . . .

I gave him stale crackers, and he filled my afternoon with greatness. I gave him slightly fermented grape juice, and he gave me freshly baked peanut-butter cookies. "Bet Students could never guess they were made from margarine," he chuckled.

These were holy cookies. I nervously munched on them all the way home.

It is finished. . . . (James P. Stobaugh)

STYLE (WRITING AND SPEAKING): PARAGRAPH (C) MAIN BODY

If the introduction is the bait, so to speak, to attract the attention of the readers, the main body is the hook that actually catches readers. It is the meal provided for the readers. Every paragraph has a topic sentence and several supporting sentences; they make up the body of the paper. Every essay has an introductory paragraph which always presents the purpose statement (or thesis) of the essay, and every essay has several supporting paragraphs (the main body).

How many sentences or paragraphs should be in the main body of this prose unit? Enough to develop thoroughly the thesis statement. That may be 3 paragraphs or it may be 300 paragraphs. However, use as few paragraphs as possible to accomplish your purpose. Writing more to just fill up the page is not indicative of good writing. Every sentence that is included in a paragraph should have a reason for being there.

The following main body paragraph comes from an essay on themes used in *Anne of Green Gables* by Lucy Maud Montgomery:

SAMPLE BODY PARAGRAPH:

What seems like a bad turn of events turns into a blessing. While the Cuthburts expected to adopt an orphan boy, by mistake they were sent a young female child. The "mistake" becomes a great blessing to the Cuthburts. Anne also becomes a blessing to others when she saves the life of a neighbor's child.

This paragraph continues the discussion about the theme of love in *Anne of Green Gables*. It states another aspect of the thesis and offers supporting evidence.

In summary, the main body is another exceptionally important part of the whole essay. It is the place where writers give readers the information that the introduction promised.

PUBLIC SPEAKING TASK: THE MAIN BODY AND THE FIRSTHAND SPEECH

The main body of a speech typically includes two-three points with several sub-points. Each point must be supported by arguments or by illustrations, all of which add credibility to each point. What sort of supporting material should you use? Facts and examples of your argument/illustrations are the best choices. Quotes from authorities, analogies (i.e., comparisons between two different items), and narrative illustrations work well too. The following is a relatively lengthy body of the speech begun in the previous lesson. By this point, the author has inspired the audience, informed the audience about the purposes of the speech, and is now ready to present the main meal of the speech.

Identify several points the speaker is making.

SAMPLE SPEECH: MAIN POINTS

After we are broken, after we know who is truly in control, we commit ourselves to reality—no matter what the cost, no matter what that reality is.

Jacob was broken and then blessed. Jacob was a conniving, selfish scoundrel. He cheated his brother out of his birthright; he tricked his aging father in order to get the paternal blessing. Then, he had no alternative except to flee the inevitable, justifiable wrath of his brother.

But God had other adventures in store for His selfish saint. In Genesis 32, we see Jacob going home. On the way, he received word that his brother, Esau, was planning to meet him with 400 men. Jacob was justifiably scared. Therefore, he divided his party for safety, and then sent most of them ahead with gifts for appeasement. Coward that he was, he even sent his family in front of him so that they, too, might be a part of the buffer between him and his cheated brother.

However, Jacob *the supplanter* was about to run out of tricks. While Jacob waited alone that last night before he was finally to meet Esau, a man came into his campsite and began to wrestle with him. What was said or why the fight began we are not told, but we do know that Jacob's opponent was no ordinary man. Hosea 12:4 indicates that the stranger was an angel of God. In fact, Genesis, 32:30 intimates that the visitor may have been an angel or, perhaps, Jesus Christ—assuming the guise of a wrestler.

Jacob was about to learn another very important lesson: a mature person is someone who knows how to accept *necessary* suffering.

Whoever this strange visitor was, he represented God. Therefore, God literally wrestled with Jacob. Jacob had reached the end of his human rope—even though it had taken twenty years or more. He could not take another step in the kingdom until he was broken—broken of his scheming and selfishness.

Sometimes we must experience the death of a vision. Many times in our lives, we seem to have it all together. Our world applauds us as we say all the right things—perhaps even *do* all the right things. But our vision is flawed. It must die. Then it can be replaced by God's vision. We cannot accept the vision, the high calling, unless God has prepared us. (James Stobaugh)

In summary, the main body of a speech develops the heart of the rhetorical experience and justifies the time and energy expended by the audience in the listening process.

SPEECH ASSIGNMENT

Present a 2-3 minute firsthand experience speech on some experience that changed your life.

WRITING ASSIGNMENTS

1. Write a firsthand experience of a life-changing event. This subject essay/oration should be on two pages and include an outline with thesis statement, rough draft, several revisions, and final copy with five new (circled) vocabulary words. Give one copy to teacher/guardian/parent and one to your peer evaluator.

2. Read 35 to 50 pages each day and keep vocabulary cards.

3. Complete the speech assignment and have a teacher complete a speech evaluation form (Appendix).

4. Pay attention to your writing style this week. Specifically consider the main body of your essay and speech.

5. Using the devotional questions as a guide, write at least three journal entries. Reflect on 1 Kings in general. Pastor Ray Stedman argues (The Ray Stedman Library, http://www.pbc.org/dp/stedman/),

> The book of 1 Kings holds the secret of success in reigning over the kingdom of your life. It is the secret of learning to be submissive to the authority and dominion of God in your own life. In other words, man can never exercise dominion over his life unless he first subjects himself to the dominion of God.

Evaluate this statement and find evidence of your view from 1 Kings. Record your reflections in essay form.

6. Complete one warm-up essay every day.

FINAL PROJECT

Correct and rewrite all essays and place them in your Final Portfolio.

WARM-UP ESSAYS:

	DAY 1	DAY 2	DAY 3	DAY 4	DAY 5
Firsthand Experience Essays	Describe your mother's reaction to your bedroom.	Describe your first day of schooling.	Describe your dad's reaction to your statement, "I lost control of the car and hit a tree because I was stung by a bee."	Describe what your dad sounds like in the shower.	Describe your mom's reaction when she discovers that you used her favorite formal silverware knife to filet a goldfish.

SUGGESTED
Weekly *Implementation*

DAY 1	DAY 2	DAY 3	DAY 4	DAY 5
Write a Warm-up Essay.	Write a Warm-up Essay.	Write a Warm-up Essay.	Write a Warm-up Essay.	Write a Warm-up Essay.
Read 35-50 pages/day.	Read 35-50 pages/day.	Read 35-50 pages/day.	Read 35-50 pages/day.	Read 35-50 pages/day.
Find five new vocabulary words.	Find five new vocabulary words.	Find five new vocabulary words.	Find five new vocabulary words.	Find five new vocabulary words.
Reflect on the speech assignment for the week.	Compose a first draft of your speech.	Revise your speech and submit to your evaluator/ parent.	Prepare and practice to present your speech tomorrow.	Present your speech to a live audience.
Write an outline and thesis for your firsthand experience.	Complete the first draft for your firsthand experience.	Revise and complete the draft of your firsthand experience.	Finish the final copy of your firsthand experience.	Submit your assignments to your evaluator/ parent.
Make a journal entry.	Make a journal entry.	Make a journal entry.	Make a journal entry.	Submit a copy of your paper to a peer for evaluation.
				Make a journal entry.
				Take Lesson 4 Test

LESSON 5

WRITING SKILL: THE DESCRIPTIVE ESSAY

The descriptive essay describes a person, place, or thing.

In the age of media-mania, good old-fashioned prose description has taken a hit. We would much prefer to take a photograph of a sunset or to record a song by our favorite artist than to describe these things with prose. However, since the whole area of apologetics is at stake, it is critical that we maintain that skill. If we can't describe a sunset, then how do we expect to explain grace to an unsaved person?

SAMPLE DESCRIPTIVE ESSAY:

East Liberty is a mean, ungenerous place to most folks, but the bag-lady fit into a different category. A person has to be strong to survive and spirit-filled to be victorious. The East Liberty area of Pittsburgh is foreboding. Enterprising entrepreneurs have made drug dealing a growth industry. Prostitution is a close second but still seasonal industry.

A homeless bag-lady visited our inner city, almost ghettoized a corner almost every day. A harbinger of hope, committed to important traditions, she gently laid neatly cut one-inch squares of white bread under the blue and white sign that warned would-be villains that there was a "Neighborhood Watch" ubiquitously guarding our community.

Some said this lady was crazy. We whose stories are so complete and well rehearsed are suspicious of those with stories we do not know, or, if we know them, we cannot comprehend. She had no story. Or, at least she was not talking.

We wanted to know who this strange woman was. She offered us very few hints—a frayed L. L. Bean two-sizes-too-big ski jacket with "j" embroidered on the right front pocket. She stuffed her pockets with West Penn Hospital brochures entitled "Cancer—Students Can Survive!"

She came to church once a year. She never said anything, never told us her name. The old woman who wandered Friendship and Roup remained an anonymous citadel.

She loved to feed the birds. She guarded her pieces of bread from unscrupulous ants, barking blue jays, and mischievous school children. Her face was all seriousness—no hint of a smile. Her work was sacred and important, even if no one else thought so.

I thought her work was important. Even if I didn't know who she was—she accepted my friendly "hellos" with a suspicious frown—I appreciated this solitudinarian who brought bird song to a community muted by hard luck. Standing alone at our corner next to two abandoned buildings ravaged and neglected by time, the homeless bag-lady brought magnificence and hope to a community that desperately needed both.

(James P. Stobaugh)

WRITING STYLE: PARAGRAPH— CONCLUSION

Stopping a paragraph is much like stopping a bicycle: there are many different options—as long as one does not merely jump off the bicycle (abandon the paragraph). The conclusion will be discussed in greater depth later in this curriculum when we discuss the Research Paper. The conclusion is the final opportunity writers have to review a point, to emphasize an argument, or to summarize an issue; the conclusion is not an opportunity to introduce a new, undeveloped point, argument, or issue. The concluding sentence in a paragraph, or the concluding paragraph in a composition, has two important functions: to end the prose construction with grace and to reiterate or bring solution to previously discussed information.

Resist the temptation to use the conclusion to "preach." If you have not already wooed the reader to your position, a final emotional plea is insulting and useless. Stay focused on the purpose of the paper and logically draw a solution or conclusion.

One final personal note: many of us attended or attend schools whose faculty is not Christian. We want to take every opportunity to share the Gospel with them. However, in my opinion, the best way to do that is to write well, to argue well, and to show excellence in everything you do. While attending Vanderbilt University eons ago, I wrote a paper for an unbelieving professor entitled "The Mosaic Authorship of the Pentateuch." Nobody in the secular world thinks that Moses wrote the first five books of the Old Testament—in spite of the fact that Jesus Christ claimed that Moses wrote the Pentateuch. However, while the professor did not believe that Moses wrote the Pentateuch, he was so impressed that I wrote a persuasive paper arguing that position that he asked me to share more about my faith. I call that *apologetics*. Write well; argue well; speak well—and let the Holy Spirit take care of the rest.

PUBLIC SPEAKING SKILL: THE CONCLUSION

The conclusion of a speech offers more latitude than the conclusion of an essay. While most speeches conclude with some sort of final statement or summary, the persuasive speech (next lesson) usually ends with a call to action. Referencing a previously used image, metaphor, or story is one good way to end a speech. Another is to use a provocative quote from a credible witness. If you

can give a personal commitment in the final statement, then you have given the most credible witness that you can. Finally, whatever ending you choose, be sure that your final thoughts are specific, direct, and crystal clear.

SPEECH ASSIGNMENT: THE DESCRIPTIVE SPEECH

Present a two-three minute descriptive speech of a person who had a great impact on your maturation as a Christian. A descriptive speech must by definition be full of numerous and well-constructed descriptions. A descriptive speech normally describes its subject *ad nauseum*. You should look for numerous ways, with multiple metaphors, to help your reader grasp what/who you are describing.

The following is a description of a wrestling match I once saw with my grandfather:

SAMPLE DESCRIPTIVE SPEECH:

People of all shapes and sizes crowded in rows of bleachers surrounding a homemade canvas ring. The ring was set off by a high intensity light fastened from the ceiling by army issue parachute cord. My grandfather and I carefully tiptoed to our seat, avoiding discarded chewing tobacco and snuff juice.

To my seven-year-old eyes it was an amazing sight. Everyone was screaming and shouting and raucously happy. The bad guys were clearly bad and really mean—350 pound overweight Big Bad Hans with his undersized black trunks and equally small muscle shirt—sported chains and a Swastika tattooed on his left arm. And our hero—225 pound svelte Gorgeous George—blond hair, blue eyed, and wearing a red, white, and blue outfit—was even more impressive.

No one had to tell us that Big Bad Hans was evil incarnate and Gorgeous George was good. Hans walked around the ring growling at us, frowning, showing off. George, on the other hand, was suitably shy, smiling, and waving at the crowd.

The fight began. Big Bad Hans had no intentions of fighting cleanly. And, so, before long Gorgeous George was in big trouble. In fact, his head was bleeding profusely, and it appeared that Big Bad Hans had won.

The referee stood over the bloodied and unconscious Gorgeous George and began to count "One, two ..."

The crowd was furious. The bad guy was going to win! And he had done it unfairly!

But, before the referee counted "three," George suddenly shook his head and managed to stand. The fight was not over after all! (James Stobaugh)

The writer uses a seven-year-old interpreter to let the reader see and feel the evening when he watched the wrestling match. He used visual, tactile, olfactory, and sensory metaphors to bring the scene alive.

WRITING ASSIGNMENTS

1. In a two-page essay, describe a person who had a great impact on your maturation as a Christian. Emphasize the following elements of descriptive essays: Starting Point, Purpose, Form, Audience, Voice, and Point of View. This description essay should include an outline with thesis statement, rough draft, several revisions, and final copy with five new (circled) vocabulary words. Your essay must pay particular attention to style (focus, content, organization). Give a copy to your peer/friend to complete a peer evaluation form (Appendix) and to your instructor to evaluate.

2. Read a book from the reading list or a book assigned in your literature and/or history elective (or another approved book). Read at least 35/50 pages/day. Make vocabulary cards from words in your reading.

3. Present your speech and have a teacher evaluate it with a speech evaluation (Appendix).

4. Using the devotional questions as a guide, write at least three journal entries. This week meditate on 1 Kings 8:22–53. Record your reflections in essay form.

5. Complete one warm-up essay every day. The warm-up essay should be one page or less; it should not take more than one-half hour. The warm-ups do not need to be edited or rewritten. Over time you will become more comfortable with writing and will see improvement in your writing if you attend to revisions from carefully evaluated papers.

FINAL PROJECT

Correct and rewrite all essays and place them in your Final Portfolio.

WARM-UP ESSAYS:

	DAY 1	DAY 2	DAY 3	DAY 4	DAY 5
Descriptive	Describe a moment that changed your life.	Describe your best friend.	Describe the causes of World War I to a four-year old.	Describe the emotion *jealousy*.	Describe the sunset.

SUGGESTED
Weekly *Implementation*

DAY 1	DAY 2	DAY 3	DAY 4	DAY 5
Write a Warm-up Essay.	Write a Warm-up Essay.	Write a Warm-up Essay.	Write a Warm-up Essay.	Write a Warm-up Essay.
Read 35-50 pages/day.	Read 35-50 pages/day.	Read 35-50 pages/day.	Read 35-50 pages/day.	Read 35-50 pages/day.
Find five new vocabulary words.	Find five new vocabulary words.	Find five new vocabulary words.	Find five new vocabulary words.	Find five new vocabulary words.
Reflect on the speech assignment for the week.	Compose a first draft of your speech.	Revise your speech and submit to your evaluator/ parent.	Prepare to present your speech tomorrow.	Present your speech to a live audience.
Write an outline and thesis for his descriptive essay.	Work on the first draft for your descriptive essay.	Revise and finish the first draft of your descriptive essay.	Finish the final copy of your descriptive essay.	Submit your assignments to your evaluator/ guardian/ parent.
Make a journal entry.	Make a journal entry.	Make a journal entry.	Make a journal entry.	Submit a copy of your paper to a peer for evaluation.
				Make a journal entry.
				Take Lesson 5 Test

LESSON 6

Writing Skill: Persuasive vs. Coercive Essay

Style (Writing and Speaking): Paragraph—Unity and Coherence

Public Speaking Skill: Delivery (A) and Converting the Persuasive Essay to a Speech

Looking Ahead: The Persuasive Advertisement Essay (Writing) and Speech Delivery (B) (Speaking)

WRITING SKILL: DESCRIPTIVE VS. COERCIVE ESSAY

A persuasive essay persuades the reader to embrace a particular course of action. Its sole purpose is to persuade. The writer must not digress to write anything that does not advance that sole purpose. The following is the end of a speech on Isaiah 35. To what position is the author persuading the audience?

The really good news of Isaiah 35, and of the Gospel, is that as we—the chosen community, today the church—rejoice, grow healthy, and find ourselves living in Zion. So also will the land and those who live in it find hope, health, and wholeness. Health to the Jew, as it was to the Greek, means far more than physical health. It means healing, wholeness. Indeed, the Greek word *salvation* has at its root the word *health*. We are the light of the world, and we can change our world as we share the good news. The Christ whom we represent is the only real hope the world has for wholeness. And we should be outspoken and unequivocal with this message. As we sing, with our words and our lives, the land

will be saved, made whole. "Say to the faint–hearted: 'Be strong; do not fear! /...Then the eyes of the blind will be opened / and the ears of the deaf unstopped" (Is. 35:4-5).

Again, this was awfully good news to a community that faced the awful King Sennacherib. King Hezekiah, Uzziah's successor, was sorely tempted to trust in Egypt, but frankly, Isaiah in chapter 35 is making an offer that Hezekiah cannot refuse. Likewise, today, when we live a holy life, when we trust in God with faith and hope, the land in which we work and live becomes holy. In this God, of whom we bear witness with our words and lives, we, like the faithful Israelites, find wholeness, health, and life. This news is good news!

The speaker is asking the audience to accept the generalization that people find their wholeness and life in Jesus Christ alone.

When you write a persuasive essay, you are creating a paper that will prove a point, which will clarify an issue, and, in the process, perhaps change readers' opinions. You won't be able to change anyone's mind, however, until you think clearly about your topic. Using the *Thinking Game* (Lesson 1) is a very effective way to clarify your thinking. Talk to your teacher, parents, and friends about the topic. Ask these folks to respond to the position you are arguing. Finally, don't insult your readers by relying only on emotion. Clearly state your case with logic and reason propelling your purpose, not veiled threats, emotion, or fear.

The latter—persuasion by means of threats, emotion,

fear—is called *coercive persuasion*. There are times when this form of persuasion is legitimate. If you were writing an essay concerning the dangers of drug abuse, it would not be inappropriate to remind readers of the consequences of drug addiction, however gruesome the details might be. On the other hand, if you were arguing vigorously that soccer is the "all American sport" and someone should be arrested for playing another sport, you would be overstating your position and definitely in the inappropriate coercive camp.

What is, then, an appropriate coercive persuasive essay? Use facts, even emotional, disturbing facts, in appropriate ways to coerce readers in a persuasive essay. While you will want to be sensitive to your audience—it is true that cigarette smoking causes millions of deaths a year, but it might not be appropriate to present this fact to a grieving widow whose husband recently died of lung cancer—you are well within your rhetorical bounds to argue persuasively, coercively, for a controversial position—as long as you use indisputable facts to support your case.

STYLE (WRITING AND SPEAKING): PARAGRAPH—UNITY AND COHERENCE

A paragraph must evidence a strategy to convey information. You must not merely "hang out" between the topic sentence and conclusion and hope everything works out. You must project a clear arrangement of ideas—or coherence—in your paragraphs. The interior life of your paragraph is up to you, and you will need to plan it carefully.

You have several options. The purpose of your essay will determine your choices. You may choose to list details according to their importance to your topic. A paragraph in a <u>persuasive essay</u> would normally implement this organizing principle. For instance, if you were arguing for the importance of completing your chores every day, because you think this is the most important reason to do chores, you might suggest first that the completion of these chores is vital to the well-being of the community. And so forth.

In another essay paragraph, you may list details according to their occurrence in your topic. An <u>expository narrative</u> would normally employ this organizing principle. For instance, if you wrote an essay paragraph about how to bake a cake, you would need to mention that eggs should be placed in the batter before yeast if that is necessary to a successful cake. If you were disorganized in your paragraph arrangement, you would have a terrible cake.

Finally, in a <u>descriptive essay</u> in particular, you may choose to describe details according to their location in your setting. For instance, if you were describing a new car, you likely would not mention the color of the upholstery before you mentioned the outside color of the car.

You must intentionally organize your paragraph. Your subject matter will not automatically fall into organizational patterns.

PUBLIC SPEAKING: DELIVERY (A) AND CONVERTING THE PERSUASIVE ESSAY TO A SPEECH

Delivery of a speech is critical to its success. The old cliché is true—sometimes people cannot hear what we say because our appearance and behavior speak too loudly. Dress appropriately for the occasion. Claiming discomfort in a suit or dress is beside the point when you are presenting a formal speech to an audience. Move around enough to show life but not so much that your movement is distracting. Engage your audience through eye contact and appropriate voice inflection. Typically, you should stand straight with one foot slightly forward to naturally focus your attention toward the audience. Posture yourself accordingly.

What if there is a podium? Don't grab it like a steering wheel and don't swing it like a dance partner. Stand behind it, if you must; move beyond it, if you can. It is not there to block you from your audience. It is there to hold your notes. Period. Move away from it. The larger the room and audience, the more animated you should be. However, don't move so close to your first row audience that you invade their body space.

Practice controlling your facial expressions. For example, you should not be smiling while you are talking about death!

In most cases your physical actions and appearance will determine how long your audience will honor you with their attention. You can write and present a highly effective, inspired speech that can end in disappointment if your physical delivery is deficient.

SPEECH ASSIGNMENT: THE PERSUASIVE SPEECH VS. THE COERCIVE SPEECH

Present a three-minute coercive speech and persuasive speech on the same topic. A speech is based on an essay, but it is not an essay. There is immediacy in a speech that forces the presenter to be precise and economical in his language. In the speech introduction clarify the goal of the speech. What are you trying to accomplish? What action do you wish to have result from this speech? A cessation of a behavior? The origination of a behavior? What is your proposition? What does your audience need to believe to be persuaded to your position? Will you be able to provide the proof to accomplish this task?

WRITING ASSIGNMENTS

1. In American society today there is much discussion about the separation of church and state. The First Amendment to the Constitution of the United States of America reads: "Congress shall make no law respecting an establishment of religion, or prohibiting the free exercise thereof." Some people argue that "under God" in the Pledge of Allegiance is a violation of the First Amendment. They argue that this phrase moves beyond persuasiveness and becomes coercion. Write a one-two page essay arguing a position concerning this debate. This essay should include an outline with thesis statement, rough draft, several revisions, and a final copy with five new (circled) vocabulary words. The essay must pay particular attention to style (focus, content, organization). Give a copy to a peer/friend to complete a peer evaluation form (Appendix) and to you instructor for evaluation.

2. Read 200-250 pages/week and make vocabulary cards.

3. Complete the speech assignment and have a teacher complete a speech evaluation form (Appendix).

4. Pay particular attention to your writing style this week.

5. With the devotional questions as a guide, write at least three journal entries. Reflect on the story of Solomon and the Queen of Sheba (1 Kings 10:1–14). What are appropriate and inappropriate ways of interacting with nonbelievers? Record your reflections in essay form. This journal is meant to be private, but you are invited to share your reflections with others.

6. Write a warm-up essay every day.

FINAL PROJECT

Correct and rewrite all essays and place them in your Final Portfolio.

WARM-UP ESSAYS:

	DAY 1	DAY 2	DAY 3	DAY 4	DAY 5
Persuasive Essay	Persuade a friend to commit his life to Christ.	Persuade your parents to give you a BMW for your birthday.	Persuade your parents to release you from doing homework.	Persuade a toll-booth operator to forgive the toll because you dropped your last quarter down the back of the seat.	Persuade your parents to let you move into your college-bound older brother's room.

SUGGESTED
Weekly *Implementation*

DAY 1	DAY 2	DAY 3	DAY 4	DAY 5
Write a Warm-up Essay.	Write a Warm-up Essay.	Write a Warm-up Essay.	Write a Warm-up Essay.	Write a Warm-up Essay.
Read 35-50 pages/day.	Read 35-50 pages/day.	Read 35-50 pages/day.	Read 35-50 pages/day.	Read 35-50 pages/day.
Find five new vocabulary words.	Find five new vocabulary words.	Find five new vocabulary words.	Find five new vocabulary words.	Find five new vocabulary words.
Reflect on the speech assignment for the week.	Compose a first draft of your speech.	Revise your speech and submit to your evaluator/ parent.	Prepare to present your speech tomorrow.	Present your speech to a live audience.
Write an outline and thesis for your persuasive essay.	Work on the first draft for your persuasive essay.	Revise and finish the first draft of your persuasive essay.	Finish the final copy of your persuasive essay.	Submit your assignments to your evaluator/ parent.
Make a journal entry.	Make a journal entry.	Make a journal entry.	Make a journal entry.	Submit a copy of your paper to a peer for evaluation.
				Make a journal entry.
				Take Lesson 6 Test

LESSON 7

Transitions are created by mentioning a previous key word or expression in a new sentence or paragraph. Transitions are also created by using such words as *however, furthermore, in addition to, consequently, next, second,* etc. Notice the way transitions are used in the following piece:

SAMPLE ESSAY EMPHASIZING TRANSITIONS:

Born in a rambling clapboard house next to the city sewage, Mom always understood limitation and constraint. Her home sat on buckshot clay that cracked and buckled every summer. The smell of feces and mildew intensified every hot summer afternoon. Behind her house was a woodlot too often the victim of unscrupulous foresters. Enchanted trails and moss-covered paths that would pique the imagination of most children were compromised in my mother's forest by young locust trees unimpeded by shade and larger competition. Sunlight was everywhere abundant. Since there was no reason to grow up and clasp sunlight, the young trees grew outward and selfishly deprived all the pretty things in the forest of light and life.

The forest was hardly a forest at all—it was a tangle of bush-size trees. Since it was warm and dry on the western edge, cane rattlers loved to slither in the shadows from the deadly Arkansas summer sun. On the eastern edge, joining the sewage reservoir, moccasins hissed warnings at mockingbirds, snapping turtles, and inquisitive little girls. Early in life, my mother

WRITING SKILL: THE PERSUASIVE ADVERTISEMENT ESSAY

The most common persuasive writings concern advertisements. Advertisements commonly rely upon the three appeals of Aristotelian rhetoric to convey their message: logos, pathos, and ethos. Logos pertains to the logical cognitive function of the argument itself; pathos involves the emotion stirred up in the audience; and ethos concerns the credibility of the advertisement. Advertisements may not include all three appeals or draw equally from them, but they are present in the advertisement in one form or another.

STYLE (WRITING AND SPEAKING): PARAGRAPHS—TRANSITIONAL DEVICES

Effective transitions perform the critical task of joining parts of a speech or a piece of writing together.

Mentioning a word, phrase, or thought from the last sentence of the previous paragraph in the first sentence of the next paragraph is a one method to transition.

learned the advantages of limitation and constraint. She learned to measure each step carefully, always looking at what was in front of her, and controlling, as much as possible, where her next step would land.

However, not all snakes were my mother's enemies. One huge, black-and-red king snake, named Uncle Roy, lived under the old piano. Actually, the piano didn't carry a tune at all. Big Mama kept it around to house Uncle Roy. An aggressive king snake brought all sorts of advantages to my mother's family: mice were noticeably absent. And no moccasin would dare show his fangs! Occasionally Uncle Roy slept behind the family toilet during the summer

Two transitions: the word However, and the mention again of snakes from the previous paragraph.

and enjoyed the only cool place in Big Mama's house. This was even too much for Uncle Roy's most fervent supporters, and eventually he retreated to the back of the ice box—a true ice box, full of block ice from Mr. Badgett's ice house. The downside of having Uncle Roy in the family was the growth of a pervasive herpephobia that appeared in all my mother's clan.

(James P. Stobaugh)

PUBLIC SPEAKING: DELIVERY (B) AND CONVERTING THE PERSUASIVE ADVERTISEMENT ESSAY TO A SPEECH

The voice is to the speaker as the ink brush is to the artist or as the pencil is to the writer. The voice is a powerful ally to communicate the message—or it can be a terrible impediment. The speaker must be aware of the speed of the speech—not too fast but not too slow. The speaker must be aware of the volume of the speech—not too low but not too loud. Speak clearly and convincingly. Use pauses to emphasize the points and vary the rhythm in order to help keep the audience's attention. Speaking smoothly, steadily, and candidly earns the audience's respect.

Delivery of the speech is obviously critical to a persuasive advertisement speech. The advertisement speech should be composed and presented like any other persuasive speech; however the delivery is absolutely crucial. Also, the speaker is acutely aware that the message is cognitive (logos), emotional (pathos), and credible (ethos).

SOME KEYS TO EFFECTIVE SPEECH DELIVERY:

Tempo: an appropriate tempo—not too fast, not too slow

Eye contact: look at your audience—make eye contact, or at least appear to make eye contact

Clarity: enunciate plainly with voice tone appropriate to the subject

Body language: face the audience with one foot forward

Facial expressions: exhibit facial responses that match the subject

SPEECH ASSIGNMENT: THE PERSUASIVE ADVERTISEMENT SPEECH

Create a persuasive advertisement speech for your favorite vacation spot.

WRITING ASSIGNMENTS

1. Write a one-page persuasive advertisement essay for your favorite vacation spot. This essay should include an outline with thesis statement, rough draft, several revisions, final copy with five new (circled) vocabulary words. Pay particular attention to style

(focus, content, organization). Give a copy to a peer/friend to complete a peer evaluation form (Appendix) and to your instructor for evaluation.

2. Read 200-250 pages/week and make vocabulary cards.

3. Complete the speech assignment and have a teacher complete a speech evaluation form (Appendix).

4. Pay particular attention to your writing style this week.

5. Using the devotional questions as a guide, write at least three journal entries. Meditate on 1 Kings 11. Consider the consequences of Solomon's choice to marry many foreign, unbelieving wives. The purpose of many of these marriages was to create political alliances. The effect on his walk with God, however, was devastating. Record your reflections in essay form.

6. Write a warm-up essay every day.

FINAL PROJECT

Correct and rewrite all essays and place them in your Final Portfolio.

WARM-UP ESSAYS:

	DAY 1	DAY 2	DAY 3	DAY 4	DAY 5
Persuasive Advertisement	Create an advertisement for your favorite meal.	Create an advertisement for your favorite line of clothing.	Create an advertisement for your favorite sport.	Create an advertisement for your favorite musician.	Create an advertisement for your favorite novel.

SUGGESTED
Weekly *Implementation*

DAY 1	DAY 2	DAY 3	DAY 4	DAY 5
Write a Warm-up Essay.	Write a Warm-up Essay.	Write a Warm-up Essay.	Write a Warm-up Essay.	Write a Warm-up Essay.
Read 35-50 pages/day.	Read 35-50 pages/day.	Read 35-50 pages/day.	Read 35-50 pages/day.	Read 35-50 pages/day.
Find five new vocabulary words.	Find five new vocabulary words.	Find five new vocabulary words.	Find five new vocabulary words.	Find five new vocabulary words.
Reflect on the speech assignment for the week.	Compose a first draft of your speech.	Revise your speech and submit to your evaluator/ parent.	Prepare to present your speech tomorrow.	Present your speech to a live audience.
Write an outline and thesis for your persuasive essay.	Work on the first draft for your persuasive essay.	Revise and finish the first draft of your persuasive essay.	Finish the final copy of your persuasive essay.	Submit your assignments to your evaluator/ parent.
Make a journal entry.	Make a journal entry.	Make a journal entry.	Make a journal entry.	Submit a copy of your paper to a peer for evaluation.
				Make a journal entry.
				Take Lesson 7 Test

LESSON 8

WRITING SKILL: SUMMARY REPORT

A summary report is an abbreviated version of a written piece, nonfiction or fiction. Typically, the summary report avoids any value analysis of the piece's argumentation (as a précis would). However, if instructed to do so, you may use a summary report as the first step of serious literary or historical analysis.

What is the difference between a summary and a précis?

A PRÉCIS

The main point of the literary piece is succinctly stated in the first paragraph, if not in the first sentence of the précis.

> On a first reading of Mark Twain's *Huckleberry Finn*, the reader is tempted to conclude that Twain is writing a humorous happy-go-lucky narrative best read on the side of a tree-covered riverbank. Such a reading is appropriate, but this reading is by a novice, an adolescent, a lover of a frog-jumping contest and of a dangerous rendezvous with Injun Joe in an eerie graveyard. Unfortunately, the more astute, more mature laureates will recognize that Twain is really writing a scathing criticism of an earlier literary movement and worldview called Romanticism. The "Arkansaw" feud, for instance, shows Twain's complete disgust with Romanticism.

This beginning paragraph of a much larger précis overviews a significant theme of the novel without offering (at this time) much analysis of its value.

A SUMMARY

A summary, on the other hand, merely summarizes the plot, offers scant comment, and gives no analysis:

> *Huckleberry Finn*, by Mark Twain, is the story of a young Southerner and his attempts to

escape with a slave. The entire novel is the narration of this journey. . . .

STYLE (WRITING AND SPEAKING SKILL): SENTENCES—OVERVIEW

In their book *Prose Style: A Handbook for Writers* (NY: McGraw-Hill, 1972), 72-73), Wilfred Stone and J. G. Bell argue that good writers prefer verbs to nouns, the active voice to the passive voice, the concrete to the abstract, the personal to the impersonal, and the shorter to the longer.

When possible, use precise, clear verbs rather than a plethora of nouns however colorful they might be: "The causes of the Civil War are related to the combination of the failure of the political system and the expansion of slavery" is less effective to "Failure of the political system to deal with slavery expansion at least partially caused the Civil War."

Use the active voice: "The skunk stampeded the herd" (active voice) is better than "The herd was stampeded by the skunk" (passive voice).

Use concrete words: "The three-hour tragedy" is better than "The long play."

Use personal nouns: "East coast, classically-educated homeschoolers are doing well on the SAT I" is better than "homeschoolers are doing better on tests."

Finally, use shorter expressions when possible to avoid excess words: "I could do nothing to stop my car from hitting the bridge" is better than "There was nothing I could do to stop my car from hitting the bridge."

PUBLIC SPEAKING: OVERCOMING FEAR AND CONVERTING A SUMMARY ESSAY TO A SPEECH

Very few of us enjoy speaking in front of a large crowd— we will be nervous, naturally. How can we overcome this fear of exposure that numbs us and makes us dysfunctional? Knowing the material and knowing the speech is of first importance. The speech doesn't have to memorized; note cards (cue cards) or other props can help you. However, cue cards or props do not substitute for absolutely knowing what you need to say. Know the material well enough that a quick glance will remind you of what comes next in the speech. Be focused and deliberate in your preparation; practice orally delivering the speech several times until presentation day.

SPEECH ASSIGNMENT: SUMMARY SPEECH

In front of an audience, present a one-minute summary of your favorite book. A summary speech has an introduction, body, and a conclusion. It carefully highlights salient components of the book that make it a good book, or, in this case, your favorite book. Remember: a summary is an overview—not an analysis—of something. Your speech will include the following literary elements (Appendix): Plot, Theme, Characters, Setting, and Tone. When you present your speech, give particular attention to your delivery.

You will gain further confidence as you practice the speech out loud—not silently—if possible in the very room where you will present it.

Most importantly, though, pray. Prepare yourself. Memorize a Scripture verse and silently quote it to yourself as you prepare.

WRITING ASSIGNMENTS

1. Summarize your favorite book, being sure to include all aspects of a good summary. Remember: a summary is an overview—not an analysis—of something. Your essay will include the following literary elements (Appendix): Plot, Theme, Characters, Setting, and Tone. This expository essay should be a two-page essay and should include an outline with thesis statement, rough draft, several revisions, final copy with five new (circled) vocabulary words. Give one copy of your paper to your teacher/parent/guardian and one copy to your peer evaluator.

2. Read a book from the reading list or a book assigned in your literature and/or history elective (or another approved book). Read at least 35/50 pages/day. Make vocabulary cards from words in your reading.

3. Present your speech and have a teacher evaluate it with a speech evaluation form (Appendix).

4. Pay attention to your stylistic tendencies this week. Make a special effort to write precisely.

5. Using the devotional questions as a guide, write at least three journal entries. Students should reflect on 1 Kings 11:14-24. In this passage, God causes enemies to come against Solomon. Reflect on this fact and ask yourself, "Why?" Record your reflections in your prayer journal. This journal is meant to be private, but you are invited to share your reflections with others.

6. Complete a warm up essay every day.

FINAL PROJECT

Correct and rewrite all essays and place them in your Final Portfolio.

WARM-UP ESSAYS:

	DAY 1	DAY 2	DAY 3	DAY 4	DAY 5
Summary Report	Summarize a favorite book.	Summarize a recent sporting event.	Summarize a typical family Christmas.	Summarize a boring book.	Summarize your reaction to this course.

SUGGESTED
Weekly *Implementation*

DAY 1	DAY 2	DAY 3	DAY 4	DAY 5
Write a Warm-up Essay.	Write a Warm-up Essay.	Write a Warm-up Essay.	Write a Warm-up Essay.	Write a Warm-up Essay.
Read 35-50 pages/day.	Read 35-50 pages/day.	Read 35-50 pages/day.	Read 35-50 pages/day.	Read 35-50 pages/day.
Find five new vocabulary words.	Find five new vocabulary words.	Find five new vocabulary words.	Find five new vocabulary words.	Find five new vocabulary words.
Reflect on the speech assignment for the week.	Compose a first draft of your speech.	Revise your speech and submit to your evaluator/ parent.	Prepare to present your speech tomor-row.	Present your speech to a live audience.
Write an outline and thesis for your summary report.	Work on the first draft for your sum-mary report.	Revise and finish the first draft of your summary report.	Finish the final copy of your sum-mary report.	Submit your assign-ments to your eval-uator/ parent.
Make a journal entry.	Make a journal entry.	Make a journal entry.	Make a journal entry.	Submit a copy of your paper to a peer for evaluation.
				Make a journal entry.
				Take Lesson 8 Test

LESSON 9

WRITING TASK: PRÉCIS

One of the most important tasks before any reader is reading and understanding difficult books. Different kinds of books require different ways of reading. Difficult books that have layers of meaning require a much closer reading than books that do not. For instance, it would be foolish to look for deep meaning in Mark Twain's *Tom Sawyer*, but it would be an entirely different matter if a person were reading Marcus Aurelius' *Meditations*.

By now you are familiar with what is meant by a paraphrase, or a summary, that merely repeats the substance of the original passage in different and usually simpler language but in approximately the same space. Paraphrasing and summarizing are processes of substituting easy phrases for those that present difficulties. In other words, a paraphrase and a summary are merely restatements of what is in the text.

A précis often requires

1. *A rearrangement of ideas.* It is not longer than the original work, but it is more profound in its analysis of a literary work than is a summary. The précis writer must apprehend and assimilate the complete thought of the passage under discussion. When writers first begin to experiment with précis writing, missing the essential meaning of the text is common.

2. *A crystallization of the text* in a precise but profound way. A précis addresses intent as well as substance.

The creation of a précis, whether of a prose or verse passage, involves certain progressive steps that should be followed in a general way by every writer.

First of all, it is necessary to read the passage attentively and usually more than once, in an effort to grasp the central idea. This preliminary reading is concerned about details.

Often it helps to read the passage aloud, for such a procedure necessitates slowness and may focus attention on some item that would otherwise be missed. At this stage it is actually quite helpful to write a paraphrase or summary of the text. Only on the second reading does the reader ferret out thematic concepts and syllogisms.

Writing Skill: Précis.

Style (Writing and Speaking): Sentences—Emphasis

Public Speaking Skill: Presentation Aids (A) and Converting a Précis to a Speech

Looking Ahead: The Character Profile (Writing) and Presentation Aids (B) (Speaking)

3. Analysis—not moralizing or preaching. The sole purpose of précis writers is to interpret the author, not judge the author. Précis writers are not critics; they are interpreters. Frequently the interpretation of an important part of a passage, or of the passage as a whole, will depend upon the clear understanding of a single word or a phrase.

For instance, the refrain "Rode the Six Hundred" by Alfred, Tennyson Lord in "Charge of the Light Brigade" is critical to an understanding of the poem:

Half a league, half a league,
Half a league onward,
All in the valley of Death
Rode the six hundred.
'Forward, the Light Brigade!
Charge for the guns!' he said:
Into the valley of Death
Rode the six hundred.

'Forward, the Light Brigade!'
Was there a man dismay'd ?
Not tho' the soldier knew
Some one had blunder'd:
Their's not to make reply,
Their's not to reason why,
Their's but to do and die:
Into the valley of Death
Rode the six hundred.

Cannon to right of them,
Cannon to left of them,
Cannon in front of them
Volley'd and thunder'd;
Storm'd at with shot and shell,
Boldly they rode and well,
Into the jaws of Death,
Into the mouth of Hell
Rode the six hundred.

Flash'd all their sabres bare,
Flash'd as they turn'd in air
Sabring the gunners there,
Charging an army, while
All the world wonder'd:
Plunged in the battery-smoke
Right thro' the line they broke;
Cossack and Russian
Reel'd from the sabre-stroke
Shatter'd and sunder'd.
Then they rode back, but not
Not the six hundred.

Cannon to right of them,
Cannon to left of them,
Cannon behind them

Volley'd and thunder'd;
Storm'd at with shot and shell,
While horse and hero fell,
They that had fought so well
Came thro' the jaws of Death,
Back from the mouth of Hell,
All that was left of them,
Left of six hundred.

When can their glory fade?
O the wild charge they made!
All the world wonder'd.
Honour the charge they made!
Honour the Light Brigade,
Noble six hundred!
(http://www.bartleby.com/246/386.html)

The refrain "Rode the six hundred" evolves into "Left of six hundred" and then to "Noble six hundred" and is a critical phrase used in the poem. Its purpose and affect on the substance and theme of the poem is central to understanding the poem. Therefore, a précis would address this element.

A skillful précis writer is on the alert for the meanings and suggestions of individual words and phrases. If they cannot be caught from the context, the dictionary should be consulted. Especially in poetry précis writers carefully examine all figures of speech to determine precisely what they clarify or illustrate. In the T.S. Eliot poem, "Hippopotamus," the Church is compared to an unlikely metaphor: a Hippopotamus!

The broad-backed hippopotamus
Rests on his belly in the mud;
Although he seems so firm to us
He is merely flesh and blood.

Hippopotamus
(about 13 ft. long)

Flesh-and-blood is weak and frail,
Susceptible to nervous shock;
While the True Church can never fail
For it is based upon a rock.

The hippo's feeble steps may err
In compassing material ends,
While the True Church need never stir
To gather in its dividends.

The 'potamus can never reach
The mango on the mango-tree;
But fruits of pomegranate and peach
Refresh the Church from over sea.

© Arttoday.com

At mating time the hippo's voice
Betrays inliexions hoarse and odd,
But every week we hear rejoice
The Church, at being one with God.

The hippopotamus's day
Is passed in sleep; at night he hunts;
God works in a mysterious way-
The Church can sleep and feed at once.

I saw the 'potamus take wing
Ascending from the damp savannas,
And quiring angels round him sing
The praise of God, in loud hosannas.

Blood of the Lamb shall wash him clean
And him shall heavenly arms enfold,
Among the saints he shall be seen
Performing on a harp of gold.

He shall be washed as white as snow,
By all the martyr'd virgins kiss,
While the True Church remains below
Wrapt in the old miasmal mist.
(http://www.classicreader.com/read.php/sid.1/bookid.8
   /sec.8/)

PREPARATION OF THE PRÉCIS

Précis writers take notes as they read the passage and then are ready to begin. Readers who will become précis writers will not merely copy sentences verbatim from the passage. A précis is not a smaller version of the text; it is itself a new creation.

Last of all, précis writers examine their creation and correct it in the light of the original, pruning it of extraneous or useless language, and making sure that it truly reproduces the intent of the author. Usually a précis should be from one-quarter to one-third the length of the original, but no inflexible rule can be laid down. In summary, précis writers meet the author halfway: While précis writers may vehemently reject the world-view of the author, they dispassionately must understand the author's point of view. Précis writers analyze; they do not moralize or preach. Their sole purpose is to interpret the author—not judge the author. Précis writers are not critics; they are interpreters.

Précis writers may be surprised at the commitment of time and effort their task requires. However, it is well worth the effort. Writing an effective précis demonstrates the fundamentals of literary criticism and great skill beneficial throughout academic life.

STYLE (WRITING AND SPEAKING SKILL): SENTENCE—EMPHASIS

Typically, write sentences that are very simple: Subject-Verb-Object. At times, though, let your rhetorical wings fly out and soar with the eagles! Experience with lots of writing in lots of genres with lots of effective evaluation informs the writer when to soar and when to remain simple. Remember: shorter is better with precision above all. Having said that, the way you craft words will determine the effectiveness of some words. After all, writers can only change the position of words and the punctuation of our sentences to gain emphasis. For example, the sentence "John, please make your bed" is much different from "John Smith, make your bed right now, or you will lose the privilege of having a bed!" Emphasis is a powerful tool in the hand of a skillful writer.

Emphasis is also a very dangerous tool. The young writer typically has a penchant to use too many coordinating and subordinating conjunctions. As one scholar warns, "Sentences of this form have neither the potential

> The précis writer analyzes; he does not moralize or preach. His sole purpose is to interpret the author, not judge the author. He is not a critic; he is an interpreter.

elegance and strength of the simple sentence nor the possibilities of emphasis afforded by the complex sentence. They have an inherently boring symmetry." Many of us would rather stay uncommitted in our writing: the compound sentence is a wonderful way to cover all the angles of an issue without committing oneself to any position. "The Romans lost Britain to the barbarians and the barbarians were too strong to conquer" is a lazy way to express this idea "The undermanned Roman army lost Britain to the aggressive barbarians."

Check compound sentences to determine if there really is a legitimate connection. "Mary went to Phoenix, Arizona, but David really likes to paint" is confusing and an example of improperly connected sentences. There is no obvious connection between Mary's trip and David's painting. Creating two separate statements is a better option in this case.

PUBLIC SPEAKING TASK: PRESENTATION AIDS (A)

Presentation aids—especially the PowerPoint © presentation—are useful and even expected in some presentations (e.g., business presentations). If you are using PowerPoint ©, be very careful to maintain eye contact with the audience as you make the presentation. Moving beyond the podium and walking more generally into your audience may be necessary but awkward unless you have a hand controller to move the presentation forward. Never allow the aid to detract from the content of the speech or the presentation.

SPEECH ASSIGNMENT: CONVERTING THE PRÉCIS ESSAY TO A SPEECH

Convert a précis of your favorite book into a speech. Remember, in your speech, you will need to follow the same guidelines established in the "Writing Skills" section of this lesson. A précis speech is based on a précis manuscript. Identify the salient points of your favorite book and emphasize them. For example, if you were presenting a précis speech on "Charge of the Light Brigade," you would be wise to memorize the refrain and maintain eye contact with your audience as you repeat phrases from it numerous times. It would also allow you to catch your thoughts as you progress through the speech.

WRITING ASSIGNMENTS

1. Write a précis of your favorite book, being sure to include all aspects of a good précis. This subject essay should be on two pages and include an outline, rough draft, thesis statement, final copy, and five new (circled) vocabulary words. Give one copy of your paper to your teacher/parent/guardian and one copy to your peer evaluator.

2. Read 35–50 pages each day and keep vocabulary cards. Finish reading your first literary work.

3. Complete the speech assignment and have a teacher complete a speech evaluation form (Appendix).

4. Pay attention to sentence emphasis in your essay and speech.

5. Using the devotional questions as a guide, write at least three journal entries. This week reflect on 1 Kings in general. Man can never exercise dominion over his life unless he first subjects himself to the dominion of God. Evaluate this statement and find evidence for your view from 1 Kings. Record your reflections in essay form.

6. Complete one warm-up essay every day.

FINAL PROJECT

Correct and rewrite all essays and place them in your Final Portfolio.

WARM-UP ESSAYS:

	DAY 1	DAY 2	DAY 3	DAY 4	DAY 5
Précis	Write a précis of your favorite song.	Write a précis of your favorite movie.	Write a précis of your favorite book.	Write a précis of a boring book.	Write a précis of a sermon you heard.

SUGGESTED
Weekly *Implementation*

DAY 1	DAY 2	DAY 3	DAY 4	DAY 5
Write a Warm-up Essay.	Write a Warm-up Essay.	Write a Warm-up Essay.	Write a Warm-up Essay.	Write a Warm-up Essay.
Read 35-50 pages/day.	Read 35-50 pages/day.	Read 35-50 pages/day.	Read 35-50 pages/day.	Read 35-50 pages/day.
Find five new vocabulary words.	Find five new vocabulary words.	Find five new vocabulary words.	Find five new vocabulary words.	Find five new vocabulary words.
Reflect on the speech assignment for the week.	Compose a first draft of your speech.	Revise your speech and submit to your evaluator/ parent.	Prepare to present your speech tomorrow.	Present your speech to a live audience.
Write an outline and thesis for your précis.	Work on the first draft for your précis.	Revise and finish the first draft of your précis.	Finish the final copy of your précis.	Submit your assignments to your evaluator/ parent.
Make a journal entry.	Make a journal entry.	Make a journal entry.	Make a journal entry.	Submit a copy of your paper to a peer for evaluation.
				Make a journal entry.
				Take Lesson 9 Test

LESSON 10

BACKGROUND

In a character profile, writers highlight the salient components of a person's life. They not only describe the physical appearance of the character, they also offer personality insights.

SAMPLE CHARACTER PROFILE:

While taking a break from my nervous Saturday night sermon review, I discovered my wife holding up to our dull attic light an archaic, but still beautiful, silver Barbie doll dress. Karen, my wife for almost fifteen years, was carefully unpacking her 1960 Barbie dolls.

"Lord," she hopefully prayed, "please don't let Jessica think these clothes are corny."

Some of these 1950ish out-of-style clothes would be part of one of my daughter's Christmas presents. With four children to purchase gifts for, Karen and I found Christmas shopping to be a painful experience. My Scottish wife never hesitated to explore creative alternatives to huge post-Christmas Visa bills. . . .

Writing Skill: The Character Profile

Style (Writing and Speaking): Sentences—Expanding Sentences

Public Speaking Skill: Presentation Aids (B) and Converting a Character Profile to a Speech

Looking Ahead: The General Analysis Essay (Writing)

I owe this woman so much, I thought to myself. (James P. Stobaugh)

WRITING STYLE: SENTENCES— EXPANDING SENTENCES

An accomplished writer should be able to expand a basic idea with a myriad of vital images and descriptions. Specifically, there are two ways to expand sentences: with cumulative sentences and with details.

Challenge: Contrast the following two paragraphs. Which one is more effective? Why?

1. The pavilion was full of happy children. They were laughing and playing. There was one man who was unhappy, though. He was crying.

2. Across the parking lot, competing with the screams from the adjoining Big Top, children could be heard laughing for at least fifty yards. As I moved closer, however, I saw a peculiar sight: a fat, aging man was crying. In his hand was a picture of a child and a woman. Behind them was the same Big Top, laughing with this frivolous juvenile multitude.

Sometimes shorter is better; however, in the above examples the second, longer passage is much better than the shorter version. Using vivid details and precise language, the second passage is much better than the first passage. The second sentence is an expanded detailed version of the first sentence. The writer develops the paragraph by expanding the details.

Challenge: Consider the following sets of sentences.

Sentences contain words in a series: *The old man was tired, sick, and lost.*

Sentences are combined using relative pronouns: *The old man, who was tired, was also sick and lost.*

Sentences are combined with an appositive or appositive phrase: *The old man, sick and tired, was also lost.*

PUBLIC SPEAKING: PRESENTATION AIDS (B) AND CONVERTING A CHARACTER PROFILE TO A SPEECH

In summary, when using any sort of presentation aids, practice using them before the presentation. This is critical in order to check for failure of equipment and to prevent lack of information for operating the equipment. Make sure the presentation aids are large enough and attractive enough. When working with Power-Point© remember that "less is more." Do not cut and paste large amounts of material for slides. Keep it simple. Finally, for dramatic effect and to prevent distraction, turn off audio-visual equipment when you are not using it.

At their heart, character profile speeches are descriptive essays. The presenter's job is to make characters come alive.

SPEECH ASSIGNMENT: CHARACTER PROFILE

In front of an audience, present a character profile of a close friend.

WRITING ASSIGNMENTS

1. Write a character profile of a close friend. Your essay should include an outline, rough draft, thesis statement, final copy, and five new (circled) vocabulary words. Pay particular attention to style (focus, content, organization). Give a copy to your peer/friend to complete a peer evaluation form (Appendix) and to your instructor for evaluation.

2. Read 35 to 50 pages each day and keep vocabulary cards.

3. Complete the speech assignment and have a teacher complete a speech evaluation (Appendix).

4. Pay attention to your stylistic tendencies.

5. Review 1 Kings 1–17 and reflect upon what God has taught you thus far.

6. Complete one warm up essay every day.

FINAL PROJECT

Correct and rewrite all essays and place them in your Final Portfolio.

WARM-UP ESSAYS:

	DAY 1	DAY 2	DAY 3	DAY 4	DAY 5
Character Profiles	Write a character profile of yourself.	Write a character profile of your pastor.	Write a character profile of your pet.	Write a character profile of a sibling.	Write a character profile of your grandmother.

SUGGESTED
Weekly *Implementation*

DAY 1	DAY 2	DAY 3	DAY 4	DAY 5
Write a Warm-up Essay. Read 35-50 pages/day. Find five new vocabulary words. Reflect on the speech assignment for the week. Write an outline and thesis for your character profile. Make a journal entry.	Write a Warm-up Essay. Read 35-50 pages/day. Find five new vocabulary words. Compose a first draft of your speech. Work on the first draft for your character profile. Make a journal entry.	Write a Warm-up Essay. Read 35-50 pages/day. Find five new vocabulary words. Revise your speech and submit to your evaluator/ parent. Revise and finish the first draft of your character profile. Make a journal entry.	Write a Warm-up Essay. Read 35-50 pages/day. Find five new vocabulary words. Prepare to present your speech tomorrow. Finish the final copy of your character profile. Make a journal entry.	Write a Warm-up Essay. Read 35-50 pages/day. Find five new vocabulary words. Present your speech to a live audience. Submit your assignments to your evaluator/ parent. Submit a copy of your paper to a peer for evaluation. Make a journal entry. Take Lesson 10 Test

LESSON 11

BACKGROUND

Analysis is a higher-level thinking process. To analyze a problem is to take it apart and understand its parts. Analysis identifies patterns in data and separates parts as a means of recognizing heretofore hidden meanings. Analysis thinking also identifies different meanings of the data. The following is an analysis of the causes of racism:

SAMPLE ANALYSIS ESSAY:

One hundred and thirty-three years after the Emancipation Proclamation, thirty years after the civil rights victories of the 1960's, there seems to be as much anger, misunderstanding, and disagreement among the races as there ever was. Blacks are fighting whites; Asians are killing blacks, and Hispanics are persecuting Asians. The motivation is anger, recrimination, unforgiveness, and despair. Little has been as enduring and damaging to the American nation as racial anger, similar to the time the first black slave stepped into Jamestown in 1619.

There exists in America a "paradox of pluralism": The American people in a nation of diversity remain ambivalent about the value of pluralism. From this tension flows the essence of the American character. Pluralism is both our greatest strength and our greatest weakness. Everyone celebrates our diversity, but no one knows how to live with it. The degree to which Christians deal with the problem of pluralism will determine the church's relevancy as a viable American institution. Indeed, the very survival of American civilization may be determined by how well the American church deals with racial issues. If there is no peace among races in the church, there will be no peace in America.

The American church must overcome many obstacles before widespread racial reconciliation can occur. The first and most challenging obstacle is racial anger.

(James P. Stobaugh)

Writing Skill: The General Analysis Essay (Writing)

Style (Writing and Speaking): Sentences—Writing Complete Sentences

Public Speaking Skill: Converting a General Analysis Essay into a Speech.

Looking Ahead: The General Synthesis Essay (Writing)

WRITING STYLE: SENTENCES—WRITING COMPLETE SENTENCES

With few exceptions, use complete sentences when you write. Avoid fragments, comma splices, run-on sentences, and rambling sentences. You will be tempted to write in fragments for the sake of emphasis. Rarely is that acceptable in academic writing.

Generally speaking, at this level, most of you know how to write complete sentences. Avoid the tendency to use fragments for emphasis except in rare instances. If there is a need to use a sentence fragment, do so with little fanfare. Do not call attention to the fragment by italics or any other unusual punctuation. The following are examples where sentence fragments may be acceptable:

RARE USE OF A FRAGMENT FOR EMPHASIS:

1. . . . And, among our own, Evangelical Professor Mark Noll unkindly observed, "The scandal of the evangelical mind is that there is not much of an evangelical mind." Indeed. Not anymore. Today, more than

Analysis means to classify, to divide, to edit, to compare, to contrast, to tell why, to map, to examine.

ever, in the garb of Christian home-schooling, Evangelicalism has gained new life.

2. Another time when a sentence fragment might be acceptable is when you ask a question and then answer it for emphasis. "Was I upset?" "Of course!" would be a sentence fragment example that is acceptable when used infrequently.

COMMA SPLICE (FUSED SENTENCE):

Commas splices occur when two or more sentences are incorrectly connected with only a comma or with only a conjunction:

"Writing poetry is my favorite, writing prose is okay too." Notice the use of the *comma without a conjunction*.

"Writing poetry is my favorite **but** writing prose is okay too." Notice the use of the *conjunction without a comma*.

"Writing poetry is my favorite**, but** writing prose is okay too." Notice the use of the *conjunction **and** the comma*. Since this example has two complete sentences being used together, they should be joined with a *comma **and** a conjunction*. With out the *comma **and** the conjunction*, the two sentences are fused together into one—incorrect mechanical construction.

ABBREVIATING SENTENCES:

Sentences may exceed their natural, useful life and may need to be shortened into two sentences, or they may need to be omitted entirely. "Slavery expansion caused the Civil War, but the Second Great Awakening and the ineffectual political process and reform movement exacerbated the situation" is too entangled. Readers forget the main point of the sentence before they finish reading it. Practice breaking this sentence down into two or three more effective sentences.

PUBLIC SPEAKING: CONVERTING A GENERAL ANALYSIS ESSAY INTO A SPEECH

You will need to analyze a problem or situation for an analysis speech. In Job 4 Eliphaz the Temanite analyzes Job's problems. He utilizes a time-honored technique commonly employed in analysis speeches: rhetorical questions. A rhetorical question states obvious truth—it is the kind of question that does not need an actual answer. A rhetorical question is used for per-

suading someone of a truth without the use of argument or to give emphasis to a supposed truth by ironically stating its opposite. For example, Temaninte asks Job, "Consider now: Who, being innocent, has ever perished? Where were the upright ever destroyed?" Additionally, rhetorical questioning is often used for comic effect as in Shakespeare's *Henry IV, Part 1*, 1597, (http://www.classicreader.com/booktoc.php/sid.5/book id.807/) when Falstaff lies about fighting off eleven men single-handedly, then responds to the prince's doubts, "Art thou mad? Is not the truth the truth?"

"If someone ventures a word with you, will you be
     impatient?
But who can keep from speaking?
Think how you have instructed many,
how you have strengthened feeble hands.
Your words have supported those who stumbled;
you have strengthened faltering knees.
But now trouble comes to you, and you are discour-
     aged;
it strikes you, and you are dismayed.
Should not your piety be your confidence
and your blameless ways your hope?

"Consider now: Who, being innocent, has ever per-
     ished?
Where were the upright ever destroyed?
As I have observed, those who plow evil
and those who sow trouble reap it.
At the breath of God they are destroyed;
at the blast of his anger they perish.
The lions may roar and growl,
Yet the teeth of the great lions are broken.
The lion perishes for lack of prey,
and the cubs of the lioness are scattered.

"A word was secretly brought to me,
my ears caught a whisper of it.
Amid disquieting dreams in the night,
when deep sleep falls on men,
	fear and trembling seized me
and made all my bones shake.
A spirit glided past my face,
and the hair on my body stood on end.
It stopped,
but I could not tell what it was.
A form stood before my eyes,
and I heard a hushed voice:
'Can a mortal be more righteous than God?
Can a man be more pure than his Maker?
If God places no trust in his servants,
if he charges his angels with error,
	how much more those who live in houses of clay,
whose foundations are in the dust,
who are crushed more readily than a moth!
Between dawn and dusk they are broken to pieces;
unnoticed, they perish forever. Are not the cords of
	their tent pulled up,
so that they die without wisdom?'"

SPEECH ASSIGNMENT

Give a three-minute analysis speech where you compare each family member to an animal. In your speech, employ as many rhetorical questions as you can.

ASSIGNMENTS

1. Analyze your family by comparing each family member to an animal. Carefully defend your choice. This essay should include an outline, rough draft, thesis statement, final copy, and five new (circled) vocabulary words. The essay must pay particular attention to style (focus, content, organization). Give a copy to your peer/friend to complete a peer evaluation form (Appendix) and to your instructor for evaluation.

2. Read 35 to 50 pages each day and keep vocabulary cards.

3. Complete the speech assignment and have a teacher complete a speech evaluation (Appendix).

4. Pay attention to your stylistic tendencies this week.

5. According to 1 Kings 16:30, "Ahab son of Omri did what was evil in the Lord's sight more than all who were before him." Why would the prophet say such an awful thing about King Ahab? Record your reflections in your prayer journal. This journal is meant to be private, but you are invited to share your reflections with others.

6. Complete one warm-up essay every day.

FINAL PROJECT

Correct and rewrite all essays and place them in your Final Portfolio.

WARM-UP ESSAYS:

	DAY 1	DAY 2	DAY 3	DAY 4	DAY 5
Analysis:	Analyze why your room is so messy.	Analyze the way one should eat a piece of pie.	Analyze the causes of your father's baldness.	Analyze one of your pastor's sermons.	Analyze the way your mother handles stress.

SUGGESTED
Weekly *Implementation*

DAY 1	DAY 2	DAY 3	DAY 4	DAY 5
Write a Warm-up Essay.	Write a Warm-up Essay.	Write a Warm-up Essay.	Write a Warm-up Essay.	Write a Warm-up Essay.
Read 35-50 pages/day.	Read 35-50 pages/day.	Read 35-50 pages/day.	Read 35-50 pages/day.	Read 35-50 pages/day.
Find five new vocabulary words.	Find five new vocabulary words.	Find five new vocabulary words.	Find five new vocabulary words.	Find five new vocabulary words.
Reflect on the speech assignment for the week.	Compose a first draft of your speech.	Revise your speech and submit to your evaluator/ parent.	Prepare to present your speech tomorrow.	Present your speech to a live audience.
Write an outline and thesis for your analysis essay.	Work on the first draft for your analysis essay.	Revise and finish the first draft of your analysis essay.	Finish the final copy of your analysis essay.	Submit your assignments to your evaluator/ parent.
Make a journal entry.	Make a journal entry.	Make a journal entry.	Make a journal entry.	Submit a copy of your paper to a peer for evaluation.
				Make a journal entry.
				Take Lesson 11 Test

LESSON 12

BACKGROUND

Whenever you report to a friend the things other friends have said about a movie or your pastor's sermon, you engage in synthesis. We synthesize information naturally to understand the connections between things; for example, you have probably stored up a mental databank of your favorite ice cream flavors. You access that data bank every time you visit an ice cream parlor. Synthesis is related to division, classification, or comparison. Instead of finding similarities and differences, synthesizing information is a matter of pulling them together into some kind of perceivable unity. In a way, all your writing is an exercise in synthesis. Synthesis searches for links between information for the purpose of constructing a thesis. It classifies, divides, and compares, and then distills the information into a thesis or purpose statement. Synthesis is a higher-level thinking process. To synthesize a problem is to put things together in another way. The following is a synthesis statement of the Stobaugh family mission.

SAMPLE FAMILY MISSION STATEMENT:

We are called to live radical Christian lives as if we belong to God and not to ourselves (Galatians 2:20). Therefore, we will seek the Lord with all our heart—knowing He will be found. We will have a heart for the lost. He has given us the ministry of reconciliation; indeed, our family is an image of this reconciliation (Romans 8; 2 Corinthians 5). We will be His ambassadors. He has given us a family to rear and people to influence for Him. We want to be world changers. The job(s) to which God has called us is requiring all we have, and it is worthy of our best and total efforts.

We will rear our four children to be world changers. We want them to accept this mission statement, and we want them to discern the times.

Pastoring, writing, lecturing, teaching—all are related to the above-mentioned mission statement.

Henceforth, the Stobaughs will make decisions based on this mission statement—not on circumstances.

Writing Skill: The General Synthesis Essay (Writing)

Style (Writing and Speaking): Sentences—Writing Clear Sentences

Public Speaking Skill: Converting a General Synthesis Essay into a Speech.

Looking Ahead: The General Evaluation Essay (Writing)

Synthesis means to combine, to speculate, to invent, to develop, to propose, to blend, to imagine, to predict.

Every new job or activity must further this mission statement or be rejected.

WRITING STYLE: SENTENCES—WRITING CLEAR SENTENCES

Students should avoid incomplete comparisons, ambiguous wording, indefinite references, misplaced modifiers, and dangling modifiers. Here are some examples:

Incomplete Comparison
> *My home is like an eighteen wheeler.* (incorrect)
> *Full of frenetic activity, my home proceeds through time like an eighteen-wheeler.* (correct)

Indefinite Reference
> *The soldier fought in the war.* (incorrect).
> *The union soldier fought in the Civil War.* (correct)

Misplaced Modifier
> *The man drove by a horse near the barn down the road.* (incorrect)
> *The man drove his car near a horse standing by the barn.* (correct)

Dangling Modifier

Standing in the rain four hours, the bus finally came. (incorrect)

After I stood in the rain for four hours, the bus finally came. (correct)

PUBLIC SPEAKING: CONVERTING A SYNTHESIS ESSAY TO A SYNTHESIS SPEECH

A synthesis speech accurately reports information about a topic using different phrases and sentences. It is organized in such a way that listeners can immediately see where the information overlaps. It defines and interprets the topic and enables the listener to understand the topic in greater depth.

The following is a synthesis essay/speech by the French author Victor Hugo, who discusses the purpose of drama by discussing all the elements that combine to make it drama.

SAMPLE SYNTHESIS ESSAY/SPEECH:

It seems to us that someone has already said that the drama is a mirror wherein nature is reflected. But if it be an ordinary mirror, a smooth and polished surface, it will give only a dull image of objects, with no relief—faithful, but colourless; everyone knows that colour and light are lost in a simple reflection. The drama, therefore, must be a concentrating mirror, which, instead of weakening, concentrates and condenses the coloured rays, which makes of a mere gleam a light, and of a light a flame. Then only is the drama acknowledged by art.

The stage is an optical point. Everything that exists in the world—in history, in life, in man—should be and can be reflected therein, but under the magic wand of art. Art turns the leaves of the ages, of nature, studies chronicles, strives to reproduce actual facts (especially in respect to manners and peculiarities, which are much less exposed to doubt and contradiction that are concrete facts), restores what the chroniclers have lopped off, harmonises what they have collected, divines and supplies their omissions, fills their gaps with imaginary scenes which have the colour of the time, groups what they have left scattered about, sets in motion anew the threads of Providence which work the human marionettes, clothes the whole with a form at once poetical and natural, and imparts to it that vitality of truth and brilliancy which gives birth to illusion, that prestige of reality which arouses the enthusiasm of the spectator,

and of the poet first of all, for the poet is sincere. Thus the aim of art is almost divine: to bring to life again if it is writing history, to create if it is writing poetry.

It is a grand and beautiful sight to see this broad development of a drama wherein art powerfully seconds nature; of a drama wherein the plot moves on to the conclusion with a firm and unembarrassed step, without diffuseness and without undue compression; of a drama, in short, wherein the poet abundantly fulfills the multifold object of art, which is to open to the spectator a double prospect, to illuminate at the same time the interior and the exterior of mankind: the exterior by their speech and their acts, the interior, by asides and monologues; to bring together, in a word, in the same picture, the drama of life and the drama of conscience.

(Victor Hugo, "Preface to Cromwell," 1827 www.Bartleby.com/39/40.html)

SPEECH ASSIGNMENT

While attending a local state university, you have written a very impressive paper entitled "A Case for the Mosaic Authorship of the Pentateuch." Your unbelieving professor is so impressed that he wants to speak to you privately. You recognize this invitation as an opportunity to share the Gospel with this professor. Write a three-minute synthesis speech organizing and presenting evidence for the Mosaic authorship of the Pentateuch.

WRITING ASSIGNMENTS

1. Last year almost a million plus Evangelical Christians graduated from high school. Many of them have gone to college and will become the next generation of leaders. Speculate about what effect this influx of graduates will have on American society and culture. This essay should include an outline with thesis statement, rough draft, revised draft, final copy, and five new (circled) vocabulary words. Pay particular attention to style (focus, content, organization). Give a copy to a peer/friend to complete a peer evaluation form (Appendix) and to your instructor to evaluate.

2. Read 200 to 250 pages this week and find vocabulary words.

3. Complete the speech assignment and have a teacher complete a speech evaluation (Appendix).

4. In 1 Kings 18:9, Obadiah said, "What sin have I committed, that you are handing your servant over to Ahab to put me to death? Meditate on this passage and others. Has God ever asked you to do something that

has put you into a place of danger? This journal is meant to be private, but you are invited to share your reflections with others.

5. Pay particular attention to your writing style this week. Watch for shifts in agreement between nouns and verbs and between pronouns and their antecedents.

6. Write a warm-up essay every day. As you experience the daily writing, you should see improvement in your ability to express your thoughts on paper. This daily writing is preparation for composing effective essays.

FINAL PROJECT

Correct and rewrite all essays and place them in your Final Portfolio.

WARM-UP ESSAYS:

	DAY 1	DAY 2	DAY 3	DAY 4	DAY 5
Synthesis	Create a new game by combining baseball and hockey.	Create a solution to your sister's/brother's long times in the bathroom.	Create a solution to your mother's/father's insistence that students eat broccoli.	Create an alternative solution to the rule that students cannot watch TV on school nights.	Create a nonviolent video game that would sell.

SUGGESTED
Weekly *Implementation*

DAY 1	DAY 2	DAY 3	DAY 4	DAY 5
Prayer journal.	**Prayer journal.**	**Prayer journal.**	**Prayer journal.**	**Prayer journal.**
Write a Warm-up Essay.	Write a Warm-up Essay.	Write a Warm-up Essay.	Write a Warm-up Essay.	Write a Warm-up Essay.
Read 35-50 pages/day.	Read 35-50 pages/day.	Read 35-50 pages/day.	Read 35-50 pages/day.	Read 35-50 pages/day.
Find five new vocabulary words.	Find five new vocabulary words.	Find five new vocabulary words.	Find five new vocabulary words.	Find five new vocabulary words.
Reflect on the speech assignment for the week.	Compose a first draft of your speech.	Revise your speech and submit to your evaluator/ parent.	Prepare to present your speech tomorrow.	Present your speech to a live audience.
Write an outline with thesis for your synthesis essay.	Work on the first draft for your synthesis essay.	Finish the first draft and then the revised draft of your synthesis essay.	Submit a copy of your paper to a peer for evaluation.	Submit your assignments to your evaluator/ parent.
Make a journal entry.	Make a journal entry.	Make a journal entry.	Finish the final copy of your synthesis essay.	Take Lesson 12 Test.
			Make a journal entry.	Make a journal entry.

LESSON 13

BACKGROUND

Literature is defined, in *Merriam Webster's Collegiate Dictionary* (10th ed., 1993), as "writings in prose or verse; especially writings having excellence of form or expression and expressing ideas of permanent or universal interest."

The person who examines, interprets, and analyzes literature is a *critic*. A critic is a guide to the reader, not a prophet or therapist. While it is the critic's right to express his preferences, and even his privilege to influence others, it is not his job to tell the reader what to like or not like. However, the critic is a helper, a guide helping the reader better to understand the author's intention and art.

In fact, the critic is concerned about the structure, sound, and meaning of the literary piece. These structures are described as genres: narrative prose, poetry, essays, drama.

Literary analysis or *criticism* is a way to talk about literature. Literary analysis is a way to understand literature better. If we really want to understand something, we need to have a common language with everyone else. If we talk about cooking, for instance, we would need to know certain terminology and use it when describing the process. How lost we might be without knowing what "to cream the butter and sugar" means!

Literary analysis employs a common language to take apart and to discuss literary pieces. The following terms are part of a language that critics use to discuss literature.

Authors—especially poets—use sounds to create a mood or to make a particularly important point. *Alliteration* is the repetition of initial consonant sounds. The repetition can be juxtaposed (side-by-side, as in simply sad). An example: "I conceive, therefore, as to the business of being profound, that it is with writers, as with wells; a person with good eyes may see to the bottom of the deepest, provided any water be there; and that often, when there is nothing in the world at the bottom, besides dryness and dirt, though it be but a yard and a half under ground, it shall pass, however, for wondrous deep, upon no wiser a reason than because it

is wondrous dark" (Jonathan Swift). Swift uses alliteration to create a satiric tone. *Allusion* is a casual and brief reference to a famous historical or literary figure or event: "You must borrow me Gargantua's mouth first. 'Tis a word too great for any mouth of this age's size" (Shakespeare). Shakespeare uses a comparison to help the reader understand his point.

Characters that appear in the story may perform actions, speak to other characters, be described by the narrator, or be remembered. An *antagonist* is the person with whom the main character has the most conflict. He is the enemy of the main character, the protagonist. In *The Scarlet Letter*, by Nathaniel Hawthorne, for instance, Chillingsworth is the antagonist. Hester, Chillingsworth's wife, the person who wears the scarlet letter, is the *protagonist*. Introduced characters whose sole purpose is to develop the main character are called *foils*. Conflict often occurs within a character. This is called *internal conflict*. An example of this occurs in Mark Twain's *Huckleberry Finn*. In this novel Huck is mentally struggling about whether to return Jim, an escaped slave and Huck's good friend, to the authorities. An *external conflict* is normally an obvious conflict between the protagonist and antagonist(s).

The *plot* is the story. The plot includes the events of the story, in the order the story gives them. A typical plot has five parts: *exposition, rising action, crisis* or *climax, falling action*, and *resolution*. Crisis or climax is the moment or event in the plot in which the conflict is most directly addressed: the main character "wins" or "loses," or the secret is revealed. After the climax, the *denouement* or *falling action* occurs.

Metaphor is a comparison that creatively identifies one thing with another, dissimilar thing and transfers or ascribes to the first thing some of the qualities of the second. Unlike a *simile* or *analogy*, which says one thing is like or as another, metaphor asserts that one thing <u>is</u> another. Frequently a metaphor is invoked by a *to be* verb: "Affliction then is ours; / We are the trees whom shaking fastens more." (George Herbert). Then Jesus declared, "I am the bread of life." (John 6:35)

The *narration* of a story is the way the author chooses to tell the story. In *first-person narration*, a character refers to himself using "I." Example: Huck Finn in *The Adventures of Huckleberry Finn* tells the story from his perspective. This creative way brings humor into the plot. In *second-person narration*, a character addresses the reader and/or the main character as "you" (and may also use first-person narration, but not necessarily). One example is the opening of each of Rudyard Kipling's *Just-So Stories*, in which the narrator refers to the child-listener as "O Best-Beloved." In *third-person narration*, the author, usually not a character in the story, refers to the story's characters as "he" and "she." This form of narration is probably the most common. In *limited narration*, the author is only able to tell what one person is thinking or feeling. Example: In *A Separate Peace*, by John Knowles, the reader only sees the story from Gene's perspective. *Omniscient narration* is when, not a character in the story; can tell what any or all characters are thinking and feeling and is what Charles Dickens employs in most of his novels. *Reliable narration* is presented with the stance that everything this story says is true, and the narrator knows everything that is necessary to the story. An *unreliable narrator* may not know all the relevant information, may be intoxicated or mentally ill, and/or may lie to the audience. Example: Edgar Allan Poe's narrators are frequently unreliable. Think of the delusions that the narrator of "The Tell-Tale Heart" has about the old man.

Onomatopoeia is the use of words which suggest their meaning through their pronunciation. Example: When spoken, hiss is intended to resemble the sound of steam or of a snake. Other examples include: slam, buzz, screech, whir, crush, sizzle, crunch, wring, wrench, gouge, grind, mangle, bang, pow, zap, fizz, roar, growl, blip, click, whimper, zip, and, of course, snap, crackle, and pop.

The *setting* is the place(s) and time(s) of the story, including the historical period, social milieu of the characters, geographical location, and descriptions of indoor and outdoor locales. The *theme* is the one-sentence major purpose of a literary piece, rarely stated but

implied. The theme is not a *moral*, which is a statement of the author's didactic purpose of his literary piece. A *thesis statement* is similar to the theme. A *précis* is a summary of the plot or a portion of the plot.

The *tone* is the mood of a literary piece. For instance, the tone or mood of Poe's poem "Annabel Lee" is quite somber.

Among others, these terms are the critic's tools to discuss and to analyze literature. As a physician defines his patient in terms of this or that syndrome or physical attribute, the critic describes his literary piece in terms of a credible narrator or an exciting plot or an effective theme.

One final word: Literary criticism papers are more frequently assigned than any other high school or college writing assignment. Therefore, developing this craft and continuing to refine it throughout your writing career is a must in academics.

SAMPLE STUDENT ESSAY

(Note any errors you find in this student's critical analysis.)

Crime and Punishment:

NARRATIVE TECHNIQUE

The book *Crime and Punishment* by the famous Russian author Fyodor Dostoyevsky is a melancholy and yet fascinating story of a young man (Raskolnikov) who commits a crime (he murders an old deceptive hag and her innocent sister) and is punished by his own conscience. It is told through omniscient narration, a nameless voice who reliably reports to the reader everything that the characters do and say and also what they think.

Most of the time the narrator keeps his opinions to himself—simply revealing the thought and actions of Raskolnikov and the other characters. The characters describe or experience the physical environment, the look on people's faces, and the level of tension among them.

However, while the author employs omniscient narration, he seems, at times, to stray into limited narration. Most of the time what the reader learns is what Raskolnikov (the protagonist) sees or feels: that's the clue that he is the central focus of the novel. Since Raskolnikov is the major character, almost everything the narrator tells the reader is about him. The other characters and events are described primarily for what they reveal about Raskolnikov. There are, for instance, only a few scenes in which he does not appear. At tough times he remains the focus, even when he is physically absent. The narrator shows the reader the warm affection Raskolinkov's family and friends feel for him in a few scenes where he is absent. While the reader decides what Raskolnikov is really like, these scenes help the reader realize that he has many good qualities after all. The author uses omniscient narration effectively to show how his protagonist develops. Therefore, while it's true that the narrator doesn't say, "Hate this character," or "Love this one," the details observed by the reader in narration lead him to the conclusion Dostoyevsky intends.

Omniscient (or all-knowing) narration is a favorite device of authors writing complicated novels, because it is an effective method for giving the reader some comprehensive views of several characters. While Dostoyevsky writes from omniscient narration, he still has his favorite interpreter: Raskolinkov.

(Jessica Stobaugh)

WRITING STYLE: SENTENCES—SENTENCE VARIETY

Use sentence variety. First, vary the beginnings of your sentences. *I was at home yesterday. I saw a television show. I did not like the show* is inferior to *While at home yesterday, I saw a boring television show.* Beginning sentences with modifiers and phrases is a good way to vary sentence structure. Another way is to vary the kinds and lengths of sentences you write.

PUBLIC SPEAKING: LITERARY ANALYSIS

It is quite challenging to convert a literary analysis essay into a literary analysis speech. For one thing, you have the arduous task of analyzing a story, characters, and other literary concepts without giving away the final resolution or even the ultimate theme. For instance, you will lose your audience fairly quickly if you begin an analysis of "The Fall of the House of Usher" by Edgar Allan Poe, with a statement that "the house killed the whole family." The profound insights of a brilliant literary analysis essay may very easily evolve into a bane, superficial discussion of a lukewarm literary piece. The truth is, writing a literary analysis speech (which is a process speech) is really challenging.

So what is one to do? It is critical that you use an outline. Devise an outline—before, not after—you write the speech. Be certain that you organize your points well. Use multiple transitions. Do not give away

your plot/theme/storyline too soon and be sure to analyze carefully each point. Use copious textual evidence. Finally, it is sometimes helpful in the written and spoken literary analysis to compare this literary piece to another piece by the same author and/or a literary piece by another author.

SPEECH ASSIGNMENT

Create a thinking game and concept map of your favorite literary piece. Use this outline to create a 1-3 minute speech to an audience.

WRITING ASSIGNMENTS

1. Write a literary analysis of your favorite novel, short story, or poem. Include an outline with thesis statement, rough draft, revised draft, final copy, and five new (circled) vocabulary words. Pay particular attention to style (focus, content, organization). Give a copy to a peer/friend who will complete a peer evaluation form (Appendix) and another copy to your parent/educator.

2. Read 150 to 200 pages this week and find vocabulary words.

3. Complete the speech assignment and have a teacher complete a speech evaluation form (Appendix).

4. In 1 Kings 18, Elijah faces the priests of Baal. Answer the question "What is the cause and effect of apostasy?" Meditate on this passage and others. Have you had a Mt. Carmel experience?

5. Pay particular attention to your writing style this week.

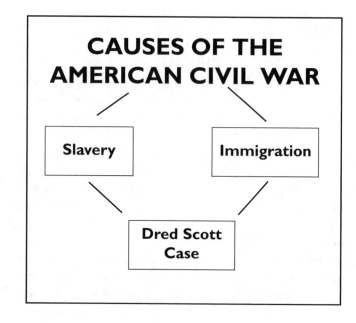

6. Write a warm-up essay every day. As you experience the daily writing, you should see improvement in your ability to express your thoughts on paper. This daily writing is preparation for composing effective essays.

FINAL PROJECT

Correct and rewrite all essays and place them in your Final Portfolio.

WARM-UP ESSAYS:

	DAY 1	DAY 2	DAY 3	DAY 4	DAY 5
Literary Analysis	Write a literary analysis of a recent sermon.	Write a literary analysis of a favorite poem.	Write a literary analysis of a favorite short story.	Write a literary analysis of a favorite movie.	Write a literary analysis of a favorite nonfiction story.

SUGGESTED
Weekly *Implementation*

DAY 1	DAY 2	DAY 3	DAY 4	DAY 5
Write a Warm-up Essay. Read 35-50 pages/day. Find five new vocabulary words. Reflect on the speech assignment for the week. Write an outline with thesis for your literary analysis. Make a journal entry.	Write a Warm-up Essay. Read 35-50 pages/day. Find five new vocabulary words. Compose a first draft of your speech. Work on the first draft for your literary analysis. Make a journal entry.	Write a Warm-up Essay. Read 35-50 pages/day. Find five new vocabulary words. Revise your speech and submit to your evaluator/ parent. Finish the first draft and then the revised draft of your literary analysis. Make a journal entry.	Write a Warm-up Essay. Read 35-50 pages/day. Find five new vocabulary words. Prepare to present your speech tomorrow. Submit a copy of your paper to a peer for evaluation. Finish the final copy of your literary analysis. Make a journal entry.	Write a Warm-up Essay. Read 35-50 pages/day. Find five new vocabulary words. Present your speech to a live audience. Submit your assignments to your evaluator/ parent. Take Lesson 13 Test. Make a journal entry.

LESSON 14

BACKGROUND

Evaluation is a higher-level thinking process. To evaluate a problem is to judge the worth of the material. Of course you must use some sort a rating system or criteria to evaluate something. Sometimes the rating criterion is given to you; other times you must set your own criteria. Then you must use evidence to show that the topic does or does not fit your criteria. You should deal with what the implications are for whether it fits or does not fit (or fits some but not others of) your criteria. Finally, you must make a value judgment concerning the material's veracity.

Your thesis is particularly important in an evaluation essay. It is the lodestone to which the rest of the paper is drawn. The thesis of the paper must be clearly stated and appropriately qualified. In other words, in an evaluation essay tell your reader what you value and why.

Next, repeat the standards of judgment you will be using in your paper. Make a judgment. Do not merely mention alternative positions; actually discuss all the alternatives. Offer supporting evidence for your judgment and be certain that your viewpoint is consistent throughout the paper—do not equivocate

WRITING STYLE: WORDS—USING THE DICTIONARY VS. THE THESAURUS

Words are the building blocks of writing. If you build your essay with precise, inspired words, you will have a precise, inspired essay.

Your friend and companion to good writing is the unabridged dictionary—not the thesaurus. The dictionary defines and uses a word in a sentence. The thesaurus gives you several analogies with no hint at their

> Evaluation means to judge, to measure, to rate, to recommend, to assess, to argue, to convince, to criticize.

usage. If you are not careful, you will use a word in the wrong way. For instance, pretend you want to find a word to use that means "bad." Your thesaurus tells you that one word for "bad" is "pejorative." You then write the sentence: "The steak was pejorative." Technically, the sentence is correct because it has a subject and a predicate and makes a complete statement; however, it is also very wrong. "Pejorative" is used to describe abstract things, not concrete things. Thus, a correct usage of "pejorative" is, "That pejorative comment hurt me deeply." An unabridged dictionary would tell you the nuances of meanings surrounding such a word as "pejorative" and would also give you a few sample sentences. Many writers make the mistake of relying on a thesaurus instead of a dictionary when they try to make their writing more sophisticated or scholarly.

PUBLIC SPEAKING: CONVERTING AN EVALUATION ESSAY TO A SPEECH

Basically an evaluation speech is constructed in a way that is very similar to the evaluation essay. You should

be very clear in your introductory comments what you are evaluating, how you are evaluating it, and what your evaluation conclusions are. As the speech unfolds, clearly state your case and evidence it well.

SAMPLE SPEECH: EVALUATION CRITERIA FOR CHOOSING THE RIGHT CURRICULUM

SPEECH ASSIGNMENT

In a three-minute speech, evaluate the significance to world history of a well-recognized individual.

WRITING ASSIGNMENTS

1. Evaluate the significance to world history of an important individual. Include an outline with thesis statement, rough draft, revised draft, final copy, and five new (circled) vocabulary words. Pay particular attention to style (focus, content, organization). For evaluation, give a copy to a peer/friend who will complete a peer evaluation form (Appendix) and another copy to your parent/educator.

2. Read 150 to 200 pages this week and find vocabulary words.

3. Complete the speech assignment and have a teacher complete a speech evaluation form (Appendix).

4. Pay particular attention to your writing style this week.

5. Read 1 Kings 16–19. The student should reflect upon who is worse: the passive and ineffective Ahab or the officious and shrewd Jezebel.

6. Write a warm-up essay every day. As you experience the daily writing, you should see improvement in your ability to express your thoughts on paper. This daily writing is preparation for composing effective essays.

FINAL PROJECT

Correct and rewrite all essays and place them in your Final Portfolio.

Curriculum Evaluation

_____ I. Inquiry Based (Does the curriculum invite the student to engage in critical thinking and student-centered activities?)

_____ II. Age Appropriate (Does the curriculum reflect a vocabulary and sentence structure appropriate to the student?)

_____ III. Colorful and Interesting (Does the curriculum appear in columns where appropriate? Are there pictures? Graphs? Is it printed on sturdy materials?)

_____ IV. Answer Key (Does the curriculum provide a clearly legible answer key?)

_____ V. Cost (Is the cost appropriate for high school curriculum? Analyze per unit costs.)

_____ VI. Multicultural (Does the curriculum seriously deal with multiculturalism?)

_____ VII. Biblically Based (Is the curriculum Christ centered?)

_____ VIII. Propagandistic (Does the curriculum reflect serious, objective, carefully researched scholarship?)

_____ IX. Need Based (Does the curriculum meet your needs? Is the curriculum college-preparatory for those students going to college? Does the curriculum satisfy requirements for an academic core course?)

_____ X. Authorship (How can you determine that the author is credentialed to offer the curriculum?)

_____ XI. Organization (Is the curriculum organized in a user-friendly manner?)

WARM-UP ESSAYS:

	DAY 1	DAY 2	DAY 3	DAY 4	DAY 5
Evaluation	Evaluate your favorite television show.	Evaluate your favorite sport.	Evaluate your favorite Bible verse.	Evaluate your favorite meal.	Evaluate your favorite movie star.

SUGGESTED
Weekly *Implementation*

DAY 1	DAY 2	DAY 3	DAY 4	DAY 5
Write a Warm-up Essay.	Write a Warm-up Essay.	Write a Warm-up Essay.	Write a Warm-up Essay.	Write a Warm-up Essay.
Read 35-50 pages/day.	Read 35-50 pages/day.	Read 35-50 pages/day.	Read 35-50 pages/day.	Read 35-50 pages/day.
Find five new vocabulary words.	Find five new vocabulary words.	Find five new vocabulary words.	Find five new vocabulary words.	Find five new vocabulary words.
Reflect on the speech assignment for the week.	Compose a first draft of your speech.	Revise your speech and submit to your evaluator/ parent.	Prepare to present your speech tomorrow.	Present your speech to a live audience.
Write an outline with thesis for your evaluation essay.	Work on the first draft for your evaluation essay.	Finish the first draft and then the revised draft of your evaluation essay.	Submit a copy of your paper to a peer for evaluation.	Submit your assignments to your evaluator/ parent.
Make a journal entry.	Make a journal entry.	Make a journal entry.	Finish the final copy of your evaluation essay.	Make a journal entry.
			Make a journal entry.	Take Lesson 14 Test

LESSON 15

BACKGROUND

What causes exorbitant fuel prices? What caused the American Civil War? A cause/effect paper invites you to consider a problem, define the problem, and offer a solution to the problem. Cause/effect papers are the most common and perhaps the most fun to write. There are two strategic points that are critical to a cause/effect paper. First, you must be clear about whether you are going to discus *causes* or *effects* or *both*. Secondly, you must be clear about the order of the causes or effects you're going to discuss. Not all causes/effects are of equal importance or impact. Will you begin with the most important or the least important cause/effect? Decide and then stick with your decision for the rest of your paper. Also, you may discuss the most important causes/effects and concede that there are less important causes/effects that you will have to overlook. Finally, one of the most challenging parts to writing cause/effect essays is ending them. Be careful to avoid a "preachy" attitude but feel free to lobby hard for one or two causes/effects or to even suggest a new one no one has noticed. Be careful, though, to avoid making this a cause/*solution* essay. Solution is beyond the scope of this particular essay.

Writing Skill: The Cause/Effect Essay

Style (Writing and Speaking): Words—Connotation vs. Denotation

Public Speaking Skill: Converting the Cause/Effect Essay into a Speech.

Looking Ahead: The Comparison/Contrast Essay

SAMPLE CAUSE/EFFECT ESSAY:

The Dialectic Process: A Struggle for Truth

Communism is a worldview in retreat. Communism in Russia has failed. However, at the heart of Communism is a reasoning process called dialectical materialism, which is very much alive. Karl Marx and Frederick Engels, fathers of Communism, base their views of communism on the works of G. W. F. Hegel.

At the heart of dialectic materialism is the notion of conflict. It is within struggle that truth emerges. The philosopher Hegel characterizes dialectic as the tendency of a notion to pass over into its own negation as the result of conflict between its inherent contradictory aspects. Karl Marx and Friedrich Engels adopt Hegel's definition and apply it to social and economic processes. To Marx, history is a process. It is dialectic, but it is not a "spirit" that drives it. In other words, Hegelian dialectics are opposed to metaphysics (the notion that a transcendent power or entity determines the course of history). It is materialism—industry—power that really drives the whole thing.

Therefore, Marx argues that if one wants to control ideals, if he wants a revolution, if he wants progress, he will have to stimulate a struggle.

Where is dialectic materialism alive in America today? Consider the way America makes policy decisions. When America decides to legalize abortion, it compromises between two positions. Truth supposedly arises out of the struggle. The pro-life position is wrong, but so are the pro-choice folks. The truth lies somewhere between these two positions. The struggle between these two polarities will bring forth the truth. Another example is the present debate over homosexuality. Some people argue that homosexuality is wrong. Others argue that it is right. Dialectic materialism leads many to conclude that neither position is right. In the struggle, a new truth emerges, a compromise. This would be the argument used by people who really love each other and are faithful to each other to allow participation in homosexual behavior.

The flaws in these arguments are obvious. Regardless of how long Americans seek to compromise, abortion will always be murder, and homosexuality will always be sinful. The struggle does not lead America to truth—it leads America into error. Truth is not found in the dialectic; it is found in the Word of God.

(Jessica Stobaugh)

WRITING STYLE: WORDS—CONNOTATION VS. DENOTATION

Words have different meanings in different contexts. In fact, the meaning of a word has two components: denotative and connotative. The word's denotation is what it actually means—according to the dictionary. The word's connotation is what it implies. For instance, the word "propaganda" means "sharing a biased position in order to convert." Originally, the word was used to describe missionaries who shared propaganda. We of course have no problem with this definition of propaganda. Unfortunately, though, during World War II, German Nazis, among others, used propaganda to influence people in adverse ways. Thus, the word gained a very negative connotation.

Exercise care with word choice. The connotation of some words may offend some people. For instance, if I said you were "absent-minded," you would probably not be offended. The connotation of "absent-minded" connotes harmless forgetfulness. On the other hand, if I called you "scatter-brained," you might be offended. Absent-minded and scatter-brained denote approximately the same thing; however, scatter-brained connotes something far more pejorative than absent-minded.

PUBLIC SPEAKING: CONVERTING THE CAUSE/EFFECT ESSAY TO A SPEECH

The cause/effect speech includes some elements of writing that might be considered more professional, even pedantic, than other process speeches might include. It is very important, for instance, that the tone of a cause/effect speech be reflective and serious and that your presentation be factual and believable. Sources are often required in a cause/effect paper, and your choice of these sources is important since they will determine whether or not your audience will accept your conclusions. Finally, in both the cause/effect essay and speech, the first-person point of view does not work. The *professional opinion* is more important than your *considered opinion*. It is important to keep your speaking voice modulated. It can be playful, even a little whimsical, but it must be authoritative. You must not sound uncertain and, above all, you must not be vitriolic.

SPEECH ASSIGNMENT

Convert a cause/effect essay into a speech.

WRITING ASSIGNMENTS

1. Evaluate the last time you made some bad choices. What were the causes of these bad choices? What was the outcome? This essay should include an outline with thesis statement, rough draft, revised draft, final copy, and five new (circled) vocabulary words. For evaluation, give a copy to a peer/friend who will complete a peer evaluation form (Appendix) and another copy to your parent/educator.

2. Read 200-250 pages this week and find vocabulary words.

3. Complete the speech assignment and have a teacher complete a speech evaluation form (Appendix).

4. Pay particular attention to style (focus, content, organization) this week.

5. Read 1 Kings 19. Have you ever felt hopeless like Elijah (19:4–5)? How does God react to Elijah? How does Elijah react to God? Record your reflections in your prayer journal. This journal is meant to be private, but you are invited to share your reflections with others.

6. Write a warm-up essay every day. Over time and as you experience the daily writing, you should see improvement in your ability to express your thoughts on paper. This daily writing is preparation for composing effective essays.

> Writing is a discipline that must be practiced frequently, or it will quickly decline in effectiveness.

FINAL PROJECT

Correct and rewrite all essays and place them in your
Final Portfolio.

WARM-UP ESSAYS:

	DAY 1	DAY 2	DAY 3	DAY 4	DAY 5
Cause/Effect	What causes inflation?	What is the cause of crime?	What were the causes of the Gulf War?	What causes snow?	What causes our country to abort millions of children?

SUGGESTED
Weekly *Implementation*

DAY 1	DAY 2	DAY 3	DAY 4	DAY 5
Write a Warm-up Essay. Read 35-50 pages/day. Find five new vocabulary words. Reflect on the speech assignment for the week. Write an outline with thesis for your cause/effect essay. Make a journal entry.	Write a Warm-up Essay. Read 35-50 pages/day. Find five new vocabulary words. Compose a first draft of your speech. Work on the rough draft for your cause/effect essay. Make a journal entry.	Write a Warm-up Essay. Read 35-50 pages/day. Find five new vocabulary words. Revise your speech and submit to your evaluator/ parent. Finish the first draft and then the revised draft of your cause/effect essay. Make a journal entry.	Write a Warm-up Essay. Read 35-50 pages/day. Find five new vocabulary words. Prepare to present your speech tomorrow. Submit a copy of your paper to a peer for evaluation. Finish the final copy of your cause/effect essay. Make a journal entry.	Write a Warm-up Essay. Read 35-50 pages/day. Find five new vocabulary words. Present your speech to a live audience. Submit your assignments to your evaluator/ parent. Take Lesson 15 Test. Make a journal entry.

LESSON 16

BACKGROUND

When you compare things, you show their similarities; when you contrast things, you show their differences. A comparison and contrast paper does both.

We can really understand only those things that are familiar to us or similar to things we already understand. Therefore, a comparison and contrast paper stretches our understanding to another level. It reaches out to the familiar to help its reader understand the unfamiliar. You may compare and contrast the unfamiliar with the familiar and vice versa. You can, and probably do, use comparison and contrast to solve problems, to describe issues, to define things, and to analyze issues; comparison and contrast is useful even to make an argument.

A good way to begin a comparison and contrast paper is to discuss the ways in which objects are similar. That is not enough, however. Within the introduction you also will need to describe the ways in which the two ideas are different.

Also, comparing and contrasting ideas can be accomplished by treating one idea thoroughly before discussing the second one. Many writers prefer this style of comparison and contrast.

The intricate plots of authors Mary Shelley and Robert Louis Stevenson, their vivid imaginations, their knowledge of science, and their whimsical, but credible characters all conspire to make their writings excellent. There are differences, though, in their writings, all of which are theistic in substance and remarkably different in tone. The following paper will examine these differences. The works being compared are the book *Frankenstein* by Mary Shelley, the poem "Dirge" by Mary Shelley, the book *Dr. Jekyll and Mr. Hyde* by Robert Louis Stevenson, and the poem "Requiem" by Robert Louis Stevenson.

> The comparison/contrast essay begins with a summary of the argument. The writer intentionally sets up a theory to be torn apart.

> **Writing Skill:** The Comparison/Contrast Essay
> **Style (Writing and Speaking):** Words—Standard and Sub-standard English
> **Public Speaking Skill:** Converting the Comparison and Contrast Essay into a Speech.
> **Looking Ahead:** The Problem/Solution Essay

> Internal comparisons are good; comparisons among different literary works are even better.

SAMPLE COMPARISON AND CONTRAST ESSAY

Both Shelley and Stevenson created protagonists who wanted to produce life outside normal human events and divine purpose. Victor Frankenstein created the monster Frankenstein, and Henry Jekyll created the monster Hyde. Both were monstrosities in physical appearance and in philosophical intent. They did not have souls. Throughout the entire undertaking, Frankenstein felt that no human has the right, even if he has the means, to create another human being. Jekyll only felt remorse at the end of his life. Victor Frankenstein and Henry Jekyll created monsters, but their author/creators had a greater purpose.

Shelley and Stevenson illustrated the excesses of the Victorian Age. Like many British subjects overburdened by Victorian morality, Frankenstein and Jekyll were discontent with the limits imposed on them as mortal humans. They wished to push beyond those limits and found themselves in an overabundance of trouble. Their vocation of "god-playing" was hazardous to their health and to everyone around them. Eventually, they regretted their excesses and tried to destroy their monsters, but it was too late. In fact, their monsters destroyed them.

In *Dr. Jekyll* and his poem "Requiem," Stevenson advances a theistic worldview. Dr. Jekyll in effect ends his life because Hyde has broken Christian moral laws, and Dr. Jekyll cannot see a way to stop Hyde unless Jekyll dies: "Henry Jekyll [was] aghast at the acts of Edward Hyde" (p. 87). In "Requiem" Stevenson writes, "Glad did I live and die. / I laid me down with a will." Stevenson's view of death is not gloomy. One could even suppose Stevenson believes in heaven. On the other hand, in her works Shelley revels in gloominess and despair. *Frankenstein* offers the reader no hope. The Romantic English writer Shelley invites readers into the deep, dreary caves of hopelessness. She obviously has no Christian theistic bent.

Shelley and Stevenson are surely grand writers. At times, though, their characters and plots seem grotesque and even evil. However, the authors promote their characters in such a way that readers feel the grotesque evil is necessary. No one escapes justice in these works. In a culture flirting with social Darwinism, it seems fitting that an author presents human nature in a monstrous, grotesque way.

(Jessica Stobaugh)

WRITING STYLE: WORDS—STANDARD AND SUBSTANDARD ENGLISH

One of the most important aspects of connotation is historical usage. There is a standard (good) and a substandard (poor) usage of most words. This standard is often determined by the purpose of and audience for the writing. For instance, the sentence "I am feeling groovy today" might be substandard English if you were presenting a sociological lecture at Harvard University. On the other hand, "I am feeling groovy today" would be entirely appropriate in Harvard Yard among other students. You have to be exceptionally discerning in your use of standard and substandard English.

Carefully avoid slang in writing. For example, using the world "ain't" in a formal, expository essay is inappropriate. So, too, is the use of vulgarity.

While avoiding slang and vulgarity, you will also need to avoid clichés and the use of contractions, except in dialogue. On the other hand, proper use of abbreviations (Ms., Dr., Mr., Mrs., and U.S. Postal Service) is expected.

PUBLIC SPEAKING: CONVERTING A COMPARISON AND CONTRAST ESSAY TO A SPEECH

The comparison and contrast speech is organized much like the comparison/contrast essay. A rhetorical question is one way to begin a comparison/contrast speech. "What is the difference between the causes of World War I and World War II?" you may ask. Another great way to begin is to use a quote: "World War II was much more violent than World War I," says Professor John Smiths. However you begin your speech, be very sure that you include a thesis statement in your introduction.

SPEECH ASSIGNMENT

In a 2-3 minute speech, compare and contrast two personal friends.

WRITING ASSIGNMENTS

1. Compare and contrast two personal friends. Your essay should include an outline with thesis statement, rough draft, revised draft, final copy, and five new (circled) vocabulary words. Pay particular attention to style (focus, content, organization). For evaluation, give a copy to a peer/friend who will complete a peer evaluation form (Appendix) and another copy to your parent/educator.

2. Read 200-250 pages/week and find vocabulary words.

3. Complete the speech assignment and have a teacher complete a speech evaluation form (Appendix).

4. Pay particular attention to your writing style this week.

5. Read 1 Kings 19:10–18. Consider where Elijah finds God. Has God appeared to you in unusual places and in unusual circumstances? Answer these questions and others in your prayer journal.

6. Write a warm-up essay every day. As you experience the daily writing, you should see improvement in your ability to express your thoughts on paper. This daily writing is preparation for composing effective essays.

FINAL PROJECT

Correct and rewrite all essays and place them in your Final Portfolio.

WARM-UP ESSAYS:

	DAY 1	DAY 2	DAY 3	DAY 4	DAY 5
Compare/ Contrast	Compare your brother to Matt Damon.	Contrast your dad to Harrison Ford.	Compare your favorite car to the car your family owns.	Contrast a movie with the book you read by the same name.	Contrast your youth director to your pastor.

SUGGESTED
Weekly *Implementation*

DAY 1	DAY 2	DAY 3	DAY 4	DAY 5
Write a Warm-up Essay. Read 35-50 pages/day. Find five new vocabulary words. Reflect on the speech assignment for the week. Write an outline with thesis for your compare/contrast essay. Make a journal entry.	Write a Warm-up Essay. Read 35-50 pages/day. Find five new vocabulary words. Compose a first draft of your speech. Work on the first draft for your compare/contrast essay. Make a journal entry.	Write a Warm-up Essay. Read 35-50 pages/day. Find five new vocabulary words. Revise your speech and submit to your evaluator/ parent. Finish the first draft and then the revised draft of your compare/contrast essay. Make a journal entry.	Write a Warm-up Essay. Read 35-50 pages/day. Find five new vocabulary words. Prepare to present your speech tomorrow. Submit a copy of your paper to a peer for evaluation. Finish the final copy of your compare/contrast essay. Make a journal entry.	Write a Warm-up Essay. Read 35-50 pages/day. Find five new vocabulary words. Present your speech to a live audience. Submit your assignments to your evaluator/ parent. Take Lesson 16 Test. Make a journal entry.

LESSON 17

BACKGROUND

A problem and solution essay is an argumentative essay. Everything, really, about a problem and solution paper is argumentative. It argues for defining a problem in a certain way, and then it argues for a specific solution or solutions to a specified problem. This paper is most common in the social sciences and business, but it is fair to say that it is one of the most important essay types in all disciplines.

A problem and solution essay inevitably begins with some sort of a problem—statement. In fact, the way the problem is introduced is extremely important with this paper.

There are several ways to introduce a problem. In the context-problem type of introduction, using references from professionals, you will offer evidence that the problem is indeed a problem recognized as such by numerous, well-informed sources. In the introduction you prove that there is indeed a major problem here. A good way to provide such proof is to demonstrate how your problem has caused a lot of other problems. For instance, you could establish that drug use is a real problem by proving that it leads to juvenile crime. In other words, a common problem-posing introduction begins with a large issue that almost all audience members will recognize as important. That gives your solution—which occurs later in the paper—a much larger target audience.

Another way to begin a problem and solution paper is to argue that there is really no problem after all. In this essay you would begin with a statement of the problem and a brief review of the solutions offered, ending with a statement about why we need to look at the problem from a different perspective and, in the process, we see that it is not a problem after all. You may even be offering an *opportunity* instead of a *solution*. For instance, the Russian intervention in Afghanistan in the late 1970s, perceived by many as a major problem, could be redefined as an opportunity because it ultimately led to the collapse of the Iron Curtain in Central Europe.

A more complicated version of a problem and solu-

tion argument evaluates the solutions currently offered as a way of arguing for a new solution rather than suggesting there is no problem. In these types of essays, you would begin with a statement of the problem and a brief review of the solutions offered, ending with a statement about why none of the solutions currently is adequate. Of course, in this instance you will want to offer alternative solutions. In other words, a critique of other solutions will provide you with the proof for an argument for a new solution. This approach can be very effective and convincing.

SAMPLE PROBLEM AND SOLUTION ESSAY:

It seems at times that Americans are lost. I am a pastor, and in spite of our hedonistic bravado, I generally find some of my congregation members—who generally are not living a life centered on Jesus Christ—are in fact desperately unhappy. No wonder. This world does not provide what we need. I once thought it did. I can remember being seduced by the august institution, Harvard University. In 1976, I really believed my university chaplain who told the incoming Harvard class, "You are the next history makers of America." I wanted to believe it. I needed to believe it. My acquaintance and colleague from Harvard Divinity School, Dr. Forrest Church, now pastor in a Unitarian Church in New York City, was fond of saying, "In our faith God is not a given; God is a question . . . God is defined by us. Our views are shaped and changed by our experiences. We create a faith in which we can live and struggle to live up to it . . . compared to love, a distant God had no allure." Indeed. This thinking has gotten us into quite a mess.

Writing Skill: The Problem and Solution Essay
Style (Writing and Speaking): Words—Idioms
Public Speaking Skill: Converting the Problem and Solution Essay into a Speech
Looking Ahead: The Definition Essay

What kind of mess? While I attended seminary, I remember hurrying to the opening ceremony of the academic year held every September at Harvard Memorial Chapel in the Yard. Spying an impressive group of Harvard Professors, decked out in all their academic robes, capes, and histrionic sententiousness, I decided to follow them to Memorial Chapel, a landmark in Harvard Yard. Although I knew one way to go there, they were not going my way, so, I trusted these sagacious gentlemen to show me a better way. Well, we got lost! And I was late! In spite of their august credentials, they did not know the way after all.

One of the most disturbing essays I have ever read is an essay by Thomas Merton entitled "A Devout Meditation in Memory of Adolf Eichmann." "One of the most disturbing facts," Merton begins, "that came out in the Eichmann trial was that a psychiatrist examined him and pronounced him perfectly sane." The fact is, given our world, we can no longer assume that because a person is "sane" or "adjusted" that he/she is ok. Merton reminds us that such people can be well adjusted even in hell itself! "The whole concept of sanity in a society where spiritual values have lost their meaning is itself meaningless."

The central symbol for every twenty-first century Christian must be the cross. At least from the second century onwards, Christians used the cross as their central symbol. I yearn, as Dietrich Bonhoeffer did at the end of his life, for the crucified Lord to return again—as the rediscovered center—to the center of the Church and American society. America does not need a new religion; it needs Jesus Christ—crucified and resurrected.

With John Stott, in *The Cross of Christ*, my prayer is that this new generation, haunted by so many bad memories, so bewitched by technology and social science theories, would again come to the cross of our Lord Jesus Christ. And, at the same time, I want us to reclaim the joy of this adventure—so persuasively presented by John Piper in *Desiring God*. Steering right into the storm, armed with God's divine presence and teachings, can affect the end results of this spiritual storm we Americans are experiencing.

(James Stobaugh).

The author establishes the problem clearly and then offers a solution. Notice how much time he spends making sure that the reader agrees with him that there is a problem.

WRITING STYLE: WORDS—IDIOMS

Idioms are special constructions of words determined by history and usage. The choice of words, or idioms, is always a knotty problem. Informal, even substandard, expressions are so common that you will be tempted to use them. In some cases this will be acceptable; in other cases it will not. First, of course, the purpose of the writing and the make-up of the audience will determine to a large degree which idioms are acceptable and which are not. A word of caution: While some idioms are acceptable in formal writing, most are not, and, as a general usage rule, if you write like you speak, you most assuredly will have too many idioms. Unless you have a pretty stiff speaking style, your writing should be much different. Thus, you might say "My opinion is the opposite *to* yours" and get away with it. In a formal essay, however, no matter how weird it may sound to you, you must write the correct form of this sentence: "My opinion is the opposite *of* yours." One more example: the idiomatic expression "You did good" might work at the beach but would never work in a formal paper. "You accomplished the task well" or even "you did well" is the correct way to express this thought in written form.

PUBLIC SPEAKING: CONVERTING A PROBLEM AND SOLUTION ESSAY TO A SPEECH

A problem and solution essay is presented much as it is written.

SPEECH ASSIGNMENT

Present a 2-3 minute speech on the topic: As this century begins, Christians are becoming a declining minority in American culture and society. In a one-page essay, answer these questions, "Is this a problem? Why? What are some solutions?"

WRITING ASSIGNMENTS

1. As this century begins, Christians are becoming a declining minority in American culture and society. In a one-page essay, answer this question, "Is this a problem? Why? What are some solutions?" Your essay should include an outline with thesis statement, rough draft, revised draft, final copy, and five new (circled)

vocabulary words. Pay particular attention to style (focus, content, organization). For evaluation, give a copy to a peer/friend who will complete a peer evaluation form (Appendix) and another copy to your parent/educator.

2. Read 200-250 pages/week and find vocabulary words.

3. Complete the speech assignment and have a teacher complete a speech evaluation form (Appendix).

4. Pay particular attention to your writing style this week.

5. First Kings 19:19–21 is a description of the call of Elisha. Elijah rebukes Elisha for returning to say goodbye to his parents. Why? Have you ever experienced such a call? Answer these questions and others in your prayer journal.

6. Write a warm-up essay every day. As you experience the daily writing, you should see improvement in your ability to express your thoughts on paper. This daily writing is preparation for composing effective essays.

FINAL PROJECT

Correct and rewrite all essays and place them in your Final Portfolio.

WARM-UP ESSAYS:

	DAY 1	DAY 2	DAY 3	DAY 4	DAY 5
Problem/ Solution	The solution to the problem of children watching too much TV violence.	The solution to the problem of teenage pregnancy.	The solution to the problem of 80 percent of urban children having no father.	The solution to the problem of Judeo-Christian morality disappearing from our culture.	The solution to the problem of ozone disappearing from the atmosphere.

SUGGESTED
Weekly *Implementation*

DAY 1	DAY 2	DAY 3	DAY 4	DAY 5
Write a Warm-up Essay.	Write a Warm-up Essay.	Write a Warm-up Essay.	Write a Warm-up Essay.	Write a Warm-up Essay.
Read 35-50 pages/day.	Read 35-50 pages/day.	Read 35-50 pages/day.	Read 35-50 pages/day.	Read 35-50 pages/day.
Find five new vocabulary words.	Find five new vocabulary words.	Find five new vocabulary words.	Find five new vocabulary words.	Find five new vocabulary words.
Reflect on the speech assignment for the week.	Compose a first draft of your speech.	Revise your speech and submit to your evaluator/ parent.	Prepare to present your speech tomorrow.	Present your speech to a live audience.
Write an outline with thesis for your problem/ solution essay.	Work on the first draft for your problem/ solution essay.	Finish the first draft and then the revised draft of your problem/ solution essay.	Submit a copy of your paper to a peer for evaluation.	Submit your assignments to your evaluator/ parent.
Make a journal entry.	Make a journal entry.	Make a journal entry.	Finish the final copy of your problem/ solution essay.	Take Lesson 17 Test.
			Make a journal entry.	Make a journal entry.

LESSON 18

BACKGROUND

A definition essay explains a common word or expression that is not easily defined. Definition is a method of analysis, as logical as possible, in which the subject is located in a general class and then distinguished from all other members of that class.

Please don't start your definition essay with either a dictionary or an encyclopedia definition of your word or comment. This approach is so often used that it is almost trite. After all, your essay is by definition (no pun intended!) your definition—not someone else's.

One good strategy of defining something is to say what it is not. The following is a portion of a sermon where the speaker has to make sure his reader understands the definition of *death*. He does this by reminding the reader what death "is not."

Jesus really died on the cross.

This was not some metaphorical event, some dramatic hoax. No, He really died. He died as in "stopped breathing." He really died.

Today, it seems to me, we have as much a problem in believing that Jesus died as we do in believing that He arose from the grave. Our ubiquitous media promises us eternal bliss and immortality—just put this cream on and the wrinkles will go away. Let's take these vitamins, and we will live forever, and so on.

It was not always so. Death was something our parents and grandparents had to face with more finality and frequency. The average life span was lower than it is now. Medical science was not as successful as now in saving human life. Infant mortality was higher. Since there were fewer hospitals and no nursing homes, sick and dying relatives died at home. Years ago it was the custom for a "wake" to be held in the family's living room. Then the deceased was buried in a local church cemetery. Every Sunday when our grandparents went to church, they were reminded of the reality of death as they passed the marble grave markers of their loved ones.

Jesus Christ was dead. And, I mean, really dead—

> **Writing Skill:** The Definition Essay
> **Style (Writing and Speaking):** Words—Adjectives and Adverbs in Comparative and Superlative Cases
> **Public Speaking Skill:** Converting the Definition Essay into a Speech
> **Looking Ahead:** The Explanatory Essay

however, he did not die quietly in bed with all His friends surrounding Him. No, He died a humiliating, messy, public death. And the world had no doubt of one salient fact on that first Easter morning: Jesus bar Joseph was very, very dead. The good news, however, is that he did not stay that way! (James P. Stobaugh)

Before you write a definition essay, you should answer these three questions: What is the term to be defined? What is the purpose for the intended definition? Who is the intended audience? Is this a general audience for whom terms must be broken down in simple sentences, or is it a special audience whose knowledge of the terminology will not require further definition?

WRITING STYLE: WORDS — ADJECTIVES AND ADVERBS IN COMPARATIVE AND SUPERLATIVE CASES

Students should avoid incomplete comparisons, ambiguous wording, indefinite references, misplaced modifiers, and dangling modifiers. Here are some examples:

> *This topic is better than that one.* (correct)
> *This topic is the best of all.* (correct)
> *Writing a research paper requires* more carefully *planned details than writing a paragraph.* (correct).

PUBLIC SPEAKING: CONVERTING A DEFINITION ESSAY INTO A SPEECH

When you present a definition speech your introduction should include the term to be defined, the definition of the term, and reason(s) for giving a more detailed definition. Also in the introduction, you should provide the listener with a notice about the kinds of additional information you will use to develop the definition. In the body of your speech use a systematic organization technique that advances your purposes. Usually there is no formal closing that is specific to the definition speech. Perhaps you will want to end with a rhetorical question, or you can conclude with a comparison/contrast with another similar/dissimilar term.

SPEECH ASSIGNMENT

Present a two or three-minute speech defining sound.

WRITING ASSIGNMENTS

1. In a one-page essay, define *sound*. Does a tree falling in the forest make sound if no human hears it? This essay should include an outline, rough draft, thesis statement, final copy, and five new (circled) vocabulary words. The essay must pay particular attention to style (focus, content, organization). Give a copy to a peer/friend to complete a peer evaluation (Appendix) and to instructor to evaluate.

2. Read 200-250 pages/week and make vocabulary cards.

3. Complete the speech assignment and have a teacher complete a speech evaluation (Appendix).

4. Pay particular attention to your writing style this week.

5. Meditate on 1 Kings 20. The student should reflect on this passage, and others, in the prayer journal.

6. Write a warm-up essay every day.

FINAL PROJECT

Correct and rewrite all essays and place them in your Final Portfolio.

WARM-UP ESSAYS:

	DAY 1	DAY 2	DAY 3	DAY 4	DAY 5
Definition	Define *immortality*.	Define *salvation*.	Define *sanctification*.	Define *grace*.	Define *judgment*

SUGGESTED
Weekly *Implementation*

DAY 1	DAY 2	DAY 3	DAY 4	DAY 5
Write a Warm-up Essay.	Write a Warm-up Essay.	Write a Warm-up Essay.	Write a Warm-up Essay.	Write a Warm-up Essay.
Read 35-50 pages/day.	Read 35-50 pages/day.	Read 35-50 pages/day.	Read 35-50 pages/day.	Read 35-50 pages/day.
Find five new vocabulary words.	Find five new vocabulary words.	Find five new vocabulary words.	Find five new vocabulary words.	Find five new vocabulary words.
Reflect on the speech assignment for the week.	Compose a first draft of your speech.	Revise your speech and submit to your evaluator/ parent.	Prepare to present your speech tomorrow.	Present your speech to a live audience.
Write an outline with thesis for your definition essay.	Work on the first draft for your definition essay.	Finish the first draft and then the revised draft of your definition essay.	Submit a copy of your paper to a peer for evaluation.	Submit your assignments to your evaluator/ parent.
Make a journal entry.	Make a journal entry.	Make a journal entry.	Finish the final copy of your definition essay.	Make a journal entry.
			Make a journal entry.	Take Lesson 18 Test.

LESSON 19

BACKGROUND

An explanatory essay explains something or advances a particular point. The following is an explanatory essay that develops a position and then argues a point. It is written in the form of an imaginary letter to an editor.

Dear Editor:

I read your article on "China's One-Child Policy," and I found it very disconcerting. Your editorial manifests bad morality and bad science.

For one thing, forced sterilization and infanticide (both practiced in China to maintain the one-child policy) are clearly against Scripture. From the very beginning, mankind was given the mandate to be fruitful and to multiply and to fulfill the earth and to subdue it (Genesis 1:28). The commandment was repeated to Noah and his sons after the Flood, which shows how important it was (Genesis 9:1). The promise of fruitfulness in procreation is an important feature of the Abrahamic covenant (Genesis 12:2). Therefore, if you are supporting China's policy of one child per family, you are supporting a policy that invites people to disobey the Word of God.

With married couples, birth control is acceptable (however, not with unwed teens) and can even be encouraged by the state. In China, as documented by many different sources, married couples are required to have one child and only one child. If they become pregnant again, many times the child is aborted, and the woman is sterilized. Abortion is murder; abortion is wrong. Therefore, again, the one-child policy is wrong.

As common in the Marxist/Leninist worldview, man is often making his own decisions and relying on his own "wisdom" to choose for the "good" (or what is thought to be good). In *Understanding the Times*, Dr. David Noebel states, "Because social and economic status are by Karl Marx's definition always changing according to the law of the dialectic, mankind's ideas about morality must also be in a state of change." Obviously, making a decision based upon what seems right, what advances the Communist agenda, does not have the moral imperative to murder unborn children

Writing Skill: The Explanatory Essay
Style (Writing and Speaking): Words—Precise Language
Public Speaking Skill: Converting the Explanatory Essay into a Speech
Looking Ahead: Fact, Inference, and Opinion

and to sterilize unwilling mothers.

Furthermore, Dr. John Jefferson Davis in his book *Evangelical Ethics* correctly argues that the population explosion is a hoax. In fact, there is no evidence to support that the world will be overpopulated any time soon. There is much evidence that the opposite is true. Most population theories of the 1960s have proven to be absolutely false. There is no reason to doubt that future agricultural advances will be able to meet the nutritional needs of a growing population. So, China is misguided in its pursuit of population decline.

Therefore, because the one-child policy violates the Word of God, I oppose it. At the same time, the policy betrays bad science—there is no evidence that the world will be overpopulated any time soon. (Jessica Stobaugh)

WRITING STYLE: WORDS—PRECISE LANGUAGE

Generally speaking, less is more in writing. In other words, if you can say it in three words, say it in three words—not in four or more. Use no more words than is absolutely necessary to express your thoughts. Use

Using the Computer Be careful when you use spell and grammar check. Since even the best computer editing programs inevitably miss some mistakes or even inadvertently cause you to make mistakes, you will still need to edit your paper.

familiar words, not esoteric, fancy words. Most of all, though, use words that exactly mean what you want to say. That means you may have to use "perfunctory" instead of "ordinary."

There are other things you can do too. To write precisely, you can:

Use action, colorful verbs.
The energetic boy kicked the slightly deflated soccer ball is better than *The boy kicked the ball.*

Use as few words as possible and give only relevant details.
The energetic boy kicked the slightly deflated soccer ball is better than *The boy with a tired look because he did not eat breakfast kicked the deflated soccer ball owned by his neighbor whose wife was in the hospital.*

Reduce the number of prepositional phrases.
The energetic, blue-clothed boy in the center of the field kicked the slightly deflated soccer ball is better than *In the center of the field, the energetic boy with a blue shirt kicked the soccer ball with a deflated appearance.*

Reduce expletive constructions.
The energetic, blue-clothed boy in the center of the field kicked the slightly deflated soccer ball is better than *Do you know what? That boy—yes, that blue-clothed boy!—kicked the slightly deflated ball.*

Avoid using vague nouns that lead to wordiness.
The energetic, blue-clothed boy in the center of the field kicked the slightly deflated soccer ball is better than *The good player on the field, the large soccer field, which is not as big as a football field, hit the ball, or at least he touched it softly with his right foot.*

Avoid big words that don't fit the context or tone of the writing.
The energetic, blue-clothed boy in the center of the field kicked the slightly deflated soccer ball is better than *The dynamical, azure-attired male in the choicest and most vital part of the sports field drove with a heavy foot the soccer sphere.*

Avoid noun strings.
The energetic, blue-clothed boy in the center of the field kicked the slightly deflated soccer ball is better than *The energetic, blue-clothed boy, son, brother, and classmate, in the center of the field kicked the slightly deflated soccer ball.*

PUBLIC SPEAKING: CONVERTING AN EXPLANATORY ESSAY TO A SPEECH

The explanatory speech (like the explanatory essay) has four components:

Introductory comments: background information on the process/controversy that your readers need to know. If the explanatory speech is less controversial, the introduction would tell readers why this subject would matter to them.

Statement of argument/belief/process: lobbies hard for your process/belief/thesis. Readers need to know why they need to continue listening to this process speech. Even if your explanatory paper is about how to bake a cake you need to make this part interesting.

Explanation/Process: explain the issue/process. Spare no detail. Assume nothing. Assume your reader needs every concept explained, every argument disclosed, and every fallacy exposed.

Conclusion: In a clever, exciting way, conclude this inspired speech.

SPEECH ASSIGNMENT

Present a 3-5 minute speech explaining the causes of World War I.

WRITING ASSIGNMENTS

1. In a one-page essay, explain what caused World War I. Include an outline, rough draft, thesis statement, final copy, and five new (circled) vocabulary words. Your essay must pay particular attention to style (focus, content, organization). Give a copy to a peer/friend to complete a peer evaluation (Appendix) and to your instructor to evaluate.

2. Read 200-250 pages/week and find vocabulary words.

3. Complete the speech assignment and have a teacher complete a speech evaluation (Appendix).

4. Pay particular attention to writing style this week.

5. Meditate on 1 Kings 20:35-41. Reflect on this passage, and others, in your prayer journal.

6. Write a warm-up essay every day.

FINAL PROJECT

Correct and rewrite all essays and place them in your
Final Portfolio.

WARM-UP ESSAYS:

	DAY 1	DAY 2	DAY 3	DAY 4	DAY 5
Explanatory	Explain how to bake a chocolate cake.	Explain how to go to your best friend's house.	Explain how to ice-skate.	Explain whether pizza should be eaten from the pointed end or the outside edge.	Explain why Brussels sprouts are wonderful to eat.

SUGGESTED
Weekly *Implementation*

DAY 1	DAY 2	DAY 3	DAY 4	DAY 5
Write a Warm-up Essay.	Write a Warm-up Essay.	Write a Warm-up Essay.	Write a Warm-up Essay.	Write a Warm-up Essay.
Read 35-50 pages/day.	Read 35-50 pages/day.	Read 35-50 pages/day.	Read 35-50 pages/day.	Read 35-50 pages/day.
Find five new vocabulary words.	Find five new vocabulary words.	Find five new vocabulary words.	Find five new vocabulary words.	Find five new vocabulary words.
Reflect on the speech assignment for the week.	Compose a first draft of your speech.	Revise your speech and submit to your evaluator/ parent.	Prepare to present your speech tomorrow.	Present your speech to a live audience.
Write an outline with thesis for your explanatory essay.	Work on the first draft for your explanatory essay.	Finish the first draft and then the revised draft of your explanatory essay.	Submit a copy of your paper to a peer for evaluation.	Submit your assignments to your evaluator/ parent.
Make a journal entry.	Make a journal entry.	Make a journal entry.	Finish the final copy of your explanatory essay.	Make a journal entry.
			Make a journal entry.	Take Lesson 19 Test.

LESSON 20

BACKGROUND

Facts can be verified or disproved. An *inference* is a statement about the unknown made on the basis of the known. *Opinion* is a statement of a writer's personal judgment. Students should recognize the difference between each type of writing and be able to create essays in each sphere. The following essay is full of inference, opinion, and a few facts. Identify each highlighted sentence as fact, inference, or opinion.

Southern Arkansas was a generous but exhausted land. Cotton grew to bountiful heights. Southwest winds permanently bent rice plants pregnant with pounds and pounds of offspring. Pecan trees cradled whole acres of antediluvian loam with their gigantic arms. **Every spring, bayous and rivers deposited a rich delta gift along the banks of grateful farmland.** It was a gift from Minnesota and Ohio, freely given by the ubiquitous Mississippi River. This was really an unselfish land, a land that seemed to give more than it took.

The house in which I now lived was a natural addition to this magnificent land. Built during the Depression years of cheap labor, "The House"—so named by Helen—reflected my grandparents' unbounded optimism. **Even to a young child, it appeared bigger than life. In fact, that mansion defied hyperbole.** They had built it with a profitable business and Depression-priced labor. They shamelessly flaunted their prosperity in a culture that was painfully impoverished. No one seemed to mind. The South has always been kind to its elitists. They were a chosen people, or so they claimed with every offering of ebullience. No one questioned their credentials—especially when my grandmother imported bricks from New Orleans streets, painted wicker chairs from replete Havana shops, and hung crystal chandeliers from abandoned Liverpool mansions. **I remember that the bricks surrounding our fireplace evoked a faint smell of horse manure as we enjoyed our winter fires.**

The House was a testimony both to my grandmother's generosity and to her eccentricity: five thousand square feet, six bedrooms, five full baths, and a full basement—the only full basement in my below-river-level community. The House appeared in *Southern Living*. The servants' quarters were above the kennel, and they were better than many of our neighbors' houses. The kitchen was built of cool New Orleans bricks and attached to The House by a closed walkway.

Our neighbors were mostly black. My grandmother had begged Old Man Parker to loan her money to build The House, but no bank would loan her money to build it. Or at least no banker would loan it to my grandfather. He had only solvency and prosperity to offer. My grandmother had other things to offer.

The problem was, as I intimated, my grandparents wanted to build their mansion too close to what my community called " — —- Town." At least my grandmother Helen wanted to built it there; my grandfather most assuredly did not. He wanted to build his house in the new Wolf Project, where all sensible, prosperous, blue-blooded white Southerners lived. **But he lacked imagination and he knew it, so he dutifully submitted the decision to Helen.** Not that he could do anything else. No one ever denied Helen anything that she really wanted.

Helen was no civil rights activist, nor did she pretend that she had any high moral standards. She was no hypocrite. Helen was a cold realist, and she cared for no one more than herself. My grandmother loved us all dearly, but she loved herself more. She knew a propitious place to build a house and was not going to let the absence of money or the pretensions of Southern society stop her.

Old Man John John Parker at first denied her request. **But Helen walked into his business, the**

Writing Skill: Fact, Inference, and Opinion
Grammar Review (Writing and Speaking): Usage – Pronoun and Subject/Verb Agreement
Public Speaking Skill: Converting the Fact, Inference, Opinion Essay into a Speech.
Looking Ahead: The Historical Profile

Fitzgerald County stock exchange, sat on his lap, kissed him on the mouth (not the cheek!), and asked in her most polished and sophisticated Southern accent, "Please, Mr. John John, will you loan me the money to build my house?" Whether from warm enticement of further benefits, or from cold fear that she would do something else to embarrass him, Old Man Parker immediately loaned her the money at no interest. The deal was sealed when Helen promised to bake him a Christmas pecan pie for the rest of his life. And she did. Parker ate pecan pie every Christmas until he died (in fact, it may have killed him: when he died he weighed a whopping 330 pounds). Only once did Helen fail to live up to her bargain; one season the pecan crop was abysmally bad and she had to substitute Vermont walnuts. Old Man Parker hardly noticed because Helen compensated the loss with her 100-proof rum cake! Helen did not like to cook, nor did she have to cook; she always had servants. But when she did anything, cooking, building a house, playing hide and seek with her grandchildren, she played and cooked to win.

Married when she was fifteen and divorced when she was sixteen, Helen was truly an iconoclast. She was the first unrepentant divorced woman my small Southern railroad town had ever known. Her first husband physically abused her once, and she nearly killed him. In fact, she would have killed him but the shotgun with which she shot him was loaded with number eight shot. She merely walked away from the marriage and the man. It was beneath her to file for divorce; but Judge Johnstown knew what she wanted, and everyone did, so he filed and granted the divorce within the week. Her first husband never remarried and suffered in ebullient regret for the rest of his life. For penance, he became a United Pentecostal pastor. As far as I know, Helen never spoke or thought of the man again.

Helen was an enigma that greatly bothered our arcane Southern society. Again, Helen was an iconoclast. She cared nothing about what others thought, except to irritate potential critics. For instance, Helen, a fourth-generation Methodist, loved to visit the Presbyterian Church because the pastor's wife wore stylish dresses. Helen wore scandalously short dresses, and while she refused to inhale, she nonetheless carried a lit cigarette in her right hand to pique scurrilous busybodies.

She had to be punished. Banished from the country club, most felt that she was sufficiently castigated. But Helen was not penitent. In fact, when she married my grandfather—the wealthiest and most eligible bachelor in town—the town was only too happy to invite my grandmother back into the country club. She refused, and all her offspring and the following generations grew up as pariahs, without the benefit of Southern country club amenities. Helen never again set a foot in the Fitzgerald County Country Club, although she loved to have garden parties and social events in The House.

Helen had three sons. My dad was the youngest. Uncle Sammy was the oldest and one of the most prosperous landowners in the area. Uncle Bobby went to Harvard and later became a Harvard Business School professor. My dad, who loved The House and Helen and black-eyed peas on New Year's Day, stayed at The House.

Daddy Bobby, my grandfather, owned The House, but Mammy Lee ran it. Mammy Lee was in a long line of distinguished women of color who had raised us "white boys," as she called us. Louise was my dad's "colored girl," so-called by my Mamaw Helen. I remember bringing my New-Jersey-born, Yankee wife and our three interracial children to meet their grandmother for the first time. "Which colored girl is raising your children?" my nursing-home Mamaw Helen innocently asked.

Armed with collard greens, black-eyed peas and a sturdy dusting cloth, my Mammy Lee single-handedly maintained this fragile world that was 1965 Arkansas. Mammy Lee was parent, servant, and benevolent despot, all rolled up into one. This 250-pound, five-foot-tall, black woman was an awesome presence. Chewing tobacco, limping slightly, and occasionally rubbing a lucky Mercury-head dime tied around her foot with kite string, Lee enveloped us in her arms and propelled us forward through all adversity. She protected us from reality and gave us false security, garnished with pecan pies and encouraging words. Lee set perimeters for all our lives. "Mistah Jim," she often scolded me, "I'se agonna spank yo' bottom if you don't pick up yo' toys." And many times she did exactly that!

I loved my Mammy Lee. I can still feel her as she held me and squeezed—as if a hug and a shake could cure anything! Lee showed me where to find the fattest fishing worms, and she helped me dig for pirate treasure.

There was a desperation about Lee. Her world was changing quickly—too quickly—and her discomfort grew. I loved Lee, I loved my homeland, this way of life, and in a way, they—Lee and my South—were one and the same. They were both grotesquely generous and subtly selfish at the same time. My mother could see it. Walter Cronkite could see it. Lyndon Baines Johnson could see it. I could see it. (James P. Stobaugh)

GRAMMAR REVIEW: USAGE—PRONOUN AND SUBJECT/VERB AGREEMENT

Match pronouns in gender and number with their antecedents. Likewise, verbs should match their subject in number. "Everyone should finish their dessert" seems accurate but actually, "everyone" is a singular indefinite pronoun antecedent that requires a singular possessive pronoun. "Everyone should finish her dessert."

PUBLIC SPEAKING: CONVERTING THE FACT, INFERENCE, OPINION ESSAY INTO A SPEECH

When you are presenting a speech, you must be able to distinguish between fact, inference, and opinion. Great speeches emerge from sound reasoning and logic. When you present your speech, ask pertinent questions, evaluate arguments, and if necessary, admit a lack of understanding. Be willing to examine beliefs, assumptions, and opinions that differ, even contrast, your own. Weigh all views against facts. Fairly and honestly tell your reader these other views. In your speech, suspend judgment until all facts have been gathered and considered, but once you have moved beyond opinion and you know your facts, state them clearly and forcefully.

SPEECH ASSIGNMENT

Present a 3-5 minute speech on some aspect of the Christian life.

WRITING ASSIGNMENTS

1. In a one-page essay, write an essay on the Lord's Supper. In your essay examine other opinions but state what you see as the facts. This essay should include an outline, rough draft, thesis statement, final copy, and five new (circled) vocabulary words. The essay must pay particular attention to style (focus, content, organization). Give a copy to a peer/friend to complete a peer evaluation (Appendix) and to your instructor to evaluate.

2. Read 200-250 pages/week and make vocabulary cards.

3. Complete the speech assignment and have a teacher complete a speech evaluation (Appendix).

4. Pay particular attention to your writing style this week.

5. Read 1 Kings 21. In your prayer journal, tell this story from the perspectives of Naboth, Ahab, Elijah, and Jezebel.

6. Write a warm-up essay every day.

FINAL PROJECT

Correct and rewrite all essays and place them in your Final Portfolio.

WARM-UP ESSAYS:

	DAY 1	DAY 2	DAY 3	DAY 4	DAY 5
Facts/ Inferences/ Opinion	You think your sister has been using your toothbrush to remove dirt from her shoes. Write a factual paper arguing your point.	You think your sister has been using your toothbrush to remove dirt from her shoes. Write an inference paper arguing your point.	You think your sister has been using your toothbrush to remove dirt from her shoes. Write an opinion paper arguing your point.	Using facts, argue that you should be allowed to go on a mission trip to Mongolia.	Using opinions, argue that you should be allowed to go on a mission trip to Mongolia.

SUGGESTED
Weekly *Implementation*

DAY 1	DAY 2	DAY 3	DAY 4	DAY 5
Write a Warm-up Essay. Read 35-50 pages/day. Find five new vocabulary words. Reflect on the speech assignment for the week. Write an outline with thesis for your fact, inference, and opinion essay. Make a journal entry.	Write a Warm-up Essay. Read 35-50 pages/day. Find five new vocabulary words. Compose a first draft of your speech. Work on the first draft for your fact, inference, and opinion essays. Make a journal entry.	Write a Warm-up Essay. Read 35-50 pages/day. Find five new vocabulary words. Revise your speech and submit to your evaluator/ parent. Finish the first draft and then the revised draft of your fact, inference, and opinion essays. Make a journal entry.	Write a Warm-up Essay. Read 35-50 pages/day. Find five new vocabulary words. Prepare to present your speech tomorrow. Submit a copy of your paper to a peer for evaluation. Finish the final copy of your fact, inference, and opinion essay. Make a journal entry.	Write a Warm-up Essay. Read 35-50 pages/day. Find five new vocabulary words. Present your speech to a live audience. Submit your assignments to your evaluator/ parent. Take Lesson 20 Test. Make a journal entry.

LESSON 21

BACKGROUND

In a history profile, you should write highlights giving the salient components of a historical person's life.

SAMPLE ESSAY

Carl Henry was born to a Roman Catholic mother and a Lutheran father, but religion was a matter of private indifference to his parents. During his early teens, Henry was baptized and confirmed in the Episcopal Church but later became a church dropout. He began a career by selling newspaper subscriptions. By 1933 he was Long Island's youngest editor of the *Port Jefferson Times Echo*. During this time he had a profound ecumenical experience. Henry said, "A Seventh-Day Adventist plied me with catastrophic forebodings from the book of Daniel. An elderly Methodist lady stressed my need to be born again. A Presbyterian minister deplored my newspaper coverage for the New York press in contrast to his coverage of Long Island for God. A university graduate in the Oxford Group pushed me to a personal decision for Christ." While he was at Wheaton College, he joined a Baptist Church. By 1949, Henry had finished his formal education (B.A. and M.A, Wheaton; B.D. and Th.D., Northern Baptist Theological Seminary; Ph.D. Boston University). He joined Harold Ockenga and Charles E. Fuller in founding Fuller Theological Seminary. (James P. Stobaugh)

GRAMMAR REVIEW: USAGE—PRONOUN USAGE

Nominative case forms of pronouns are used in subject and nominative positions. Objective case forms of pronouns are used as objects.

Him and me went to the store is incorrect.

He and I went to the store is correct.

> **Writing Skill:** Historical Profile
> **Grammar Review (Writing and Speaking):** Usage—Pronoun Usage
> **Public Speaking Skill:** Converting the Historical Profile into a Speech
> **Looking Ahead:** Final Project is due

Mary and Susan spoke to he and I is incorrect.

Mary and Susan spoke to him and me is correct.

PUBLIC SPEAKING: CONVERTING THE HISTORICAL PROFILE ESSAY INTO A SPEECH

The historical profile speech is basically the historical profile essay in speech form. You must be careful to give the details in some sort of order—sequential or temporal.

SPEECH ASSIGNMENT

Present a 1-3 minute historical profile of a William Wilberforce.

WRITING ASSIGNMENTS

1. Write a historical profile of William Wilberforce. This essay should include an outline, rough draft, thesis statement, final copy, and five new (circled) vocabulary words. Pay particular attention to style (focus, content, organization). Give a copy to your peer/friend to complete a peer evaluation (Appendix) and to your instructor to evaluate.

2. Read 100-250 pages/week and keep vocabulary cards.

3. Complete the speech assignment and have a teacher complete a speech evaluation (Appendix).

4. Pay attention to stylistic tendencies this week.

Practice combining sentences to make your paper more interesting.

    5. In the book of 1 Kings there is a despicable character named Jezebel. Meditate upon why she is so despicable and record reflections in your prayer journal.

    6. Complete one warm-up essay every day.

FINAL PROJECT

Correct and rewrite all essays and place them in your Final Portfolio.

WARM-UP ESSAYS:

	DAY 1	DAY 2	DAY 3	DAY 4	DAY 5
Historical Profile	Write a historical profile of your next door neighbor.	Write a historical profile your pastor.	Write a historical profile of your teacher.	Write a historical profile of the president.	Write a historical profile of the apostle Paul.

SUGGESTED
Weekly *Implementation*

DAY 1	DAY 2	DAY 3	DAY 4	DAY 5
Write a Warm-up Essay.	Write a Warm-up Essay.	Write a Warm-up Essay.	Write a Warm-up Essay.	Write a Warm-up Essay.
Read 35-50 pages/day.	Read 35-50 pages/day.	Read 35-50 pages/day.	Read 35-50 pages/day.	Read 35-50 pages/day.
Find five new vocabulary words.	Find five new vocabulary words.	Find five new vocabulary words.	Find five new vocabulary words.	Find five new vocabulary words.
Reflect on the speech assignment for the week.	Compose a first draft of your speech.	Revise your speech and submit to your evaluator/ parent.	Prepare to present your speech tomorrow.	Present your speech to a live audience.
Write an outline with thesis for your historical profile.	Work on the first draft for your historical profile.	Finish the first draft and then the revised draft of your historical profile.	Submit a copy of your paper to a peer for evaluation.	Submit your assignments to your evaluator/ parent.
Make a journal entry.	Make a journal entry.	Make a journal entry.	Finish the final copy of your historical profile.	Make a journal entry.
			Make a journal entry.	Take Lesson 21 Test.

LESSON 22

FINAL PORTFOLIO DUE

You will give to your teacher your corrected essays, speech evaluations, peer evaluations, and other material in an attractive organized and labeled folder.

You should include fifteen to twenty book reviews.

You will submit at least three warm-up essays for each week (a total of sixty-three) and show evidence of others.

You will include evidence that you have produced at least three weekly journal entries (a total of sixty-three). A sample cover sheet for your Final Portfolio is shown below.

Skills for
Rhetoric
Folder

Name
Month day, year

Research Paper Overview: Writing the Research Paper

Each lesson will emphasize a separate aspect of the research paper.

Writing Style: Different writing styles will continue to be emphasized.

Journal Writing: You should continue to journal.

Writing Assignments: Over the next twelve lessons, you will write a research paper. At the same time, you should continue to read classics and complete book review sheets (Appendix). The best writers inevitably read vast amounts of good books during their careers. You should also continue to write warm-up essays.

THE RESEARCH PAPER

Rarely, if ever, are college students evaluated through objective tests (e.g., multiple choice, true-false). Most professors prefer to have their students write two or three short papers (or three to five papers) and one large, final research paper. Therefore, the ability to read vast amounts of material (500–1,500 pages per week) and to write large numbers of manuscripts is part of the American college scene. Prepare now!

LESSON 23

BACKGROUND

For the next few weeks, you will be writing a research paper. The research paper is really only a long explanatory paper. Like all papers, it has prewriting, writing, and rewriting phases. The prewriting part of preparing a research paper includes the following: selecting an interesting topic, gathering information, and limiting the topic.

In a few weeks, when you finish your research paper, you will have a thesis statement, preliminary outline, many notes, a thorough outline, an inspiring outline, a thoroughly developed main body, a satisfying conclusion, and a complete works cited page. You will write and rewrite this research paper until you are a specialist in your topic.

THE THINKING GAME

Issue
State problem/issue
in five sentences.
in two sentences.
in one sentence.

Name three or more subtopics of problem.

Name three or more subtopics of the subtopics.

What information must be known in order to solve the problem or to answer the question?

State the answer to the question/problem
in five sentences.
in two sentences.
in one sentence.

Stated in terms of outcomes, what evidences will I see to confirm that I have made the right decision?

Once the problem/question is answered/solved, what one or two new problems/answers will arise?

Writing Skill: Research Paper: Designing a Working Plan by Choosing a Topic; Initial Research; and Organization

Style (Writing and Speaking): Usage – *Fewer vs. Less, Good vs. Well*, and Double Negatives

Public Speaking Skill: Effective Listening

Looking Ahead: The Research Paper: Thesis Statement

Use the Thinking Game (Appendix) to help you narrow your topic, and, later, to sharpen your thesis statement. *The first step in all prewriting is articulating a thesis statement.* Next, even though it is still early, you should begin to collect resources about your topic and even begin to take notes.

Let's begin!

STYLE (WRITING AND SPEAKING): USAGE – FEWER VS. LESS, GOOD VS. WELL, AND DOUBLE NEGATIVES

Fewer refers to the number of separate units; *less* refers to bulk quantity. If you can count the item, it is fewer; if you cannot, it is less.

Good is used as an adjective; *well* is used as an adverb.

Avoid double negatives:
I can't hardly read the signs (incorrect).
I can hardly read the signs (correct).

PUBLIC SPEAKING: EFFECTIVE LISTENING

Every great orator is a great listener. First, you must desire to become a better listener. Stop talking. Look at the speaker. Listening is an active process. Try to listen objectively. Get rid of distractions. As you listen, make a note of the main points. Don't be quick to judge. Don't mentally offer a response until you have heard

everything. Avoid jumping to conclusions. Finally, most importantly, decide what is not said. Only respond to what is said, not what is unsaid.

The inability to listen may have disastrous results. At the end of the Civil War, knowing that the end of the Civil War was near, Jefferson Davis, the president of the southern Confederacy, was greatly encouraged by President Abraham Lincoln's Second Inaugural Speech. After this speech, Davis saw Lincoln as the South's best friend and the only hope that the South had to obtain a just peace. On the other hand, the misguided, southern patriot John Wilkes Booth heard the following speech and decided that Abraham Lincoln was the South's worst enemy. As a result, Booth assassinated President Lincoln a month after this speech was presented. Listen to the following speech and decide who was a better listener: Jefferson Davis or John Wilkes Booth.

Fellow countrymen: At this second appearing to take the oath of the presidential office, there is less occasion for an extended address than there was at the first. Then a statement, somewhat in detail, of a course to be pursued, seemed fitting and proper. Now, at the expiration of four years, during which public declarations have been constantly called forth on every point and phase of the great contest which still absorbs the attention and engrosses the energies of the nation, little that is new could be presented. The progress of our arms, upon which all else chiefly depends, is as well known to the public as to myself; and it is, I trust, reasonably satisfactory and encouraging to all. With high hope for the future, no prediction in regard to it is ventured.

On the occasion corresponding to this four years ago, all thoughts were anxiously directed to an impending civil war. All dreaded it—all sought to avert it. While the inaugural address was being delivered from this place, devoted altogether to saving the Union without war, insurgent agents were in the city seeking to destroy it without war—seeking to dissolve the Union, and divide effects, by negotiation. Both parties deprecated war; but one of them would make war rather than let the nation survive; and the other would accept war rather than let it perish. And the war came.

One-eighth of the whole population were colored slaves, not distributed generally over the Union, but localized in the Southern part of it. These slaves constituted a peculiar and powerful interest. All knew that this interest was, somehow, the cause of the war. To strengthen, perpetuate, and extend this interest was the object for which the insurgents would rend the Union, even by war; while the government claimed no right to do more than to restrict the territorial enlargement of it.

Neither party expected for the war the magnitude or the duration which it has already attained. Neither anticipated that the cause of the conflict might cease with, or even before, the conflict itself should cease. Each looked for an easier triumph, and a result less fundamental and astounding. Both read the same Bible, and pray to the same God; and each invokes his aid against the other. It may seem strange that any men should dare to ask a just God's assistance in wringing their bread from the sweat of other men's faces; but let us judge not, that we be not judged. The prayers of both could not be answered—that of neither has been answered fully.

The Almighty has his own purposes. "Woe unto the world because of offenses! for it must needs be that offenses come; but woe to that man by whom the offense cometh." If we shall suppose that American slavery is one of those offenses which, in the providence of God, must needs come, but which, having continued through his appointed time, he now wills to remove, and that he gives to both North and South this terrible war, as the woe due to those by whom the offense came, shall we discern therein any departure from those divine attributes which the believers in a living God always ascribe to him? Fondly do we hope—fervently do we pray—that this mighty scourge of war may speedily pass away. Yet, if God wills that it continue until all the wealth piled by the bondsman's two hundred and fifty years of unrequited toil shall be sunk, and until every drop of blood drawn by the lash shall be paid by another drawn with the sword, as was said

SENATE CHAMBER U.S.A. CONCLUSION OF CLAY'S SPEECH IN DEFENCE OF SLAVERY.

three thousand years ago, so still it must be said, "The judgments of the Lord are true and righteous altogether."

With malice toward none; with charity for all; with firmness in the right, as God gives us to see the right, let us strive on to finish the work we are in; to bind up the nation's wounds; to care for him who shall have borne the battle, and for his widow, and his orphan—to do all which may achieve and cherish a just and lasting peace among ourselves, and with all nations. (Abraham Lincoln. http://www.bartleby.com/124/pres32.html)

Public Speaking: Controversial Subjects

It is important for the speaker to clarify his goals and to make sure that his audience knows his goals. The amount of controversy surrounding the proposition and the attitudes of the audience will determine how much time and rhetoric the speaker devotes to convincing the audience of the veracity of his position. How persuasive is the following Christmas Eve sermon?

I want to suggest something so obvious, but so radical, that it seems silly for me to say it: God is always with us; God is everywhere; God can do all things. If I can convince you that this is true, I want to show you through the Christmas story that this omniscient, omnipresent God loves us too.

We wonder, I fear, whether it is true—whether or not God is real, whether or not He is here among us. We can believe in the stock market, in the Pittsburgh Pirates, in post-Christmas sales, but can we believe that God is right here, right now, in our midst, right next to us even in our hearts? Can we believe this? I hope we

can. Statisticians tell us that almost 75 percent of us believe in miracles, and more that that believe that there is a God. But how many of us live our lives as though God knew everything that we are doing, thinking, saying? I imagine if we really understood, our actions and words would probably change!

No doubt Joseph and Mary's generation wondered if there was a God at all. That is, I fear, a perennial question. As Gideon watched his people being persecuted by enemy armies, he wondered where God had gone. David, as he grieved over the death of his son Absalom, wondered if God really cared. Thomas Jefferson, the author of the Declaration of Independence, sincerely held that God was no longer present or concerned about the world He had created. Jefferson thought God had placed the world in the universe, wound up as a clock, and then backed off to let things happen according to natural law. The great Colonial Awakening preacher Jonathan Edwards shared genuine concern that God was still active in his world—at least, he lamented that no one seemed to act like it!

The great English Christian apologist C. S. Lewis, when his cherished wife Joy Davidman died, wished that God were not so present! Listen to Lewis—and remember that this is a man who loved Jesus Christ with all his heart.

Where is God? This is one of the most disquieting symptoms. When you are happy, so happy that you have no sense of needing Him, so happy that you are tempted to feel His claims on you as an interruption, if you remember yourself and turn to Him with gratitude and praise, you will be welcomed with open arms. But go to Him when your need is desperate, when all other help is in vain, and what do you find? . . . Silence. . . . There are no lights in the window.

Are there no lights in your windows? Have you given up on God? Surely the generation in our Gospel lesson had reason to give up, to lose hope. Why not? When is the last time God had done anything for them? From their perspective, the hated Romans had subjected God's people to unthinkable indignities, with no end in sight. Where was God? Where was the light?

This generation, as our own, echoes the words of C. S. Lewis, "Not that I am thinking that there is no God. . . . The real danger is of coming to believe such dreadful things about Him." How is God doing in your book? Do you still believe in Him? How near is God? As near as one born as we were born, albeit in a stable, among most primitive conditions. As near as one who announces a new Way, a new Life, a new Hope. As near as one who died a horrible death on a cross—because He loved me—and then arose from the grave. . . . He is here.

He came with singing angels, dirty shepherds, and glowing wise men. He came to Joseph and Mary—hardly older than many of the children in this place. He came. He is. He lives. Perhaps tonight you can discover, for yourself, God's inescapable nearness. . . . (James P. Stobaugh)

SPEECH ASSIGNMENT

Listen carefully to a speech or sermon and relate the main points to your teacher/parent/ guardian.

WRITING ASSIGNMENTS

1. You will be assigned a research topic this week. After being assigned a paper topic, narrow that topic by using the Thinking Game (Appendix).

2. Read 150 to 200 pages this week and create vocabulary cards.

3. Complete the speech assignment and have a teacher complete a speech evaluation of your speech (Appendix).

4. While preparing the warm-up essays, pay particular attention to your writing style this week.

5. Meditate on 1 Kings 21:29 and imagine how Elijah felt when his archenemy King Ahab was shown mercy by God. Meditate on this passage and others. Has God ever disappointed you?

6. Write a warm-up essay every day.

RESEARCH PAPER BENCHMARK

In the next 11 lessons you will write a research paper. If you complete the assignments for each lesson, by Lesson 34 you will have a complete research paper. Do not skip any step! During this lesson you will obtain/choose and narrow your research paper topic.

WARM-UP ESSAYS:

	DAY 1	DAY 2	DAY 3	DAY 4	DAY 5
Narrow a topic in the first paragraph of a research paper.	Topic: Adolescent pimples.	Topic: Drinking milk with pizza.	Topic: Pesky little brothers/ sisters.	Topic: Should curfew be negotiated?	Topic: Is there a pot of gold at the end of a rainbow?

SUGGESTED
Weekly *Implementation*

DAY 1	DAY 2	DAY 3	DAY 4	DAY 5
Write a Warm-up Essay.	Write a Warm-up Essay.	Write a Warm-up Essay.	Write a Warm-up Essay.	Write a Warm-up Essay.
Read 35-50 pages/day.	Read 35-50 pages/day.	Read 35-50 pages/day.	Read 35-50 pages/day.	Read 35-50 pages/day.
Find five new vocabulary words.	Find five new vocabulary words.	Find five new vocabulary words.	Find five new vocabulary words.	Find five new vocabulary words.
Reflect on the speech assignment for the week.	Narrow your topics to one or two by using the Thinking Game.	Discuss your topic with a parent/ teacher/ Guardian	Write a short summary or present orally a synopsis of the listening assignment you had this week.	Review your speech assignment.
List a few possible topics for your research paper.	Make a journal entry.	Make a journal entry.	Finalize your topic.	Determine the topic of your research paper.
Make a journal entry.			Make a journal entry.	Take Lesson 23 Test.
				Make a journal entry.

CHOOSING A TOPIC

Sometimes the general topic is *given* to you—you do not *choose* it. However, if you have a choice, choose a topic that is sufficiently narrow to keep you focused but sufficiently broad to be relevant. For instance, a topic like "Civil War Weaponry" would be a better research topic than "The Civil War Repeater Rifle" only if your goal is to give a broad overview of weaponry.

LESSON 24

BACKGROUND

The first step in all prewriting is the articulation of a thesis statement, which states the main idea of an essay. It usually appears toward the end of the introduction. The thesis statement is the main idea or point of the essay. A thesis statement is a one or two-sentence statement or an answer to a question concerning the purpose of the writing assignment. All writing assignments, no matter how complicated or how long, can be reduced to a single statement. For example, if the paper topic assigned is "The Causes of the American Civil War," the thesis statement must answer the question "What Caused the American Civil War?" Again, the answer to this question is the thesis statement for the paper. A thesis statement must be interesting, as specific as possible, and manageable in scope. A good way to ferret out a thesis statement is to write something like this:

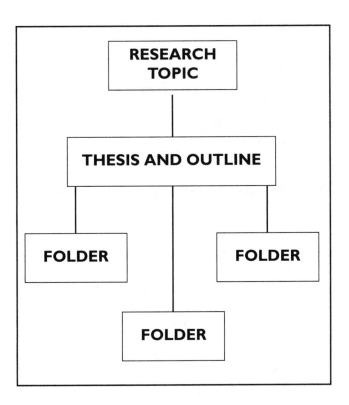

> **Writing Skill:** Research Paper: Thesis Statement
>
> **Style (Writing and Speaking):** Usage – *Who* vs. *Whom*
>
> **Public Speaking Skill:** Oratory
>
> **Looking Ahead:** The Research Paper: Preliminary Bibliography and Works Cited Page

In this essay, I plan to explain or argue that

_____

_____ because of

(1) _____ ,

(2) _____ ,

(3) _____ , and

(4) _____ .

In summary, an effective thesis statement is a one-sentence statement of truth about a topic. "Slavery caused the Civil War" is a correctly formed thesis statement, but it is too broad and incomplete. "The failure of the American political system to manage the problem of slavery expansion in antebellum America caused the Civil War" is more defined. This statement presents a topic and an opinion about a topic in a sufficiently broad way to summarize the purpose of the research paper and in a sufficiently narrow way to have precise application to this particular research paper.

WRITING STYLE: USAGE – WHO VS. WHOM

The case of the pronoun beginning a subordinate clause is determined by its use in the clause that it begins. The case and number of the pronoun is not affected by any word outside the clause. In the case of *who* and *whom*, *who* functions in the subjective case (subject, predicate noun) and *whom* functions in the objective case (direct object, indirect object, object of a preposition).

> *The new Sunday school teacher, whom came from Chicago, was very effective.* (incorrect)
>
> *The new Sunday school teacher, who came from Chicago, was very effective.* (correct)

PUBLIC SPEAKING: THE GREAT ORATORY

Have you ever heard a speech/sermon that changed your life? An oratory is a speech that communicates a truth or information to the listener. It persuades the reader to accept a particular view of reality. One of the best oratories is the "Gettysburg Address" by Abraham Lincoln:

Four score and seven years ago our fathers brought forth, upon this continent, a new nation, conceived in Liberty, and dedicated to the proposition that all men are created equal.

Now we are engaged in a great civil war, testing whether that nation, or any nation so conceived, and so dedicated, can long endure. We are met here on a great battlefield of that war. We have come to dedicate a portion of it as a final resting place for those who here gave

their lives that that nation might live. It is altogether fitting and proper that we should do this.

But in a larger sense we can not dedicate—we can not consecrate—we can not hallow this ground. The brave men, living and dead, who struggled here, have consecrated it far above our poor power to add or detract. The world will little note, nor long remember, what we say here, but can never forget what they did here. It is for us, the living, rather to be dedicated here to the unfinished work which they have, thus far, so nobly carried on. It is rather for us to be here dedicated to the great task remaining before us—that from these honored dead we take increased devotion to that cause for which they here gave the last full measure of devotion—that we here highly resolve that these dead shall not have died in vain; that this nation shall have a new birth of freedom; and that this government of the people, by the people, for the people, shall not perish from the earth. (http://www.geocities.com/way2anand/Speech/gb.html)

SPEECH ASSIGNMENT: PRESENTING AN ORATORY

Write and then present a three-minute oratory on a subject of your choice.

The Roman statesman Cicero, in "To Cerealis," discusses how you should create your oratory (www.bartleby.com/9/4/1024.html):

1. The entrance, or the introduction
2. The narration, or the background details
3. The proposition, or the thesis
4. The division, or a brief list of your points
5. The confirmation, or the evidence for these points
6. The confutation, or anticipation of the rebuttal
7. The conclusion

WRITING ASSIGNMENTS

1. After being assigned a paper topic by your educator/teacher, write a thesis statement.

2. Read 150 to 200 pages this week and create vocabulary cards.

3. Complete the speech assignment and have a teacher complete a speech evaluation (Appendix).

4. While preparing the warm-ups, pay particular attention to your writing style this week.

5. Meditate on 1 Kings 22 and reflect on the story of Micaiah.

6. Write a warm-up essay every day.

RESEARCH PAPER BENCHMARK

Last lesson you determined and narrowed your topic. During this lesson you will write your research paper thesis statement.

WARM-UP ESSAYS:

	DAY 1	DAY 2	DAY 3	DAY 4	DAY 5
Write a thesis statement for the following research paper topics.	Topic: Soccer is a game for the intelligent.	Topic: Home-schoolers should have a snow day.	Topic: The theory of relativity is relative.	Topic: Why do home-schooled girls score as well as home-schooled boys on the SAT I?	Topic: Why do bad things happen to good people?

SUGGESTED
Weekly *Implementation*

DAY 1	DAY 2	DAY 3	DAY 4	DAY 5
Write a Warm-up Essay.	Write a Warm-up Essay.	Write a Warm-up Essay.	Write a Warm-up Essay.	Write a Warm-up Essay.
Read 35-50 pages/day.	Read 35-50 pages/day.	Read 35-50 pages/day.	Read 35-50 pages/day.	Read 35-50 pages/day.
Find five new vocabulary words.	Find five new vocabulary words.	Find five new vocabulary words.	Find five new vocabulary words.	Find five new vocabulary words.
Reflect on the speech assignment for the week.	Compose a first draft of your speech.	Revise your speech and submit to your evaluator/ parent.	Prepare to present your speech tomorrow.	Present your speech to a live audience.
Review information on how to write a thesis statement.	Make a journal entry.	Write several thesis statements for your research paper. Narrow your choices.	Submit a copy of your thesis statement to a peer for evaluation.	Submit your assignments to your evaluator/ parent.
Make a journal entry.		Make a journal entry.	Make your final choice for your thesis statement.	Take Lesson 24 Test.
			Make a journal entry.	Make a journal entry.

LESSON 25

BACKGROUND

The prewriting part of writing a research paper includes the following: selecting an interesting topic, gathering information, and limiting a subject. Presumably, your paper topic and thesis statement have already been established. Your job now is to continue the process of gathering information and taking notes. At this point, even if you create computer generated files later, it would be advantageous to create a physical file where you can keep such hard evidence as magazine articles and pictures.

Now that you know where you are going, and why, and you have a fairly good idea of what problem you are going to address, the next step is to find the sources you

> **Writing Skill:** Research Paper: Preliminary Bibliography and Works Cited Page
>
> **Style (Writing and Speaking):** Usage— *Further* vs. *Farther*; *Than* vs. *As*.
>
> **Public Speaking Skill:** Dramatic Readings
>
> **Looking Ahead:** The Research Paper: Taking Notes (A)

will need to answer the question you have asked in your Thinking Game and your thesis statement. This means developing a preliminary bibliography. It is the "preliminary" bibliography, but since it will become a works cited page at the end of the research paper, be thorough.

What is the difference between a preliminary bibliography and a works cited page? A preliminary bibliography will not be submitted with the final project and lists all the sources you anticipate using. The preliminary bibliography is the whole salad bar; the works cited page is what you actually put on your plate. The works cited page is included with the final research paper and lists all the sources that you actually used in your paper. So, you can see how the preliminary bibliography naturally evolves into the works cited page. What makes this so nice is that the punctuation and style of the preliminary bibliography is exactly the same as the works cited page.

Where does one begin? Most contemporary research begins with an online search engine. There are hundreds but one of the best is http://www.dogpile.com. Next, visit your local library. Typically, many of you might prefer to skip the library visit and merely use internet resources. Don't. The library may have a video, book tape, or rare manuscript that you will not find online. Additionally, online sources must be carefully evaluated for validity.

Use the card catalog and *Reader's Guide for Periodical Literature*. Also, you may find several computer collections that will be beneficial (e.g., ERIC). Ask the librarian to help you. A public library is a good beginning, but a university library, if available, is better.

STYLE (WRITING AND SPEAKING): USAGE – FURTHER VS. FARTHER; THAN VS. AS.

Farther refers to physical distance; *further* refers to quantity or degree.

After *than* and *as* introducing an incomplete construction, the student should use the form of the pronoun he would use if the sentence construction were actually completed.

John is a better soccer player than him is incorrect.

John is a better soccer player than he is correct. Think of the sentence this way: *John is a better soccer player than he (is).*

PUBLIC SPEAKING: DRAMATIC READINGS

Reading is a more difficult chore than may be supposed. In fact, reading effectively is extremely difficult. Familiarize yourself with the material, or even better, memorize the piece. Observe the places that require accents, pauses, and other punctuation. Finally, you must be careful to speak slowly and clearly. Narration is simply the verbal telling of a story, as opposed to telling it in other ways—through the media for instance. Dramatic readings tell the audience things that are not obvious from the acting alone.

SPEECH ASSIGNMENT

Read the following biblical passages to an audience:

Daniel 5:1–30

King Belshazzar held a great feast for 1,000 of his nobles and drank wine in their presence. Under the influence of the wine, Belshazzar gave orders to bring in the gold and silver vessels that his predecessor Nebuchadnezzar had taken from the temple in Jerusalem, so that the king and his nobles, wives, and concubines could drink from them. So they brought in the gold vessels that had been taken from the temple, the house of God in Jerusalem, and the king and his nobles, wives, and concubines drank from them. They drank the wine and praised their gods made of gold and silver, bronze, iron, wood, and stone.

At that moment the fingers of a man's hand appeared and began writing on the plaster of the king's palace wall next to the lampstand. As the king watched the hand that was writing, his face turned pale, and his thoughts so terrified him that his hip joints shook and his knees knocked together.

The king called out to bring in the mediums, Chaldeans, and astrologers. He said to these wise men of Babylon, "Whoever reads this inscription and gives me its interpretation will be clothed in purple, have a gold chain around his neck, and have the third highest position in the kingdom."

So all the king's wise men came in, but none could read the inscription or make known its interpretation to him. Then King Belshazzar became even more terrified, his face turned pale, and his nobles were bewildered.

Because of the outcry of the king and his nobles, the queen came to the banquet hall. "May the king live forever," she said. "Don't let your thoughts terrify you or your face be pale. There is a man in your kingdom who has the spirit of the holy gods in him. In the days of your predecessor he was found to have insight, intelligence, and wisdom like the wisdom of the gods. Your predecessor, King Nebuchadnezzar, appointed him chief of the diviners, mediums, Chaldeans, and astrologers. Your own predecessor, the king, [did this]* because Daniel, the one the king named Belteshazzar, was found to have an extraordinary spirit, knowledge and perception, and the ability to interpret dreams, explain riddles, and solve problems. Therefore, summon Daniel, and he will give the interpretation."

Then Daniel was brought before the king. The king said to him, "Are you Daniel, one of the Judean exiles that my predecessor the king brought from Judah? I've heard that you have the spirit of the gods in you, and that you have insight, intelligence, and extraordinary wisdom. Now the wise men and mediums were brought before me to read this inscription and make its interpretation known to me, but they could not give its interpretation. However, I have heard about you that you can give interpretations and solve problems. Therefore, if you can read this inscription and give me its interpretation, you will be clothed in purple, have a gold chain around your neck, and have the third highest position in the kingdom."

Then Daniel answered the king, "You may keep your gifts, and give your rewards to someone else; however, I will read the inscription for the king and make the interpretation known to him.

Your Majesty, the Most High God gave sovereignty, greatness, glory, and majesty to your predecessor Nebuchadnezzar. Because of the greatness He gave him, all peoples, nations, and languages were terrified and fearful of him. He killed anyone he wanted and kept alive anyone he wanted; he exalted anyone he wanted and humbled anyone he wanted. But when his heart was exalted and his spirit became arrogant, he was deposed from his royal throne and his glory was taken from him. He was driven away from people, his mind was like an animal's, he lived with the wild donkeys, he was fed grass like cattle, and his body was drenched with dew from the sky until he acknowledged that the Most High God is ruler over the kingdom of men and sets anyone He wants over it.

"But you his successor, Belshazzar, have not humbled your heart, even though you knew all this. Instead, you have exalted yourself against the Lord of heaven. The vessels from His house, were brought to you, and as you and your nobles, wives, and concubines drank wine from them, you praised the gods made of silver and gold, bronze, iron, wood, and stone, which do not see or hear or understand. But you have not glorified the God who holds your life-breath in His hand and who controls the whole course of your life. Therefore, He sent the hand, and this writing was inscribed.

"This is the writing that was inscribed:

MENE, MENE, TEKEL, PARSIN

This is the interpretation of the message:

Mene: God has numbered [the days of] your kingdom and brought it to an end.

Tekel: You have been weighed in the balance and found deficient.

Peres: Your kingdom has been divided and given to the Medes and Persians."

Then Belshazzar gave an order, and they clothed Daniel in purple, a gold chain around his neck, and issued a proclamation concerning him that he should be the third ruler in the kingdom.

That very night Belshazzar the king of the Chaldeans was killed, and Darius the Mede received the kingdom at the age of 62. (Holman CSB)

Isaiah 6:1–8

In the year that King Uzziah died, I saw the Lord seated on a high and lofty throne, and His robe filled the temple. Seraphim were standing above Him; each one had six wings: with two he covered his face, with two he covered his feet, and with two he flew. And one called to another:

"Holy, holy, holy is the Lord of Hosts;
His glory fills the whole earth."

The foundations of the doorways shook at the sound of their voices, and the temple was filled with smoke.

Then I said: "Woe is me, for I am ruined, because I am a man of unclean lips and live among a people of unclean lips, [and] because my eyes have seen the King, the Lord of Hosts." Then one of the seraphim flew to me, and in his hand was a glowing coal that he had taken from the altar with tongs. He touched my mouth [with it] and said: "Now that this has touched your lips, your wickedness is removed, and your sin is atoned for."

Then I heard the voice of the Lord saying: "Who should I send? Who will go for Us?"

I said: "Here I am. Send me." (Holman CSB)

WRITING ASSIGNMENTS

1. Prepare a preliminary bibliography of at least ten sources of information. At least one of these sources must be a primary source and at least one must be a journal article. While you may use encyclopedias and indexes in preparing this bibliography, they will not count as sources. Each bibliographic entry should be typed and contain all the necessary bibliographic infor-

mation: author's name, title, translator's name, editor's name, place of publication, publisher's name, date of publication, and page numbers. At this point, format is not important. Create bibliography cards on note cards, or you may use files created on your computer's word-processing software.

2. Read 150 to 200 pages this week and create vocabulary cards.

3. Complete the speech assignment and have a teacher complete a speech evaluation of your speech (Appendix).

4. While preparing the warm-ups, pay particular attention to your writing style this week.

5. Meditate on 1 Kings 22. Reflect on righteous Jehoshaphat's decision to ally himself with evil Ahab.

6. Write a warm-up essay every day.

RESEARCH PAPER BENCHMARK

So far you have determined and narrowed your topic and written your thesis statement. During this lesson you will write your research paper preliminary bibliography.

WARM-UP ESSAYS:

	DAY 1	DAY 2	DAY 3	DAY 4	DAY 5
Write an essay on what happens to you at the library	You knock over the potted plant next to the reference librarian.	You stand in line to check out library books, then happen to notice than a crucial resource is being checked out by another classmate.	You notice that an important (priceless) video, borrowed from the rare archives section, has been chewed up by your dog. What do you tell the librarian?	Your cheese sandwich is mistakenly caught in the microfiche machine.	Delayed by traffic, You arrive at 5:01, but the library closed at 5:00. Try to persuade a librarian, locking the door, to let you grab one book.

SUGGESTED
Weekly *Implementation*

DAY 1	DAY 2	DAY 3	DAY 4	DAY 5
Write a Warm-up Essay.	Write a Warm-up Essay.	Write a Warm-up Essay.	Write a Warm-up Essay.	Write a Warm-up Essay.
Read 35-50 pages/day.	Read 35-50 pages/day.	Read 35-50 pages/day.	Read 35-50 pages/day.	Read 35-50 pages/day.
Find five new vocabulary words.	Find five new vocabulary words.	Find five new vocabulary words.	Find five new vocabulary words.	Find five new vocabulary words.
Reflect on the speech assignment for the week.	Practice your dramatic reading. Start to memorize the passage.	Practice your dramatic reading. Memorize the passage.	Prepare to present your dramatic reading tomorrow.	Present your dramatic reading to a live audience.
Write a preliminary bibliography for your research paper.	Write a preliminary bibliography for your research paper.	Write a preliminary bibliography for your research paper.	Write a preliminary bibliography for your research paper.	Submit your assignments to your evaluator/ parent.
Make a journal entry.	Make a journal entry.	Make a journal entry.	Make a journal entry.	Make a journal entry.
				Take Lesson 25 Test

WRITING YOUR PAPER ON THE COMPUTER

Virtually all college papers will be written on computers. Two basic computer word-processing programs are used: Microsoft Word© and WordPerfect©. You should be comfortable working with both.

Create a folder (not a file) with the title of your paper. Include a thesis statement in the title or on top of the outline.

Create a preliminary bibliography.

Organize your paper into several relevant topics. Make computer files on each topic in your folder. These topics will become outline headings.

Create an outline based on file headings.

Take notes on relevant topics from the preliminary bibliography. Type these notes in sentence form in the files you have created. If they are written well, you will be ready to import the material into your document at a later time. Be sure to record page numbers and references for future footnoting (or endnoting). When you finish, most of the paper should already have been written.

When you are ready, write your rough draft. "Writing the rough draft" basically should mean importing information from your files.

Write and rewrite as often as necessary.

LESSON 26

BACKGROUND

The prewriting part of composing a research paper includes selecting an interesting topic, gathering information, and limiting your subject. A subject for your paper has already been given. You job this week will be to begin gathering information. Place this information in sentence form into your computer files or other organizational modes. If you take notes efficiently, you can read with more understanding and thereby gather information more efficiently. This technique will also save time and frustration when you actually write your research paper. You can invest a lot of time now and things will run smoother and more efficiently later—that is you will have less difficulty writing your first draft—or you can fudge references, skimp on note taking, and not bother to keep note files now, but eventually you will spend more time finding your sources later than now.

First, focus your approach to the topic before you start detailed research. Familiarize yourself with public facts about your topic. Determine the breath of controversy surrounding your topic and, if possible, decide on which side you stand on an issue. At this point, it is helpful to begin with an encyclopedia. How does the encyclopedia divide the subject? You could use a similar organizing principle. Again, use the Thinking Game as a resource. List the subtopics you would expect to find in your readings. These may become handy as labels for notes.

At this point, resist recording a great deal of information until you are ready to structure your arguments. This is an important step on the way to making your research paper as an expression of your own thinking, not merely a grid of other theories. Therefore, first summarize rather than quote. Write a paraphrase of the information in your notes. Whether you use standard note cards or employ a computer program, you should

Writing Skill: Research Paper: Taking Notes (A)

Style (Writing and Speaking): Usage— *There, And/Nor/Or, There/Their/They're*

Public Speaking Task: Poetry Reading

Looking Ahead: The Research Paper: Taking Notes (B)

take notes in a way that you will be able to use. Save yourself some time later by recording bibliographic information in multiple locations: on a master list *and* on the note card. No matter how much extra time and material it requires, you should put notes on separate cards, files, or sheets. This will allow for synthesizing and ordering the material later. Finally, as you gather material, cross-reference related material.

Master List

Reference:

Title of Book, Author

Sub-topic (in paper)

Material For Paper:

Master List

Note Cards

Desktop

My Computer

C Drive

Research Paper

Prewriting

Notes

Topic A:

Topic B:

Organization Chart   Computer

STYLE (WRITING AND SPEAKING): USAGE—THERE, AND/NOR/OR, THERE/THEIR/THEY'RE

Rarely, if ever, should you use the expression *there is* in your paper. It is a weak, uneconomical expression.

Two subjects connected by *and* require a plural form of the verb. When two or more subjects are connected by *or* or *nor*, the subject closest to the verb determines the number/form of the verb.

He and I is ready to depart. (incorrect)
He and I are ready to depart. (correct)

Avoid using *would have* in "if" clauses that express the earlier of two past actions:

If he would have done what his parents asked him to do, he would have finished the work sooner (incorrect).

If he had done what his parents asked him to do, he would have finished the work sooner (correct).

Their is a possessive pronoun. *There* is an adverb. *They're* is a contraction for *they are.*

PUBLIC SPEAKING: ORAL POETRY READING

Oral poetry reading is more difficult than orally reading prose. It demands that you become very familiar with the passage (and maybe even memorize most, if not all, of it). In effect, you must take words and make them poetical. The words must have rhythm and rhyme. Readers of poetry must be careful to put pauses in appropriate places.

Mark a poem; write in the margins; react to it; get involved with it. Circle important, striking, or repeated words. Draw lines to connect related ideas.

What is your initial impression of the poem's subject? What is the poem saying about its subject?

What words are difficult or confusing? Can you pronounce them?

What mood does the poem evoke? How is this accomplished? Consider the means by which the poet creates the poem's mood: meanings of words, their sound, and rhythms.

What word patterns are consistent?

Consider the sound and rhythm of the poem. Does it have a metrical pattern? If so, how regular is it? Does the poet use rhyme? What do the meter and rhyme emphasize? Does the poem have alliteration? Assonance? What effect do they create in the poem?

Are there divisions within the poem? Marked by stanzas? By rhyme? By shifts in subject? How can you communicate these divisions to the reader?

SPEECH ASSIGNMENT

In front of an audience, Read the following ending of "The Rime of the Ancient Mariner" by the British poet Samuel Taylor Coleridge:

This Hermit good lives in that wood
Which slopes down to the sea.
How loudly his sweet voice he rears!
He loves to talk with marineres
That come from a far countree.

He kneels at morn and noon and eve—
He hath a cushion plump:
It is the moss that wholly hides
The rotted old oak-stump.

The skiff-boat neared: I heard them talk,
"Why this is strange, I trow!
Where are those lights so many and fair,
That signal made but now?"

"Strange, by my faith!" the Hermit said—
"And they answered not our cheer!
The planks looked warped! and see those sails,
How thin they are and sere!
I never saw aught like to them,
Unless perchance it were

"Brown skeletons of leaves that lag
My forest-brook along;
When the ivy-tod is heavy with snow,
And the owlet whoops to the wolf below,
That eats the she-wolf's young."

"Dear Lord! it hath a fiendish look—
(The Pilot made reply)
I am a-feared"—"Push on, push on!"
Said the Hermit cheerily.

The boat came closer to the ship,
But I nor spake nor stirred;
The boat came close beneath the ship,
And straight a sound was heard.

Under the water it rumbled on,
Still louder and more dread:
It reached the ship, it split the bay;
The ship went down like lead.

Stunned by that loud and dreadful sound,
Which sky and ocean smote,
Like one that hath been seven days drowned
My body lay afloat;
But swift as dreams, myself I found
Within the Pilot's boat.

Upon the whirl, where sank the ship,
The boat spun round and round;
And all was still, save that the hill
Was telling of the sound.

I moved my lips—the Pilot shrieked
And fell down in a fit;
The holy Hermit raised his eyes,
And prayed where he did sit.

I took the oars: the Pilot's boy,
Who now doth crazy go,
Laughed loud and long, and all the while
His eyes went to and fro.
"Ha! ha!" quoth he, "full plain I see,
The Devil knows how to row."

And now, all in my own countree,
I stood on the firm land!
The Hermit stepped forth from the boat,
And scarcely he could stand.

"O shrieve me, shrieve me, holy man!"
The Hermit crossed his brow.
"Say quick," quoth he, "I bid thee say—
What manner of man art thou?"

Forthwith this frame of mine was wrenched
With a woeful agony,
Which forced me to begin my tale;
And then it left me free.

Since then, at an uncertain hour,
That agony returns;

And till my ghastly tale is told,
This heart within me burns.

I pass, like night, from land to land;
I have strange power of speech;
That moment that his face I see,
I know the man that must hear me:
To him my tale I teach.

What loud uproar bursts from that door!
The wedding-guests are there:
But in the garden-bower the bride
And bride-maids singing are:
And hark the little vesper bell,
Which biddeth me to prayer!

O Wedding-Guest! this soul hath been
Alone on a wide wide sea:
So lonely 'twas, that God himself
Scarce seemed there to be.

O sweeter than the marriage-feast,
'Tis sweeter far to me,
To walk together to the kirk
With a goodly company!—

To walk together to the kirk,
And all together pray,
While each to his great Father bends,
Old men, and babes, and loving friends,
And youths and maidens gay!

Farewell, farewell! but this I tell
To thee, thou Wedding-Guest!
He prayeth well, who loveth well
Both man and bird and beast.

He prayeth best, who loveth best
All things both great and small;
For the dear God who loveth us
He made and loveth all.

The Mariner, whose eye is bright,
Whose beard with age is hoar,
Is gone: and now the Wedding-Guest
Turned from the bridegroom's door.

He went like one that hath been stunned,
And is of sense forlorn:
A sadder and a wiser man,
He rose the morrow morn.
(www.classicreader.com/read.php/sid.1/bookid.143/sec
   .7/)

WRITING ASSIGNMENTS

1. For the next two lessons you will be taking notes on your topic. You will create 3-by-5 note cards, or you may create files on your computer's word-processing software.

2. Read 150 to 200 pages this week and create vocabulary cards.

3. Complete the speech assignment and have a teacher complete a speech evaluation of your speech (Appendix).

4. While preparing the warm-ups, pay particular attention to your writing style this week.

5. Meditate on 1 Kings 22. Reflect on the pattern created by King Ahaziah.

6. Write a warm-up essay every day.

RESEARCH PAPER BENCHMARK

You should have your topic, thesis statement, and preliminary bibliography. During this lesson you will begin to take notes on your research paper topic.

WARM-UP ESSAYS:

	DAY 1	DAY 2	DAY 3	DAY 4	DAY 5
Warm-ups The student should solve these problems	You can find no books on your topic.	Your topic is too narrow.	Your topic is too broad.	You lost your preliminary bibliography two days before the paper was due.	You wish you had never enrolled in this course.

SUGGESTED
Weekly *Implementation*

DAY 1	DAY 2	DAY 3	DAY 4	DAY 5
Write a Warm-up Essay.	Write a Warm-up Essay.	Write a Warm-up Essay.	Write a Warm-up Essay.	Write a Warm-up Essay.
Read 35-50 pages/day.	Read 35-50 pages/day.	Read 35-50 pages/day.	Read 35-50 pages/day.	Read 35-50 pages/day.
Find five new vocabulary words.	Find five new vocabulary words.	Find five new vocabulary words.	Find five new vocabulary words.	Find five new vocabulary words.
Reflect on the speech assignment for the week.	Practice reading your poetry selection.	Memorize your poetry selection.	Prepare to present your poetry reading tomorrow.	Present your poetry reading to a live audience.
Take notes on your topic.	Take notes on your topic.	Take notes on your topic.	Take notes on your topic.	Submit your assignments to your evaluator/ parent
Make a journal entry.	Make a journal entry.	Make a journal entry.	Make a journal entry.	Make a journal entry.
				Take Lesson 26 Test

Revivalism

II. C. The Second Great Awakening
1. Cane Ridge revival 1800
2. Finney Revival

The Cane Ridge revival was formed by a Presbyterian minister named James McGready. McGready preached out against formalit, and darkness of the churches. Many people were touched. Even the "boldest and most daring sinners in the country covered their faces and wept bitterly," and "many fell to the ground, and lay powerless, groaning, praying and crying for mercy." In 1800 McReady was joined by two other pastors, William Hodges and John Rankin, both Presbyterian ministers, along with two brothers, John and William Mcgee. This was the beginning of the great Revivalism. . . . Revivalism sparked individuality and self-purposes. Weisberger, p. 24.

The Finney Revival was constructed by Charles Grandison Finney. He was known as a "soul-winner" and a man who "made good" in his chosen work, which was bringing men to Christ. Weisberger, p. 87; Ahlstrom, pp. 459-460.

Computer Generated File

LESSON 27

BACKGROUND

You started taking notes during your last lesson. You should continue to do the same during this lesson. In summary: start taking notes as soon as you receive your topic. Be careful to record all pertinent information—author, title, publication information, and page numbers. Follow the same format of note-taking throughout the project.

An important part of note-taking is the preliminary outline. A preliminary outline will help you focus in note taking. It is the rubric of your note-taking. It is the skeleton on which you build your paper. The notes, as they are placed on the preliminary outline, become the research paper itself.

An important step for all writers is to create a preliminary outline. While this outline is only preliminary and probably will be expanded or be replaced later, it is an important resource to reference when you take notes. "Why didn't I need to create a preliminary outline before I started taking notes (during last lesson)?" you might ask. The answer is that you needed to enter the stream of research unprejudiced by any agenda. You have a thesis to guide you into the evidence but you did not need to make a writing strategy at that point. If you had, it would have been like creating a map to Toledo, Ohio, from Pittsburgh, Pennsylvania, without knowing exactly where Toledo was or how you were going to get there. A preliminary outline may be discarded later, and it most certainly will be revised, but for now it serves an important purpose: it guides your note-taking journey.

A typical preliminary outline might look like this:

> **Writing Skill:** Research Paper: Taking Notes (B) and Preliminary Outline
> **Style (Writing and Speaking):** Usage—Comparisons and Superlatives
> **Public Speaking Skill:** Debate (A)
> **Looking Ahead:** Research Paper: Designing a Working Plan

I. What I know.
   A. Source 1
   B. Source 2

II. What I wish to prove.
   A. Source 1
   B. Source 2
   C. Source 3

III. What I need to know to support what I wish to prove.
   A. Source 1
   B. Source 2
   C. Source 3
   D. Source 4

IV. What I will conclude.

Again, this is merely a preliminary outline to guide you as you organize your thoughts. You will know more about the subject and be ready for a permanent outline next lesson.

I-A. Introduction
I-B. Thesis: Japan had to attack Pearl Harbor because of expansion, resources, and to take America out of the war.

II-A. Body
II-B. Arguments (overview)
II-C. Overpopulated Japan

1. Japan's need for more land
2. Japan's effort to get parts of China and Alaska.

II-D. Resources
1. When Japan joined the Nazis, America stopped selling coal and oil to Japan.
2. Japan was at war with China, and they needed coal and oil.
3. For Japan to safely get coal and oil from the Pacific, they would have to annul the American and British presence in the Pacific.

II-E. To cripple America
1. Japan tried to destroy the entire American Navy.
2. It would take decades for America to build it back up enough to fight a war

sample outline

STYLE (WRITING AND SPEAKING): USAGE – COMPARATIVES AND SUPERLATIVES

Use the comparative degree when you compare two things. Use the superlative degree when you compare more than two.

Comparison of two things

Although Robert E. Lee was the **more talented** general, Ulysses S. Grant had the **stronger** army.

Comparison of more than two things

In spite of the commanding popularity of soccer in Europe and the widespread popularity of football in the United States, baseball is by far the **most popular** sport in the United States.

PUBLIC SPEAKING: DEBATE

Debate is the practice of comparing and contrasting ideas. At the beginning of the twenty-first century when our nation is in such turmoil and discord, when we have come so far from our Christian roots, this generation will be called to take a stand for Christ. In a nation increasingly confused about what truth is, it will be asked to state the truth clearly. Formal debate will equip this generation to argue the truth effectively in real life. A commitment to debate is a commitment to work two to three hours per week to research a topic. To the Christian, debate is not simply another speech-making or educational activity. Debate can become a life-changing entity that empowers critical advocacy for change. Akin to debate is apologetics, the tool Christians use to authenticate the claims of Christ in a hostile world. By nature, debate is about change

How does formalized debate occur?

Two people form a "debate team." Sometimes the team will have to be for the issue (the affirmative) and sometimes it will have to be against the issue (negative).

Debaters deliver speeches in a format that is unique to debate. The speeches are called constructives and rebuttals. Each person on each team will speak twice. There are affirmative constructives and negative constructives. There are affirmative rebuttals and negative rebuttals.

All speeches are presented to the judges, who will determine who wins the debate.

Debaters argue the same resolution throughout the course of the debate.

Debate Suggestions

The simpler the argument, the better the argument. Even complex arguments can be made simple. Keep it simple.

Arguments must be repeated at least three times.

Avoid using statistics and lengthy quotes—especially of unknown persons. If you do, put them on an overhead or provide a handout.

Never, never contradict yourself.

In all parts of the debate, brevity brings better results than lengthy discourses.

If one is unprepared, it will hurt one's argument—no matter how good the argument is. Memorize. Speak clearly and slowly. Never assume the existence of a particular body of information.

Never speak when your opponent is speaking.

In rebuttal, remind the other team and audience of the question asked and the purpose of the question. It is all right to say, "I do not know," but never ignore a question.

Never show disrespect toward your opponent and never engage in conversation with him/her while he is speaking.

Closing remarks can rarely win a case, but they can surely lose it.

SPEECH ASSIGNMENT

Conduct some research and argue affirmatively about the following resolution: Resolved, whereas, in a time of national crisis, for the sake of national security, in the face of overwhelming danger, profiling of possible terrorists should be legal.

WRITING ASSIGNMENTS

1. Create a preliminary outline and continue to take notes on your research topic. Create note cards or you use files created on your computer word-processing software.

2. Read 100-250 pages this week and create vocabulary cards.

3. Create speech assignment and have a teacher complete a speech evaluation (Appendix).

4. While preparing the warm-ups, pay particular attention to your writing style this week.

5. Meditate on 1 Kings 22. Reflect on the difference between King Jehoshaphat and King Ahaziah's characters and explain the source of this difference.

6. Write a warm-up essay every day.

RESEARCH PAPER BENCHMARK

You should have your topic, thesis statement, preliminary bibliography, and some notes. During this lesson you will create a preliminary outline and continue to take notes on your research paper topic.

WARM-UP ESSAYS:

	DAY 1	DAY 2	DAY 3	DAY 4	DAY 5
Summarize these topics:	Happiness.	Warmth.	Trepidation.	Coldness.	Jealousy.

USING THE INTERNET AS A SOURCE

One of the most common resources to modern research—at least preliminary research—is the Internet. Quick and accessible, Internet resources can be very helpful, but words of caution are in order:

Internet sources can be heavily biased. The Amerian Civil Liberties Union has a radically different take on the issue of criminal rights than the Brookings Institute. Be aware of a source's agenda.

Internet resources can be easily plagiarized. "Block-copy-paste"—it's that simple, but who is the author? If you err, err on the side of having too many footnotes/endnotes.

Stay away from "adult" sites. A search engine can easily pull you into areas you should avoid. It is wise to invite parents into an Internet site with you. An excellent search engine is www.dogpile.com, which includes results from www.google.com.

SUGGESTED
Weekly *Implementation*

DAY 1	DAY 2	DAY 3	DAY 4	DAY 5
Write a Warm-up Essay.	Write a Warm-up Essay.	Write a Warm-up Essay.	Write a Warm-up Essay.	Write a Warm-up Essay.
Read 35-50 pages/day.	Read 35-50 pages/day.	Read 35-50 pages/day.	Read 35-50 pages/day.	Read 35-50 pages/day.
Find five new vocabulary words.	Find five new vocabulary words.	Find five new vocabulary words.	Find five new vocabulary words.	Find five new vocabulary words.
Reflect on the speech assignment for the week.	Compose a first draft of your speech.	Revise your speech and submit to your evaluator/ parent.	Prepare to present your speech tomorrow.	Present your speech to a live audience.
Create a preliminary outline and continue to take notes on your topic.	Create a preliminary outline and continue to take notes on your topic.	Create a preliminary outline and continue to take notes on your topic.	Create a preliminary outline and continue to take notes on your topic.	Submit your assignments to your evaluator/ parent.
Make a journal entry.	Make a journal entry.	Make a journal entry.	Make a journal entry.	Take Lesson 27 Test
				Make a journal entry.

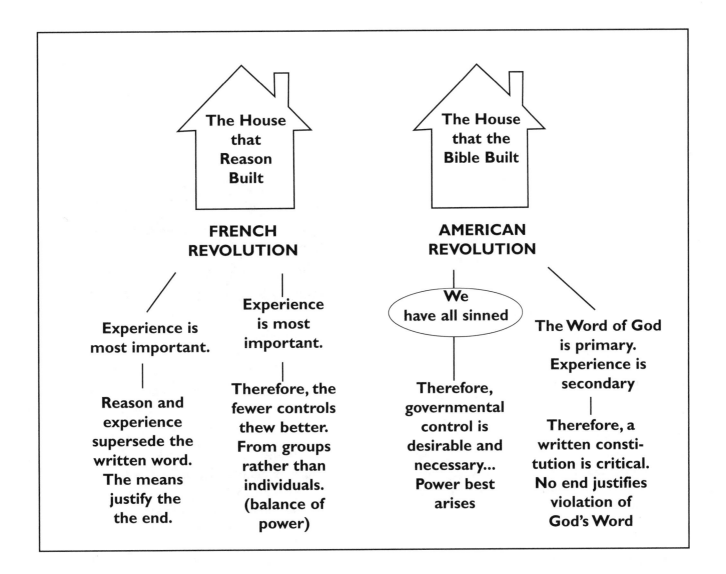

The House that Reason Built

FRENCH REVOLUTION

Experience is most important.

Reason and experience supersede the written word. The means justify the the end.

Experience is most important.

Therefore, the fewer controls thew better. From groups rather than individuals. (balance of power)

The House that the Bible Built

AMERICAN REVOLUTION

We have all sinned

Therefore, governmental control is desirable and necessary... Power best arises

The Word of God is primary. Experience is secondary

Therefore, a written consti- tution is critical. No end justifies violation of God's Word

LESSON 28

BACKGROUND

This week you will write a working outline, continue developing your research, and revise your outline. The research paper outline is also a plan for the research. In other words, it is an organized description of your research. Don't even think about skipping this step.

The following is an example of an outline for a research paper entitled "Racial Anger."

Outline

I. Introduction: unexplored lands

II. Body
A. Paradox of pluralism
B. Race mixing
C. The promised land, or Babylon revisited
D. So much time, so little change
E. Positive liberal state

III. Conclusion
A. Patterns of racial accommodation
B. Power of forgiveness

An outline is a tool that organizes your material. It is nothing more and nothing less. It shapes information into a pattern you can follow as you write your research paper. It is a road map that guides you to your goal. Once your thoughts are organized, it will be easy for you to write your first draft. More detail in the outline makes it easier to write the first draft.

Each heading in the outline is tied to several note cards. The following is the outline of a paper on the causes of the American Civil War.

Outline

Thesis Statement: The combination of an expanding economy, a flood of immigrants, the   Second Great Awakening, the Manifest Destiny, the rise of nativism, and the   failure of the American political system doomed the young Republic to a Civil War.

Writing Skill: Research Paper: Designing a Working Plan

Style (Writing and Speaking): Punctuation – Quotation Marks

Public Speaking Skill: Debate (B)

Looking Ahead: Introduction (A)

I. Introduction
A. Sectionalism assured by the U.S. Constitutional Convention.
B. "Slavery was the sleeping serpent coiled up under the table at the Constitutional Convention." (Abraham Lincoln)

II. Body
A. Economic explosion in The United States from 1812 to 1860
1. Invention of the cotton gin.
2. Industrial revolution in the North.
3. Problem with tariffs
B. Immigrant explosion in The United States from 1800 to 1860 (population doubled every 20 years)
1. Immigrants from Northern Europe
2. Immigrants from Ireland
3. Very few immigrants into the South (stagnant economy)
4. Rise of nativism
C. The Second Great Awakening
1. Cane Ridge Revival, 1800
2. Finney Revival
D. The Manifest Destiny: Mexican War
E. Failure of American political system
1. Jacksonian democracy
2. Rise of Republican Party
F. Slavery and slavery expansion

III. Conclusion

> The more detail in the outline, the easier it will be to write the first draft.

134

STYLE (WRITING AND SPEAKING): PUNCTUATION—QUOTATION MARKS

Introduce a quotation either by indicating what it is intended to show, by naming its source, or both. For poetry that is not narrative, it is customary to attribute quotations to "the speaker"; for a story with a narrator, to "the narrator." For plays, novels, and other works with characters, identify characters as they are quoted.

For example, "The speaker in Robert Frost's 'Death of a Hired Hand' guides the reader through the intricacies of growing old." Another example is "The reader has serious questions about the saneness of the narrator in Edgar Allan Poe's 'Tell-Tale Heart.'"

PUBLIC SPEAKING: DEBATE (B)

At the heart of debate is argument. Argument is communication in which logic is used to influence others. Normally argument is used to change attitudes or to establish new ones. Much that is called argument is not that; it is merely the expression of opinion over and against another's opinion. The real process of argument is the demonstration of conclusions from facts or premises that the debater has established as truths. (It is beyond the scope of this course to teach students everything they need to know about debate. Interested students can find ample information online.)

SPEECH ASSIGNMENT

The student should outline and present an affirmative speech and then a negative speech for the following resolution: Resolved, capital punishment should be banned.

WRITING ASSIGNMENTS

1. Write your outline for your research paper.

2. Read 200-250 pages this week and create vocabulary cards.

3. Complete the speech assignment and have a teacher complete a speech evaluation (Appendix).

4. While preparing the warm-ups, pay particular attention to your writing style this week.

5. Meditate on 2 Kings 1. What is the mistake that Ahaziah makes?

6. Write a warm-up essay every day. Over the next few weeks, you will gradually be developing a "practice" paper on each topic. Add to the same topic each week as you build the paper. For instance: On Day 1, Lesson 28, you will compare a research paper with a cold shower. On Day 1, Lesson 29, you will continue writing on the same topic but will add more information. On Day 1, Lesson 30, you will add even more information to the same topic, etc.

RESEARCH PAPER BENCHMARK

You should have your topic, thesis statement, preliminary bibliography, a preliminary outline to guide you in your note-taking, and many notes. During this lesson you will create an outline.

WARM-UP ESSAYS:

	DAY 1	DAY 2	DAY 3	DAY 4	DAY 5
Comparison/ Contrast Monday	Compare a research paper with a cold shower.	Compare a research paper with your favorite CD.	Compare a footnote and an endnote. Which do you prefer? Why?	Compare a question mark with a colon.	Compare active voice with passive voice writing.

SUGGESTED
Weekly *Implementation*

DAY 1	DAY 2	DAY 3	DAY 4	DAY 5
Write a Warm-up Essay.	Write a Warm-up Essay.	Write a Warm-up Essay.	Write a Warm-up Essay.	Write a Warm-up Essay.
Read 35-50 pages/day.	Read 35-50 pages/day.	Read 35-50 pages/day.	Read 35-50 pages/day.	Read 35-50 pages/day.
Find five new vocabulary words.	Find five new vocabulary words.	Find five new vocabulary words.	Find five new vocabulary words.	Find five new vocabulary words.
Reflect on the speech assignment for the week.	Compose a first draft of your speech.	Revise your speech and submit to your evaluator/ parent.	Prepare to present your speech tomorrow.	Present your speech to a live audience.
Create an outline.	Create an outline.	Create an outline.		Submit your assignments to your evaluator/ parent.
Make a journal entry.	Make a journal entry.	Make a journal entry.	Create an outline.	Take Lesson 28 Test
			Make a journal entry.	Make a journal entry.

LESSON 29

BACKGROUND

The introduction is one of the most important parts of a research paper. It invites the reader into the paper; it can also warn the reader that he is in for a difficult, if not boring, reading! Every essay creates a new world in a new universe. The new world has a tone, theme, prejudice, and, above all, an argument(s). The reader can choose whether or not to go into the world, staying in this universe for a while. It is the reader's choice. You can help readers decide to enter your world if you have an effective introduction. What in this paper is going to change the reader's life? What new revelation will be discovered? Let readers know that it is well worth their time to proceed. If your three paragraph introduction is boring, then do you really think readers will want to read your 15 page main body? The introduction, in other words, is a hook to the rest of the paper.

An introduction can begin with a quote or a rhetorical question. Don't be trite by beginning your essay with "Webster defines so and so as . . ." and don't be redundant and shy by beginning with "I think so and so is true . . ." Of course you think it, or you wouldn't write it!

Then, you should state precisely, with no equivocation, or fanfare, your thesis statement. We have already talked about a thesis. If I am reading your paper, for better or for worse, I want to know within 25 words what I am reading and why I am reading it.   Finally, state your arguments. There are no surprises in academic writing. Surprises belong to cheap fiction, like that written by O. Henry, for instance, who loved to trick his reader. His cheap tricks were a camouflage for mediocre rhetoric. Good story; bad writing.

Anyway, your introduction should state your arguments. You don't have to evidence them yet, but state all your arguments. I can't say this enough: In your introduction, state all the arguments that will be argued in your research paper.

Then, end the introduction with a catch summary, even provocative statement.

A fairly typical introduction then would look something like this:

Writing Skill: Research Paper: The Introduction (A)
Style (Writing and Speaking): Introductory Words and Phrases
Public Speaking Skill: The Spoken Introduction
Looking Ahead: Introduction (B)

A. Rhetorical Question or Quote or some other Catchy Beginning Sentence
 B. Thesis
 C. Evidence
 D. Catchy Summary Statement
How effective is the following introduction?

I. INTRODUCTION: A TRAGEDY THAT COULD HAVE BEEN AVOIDED

For years the question "What caused the Civil War?" has puzzled historians. They suggest many reasons, but what is the main cause? Slavery was the chief irritant, but it did not cause the conflict. Both Rachel and Samuel Cormany, Civil War contemporaries, supported their government's efforts to quell the Southern rebellion, but neither of them was irritated by slavery. Rachel blamed the war on the "hotheadedness of the South, and the invisibleness of the North." (http://www.civilwarmonthly.homestead.com/RCormanyDiary.html) In fact, there were many things that contributed to the Civil War—some more than others. Certainly slavery was *a* cause but not *the* cause.

The Civil War was caused because Southern and

> The Introduction is not a place to hold back. The reader needs to know that this subject is vitally important and worth his effort to read about it. Using a contemporary quote is actually a pretty good idea.

137

The author is forthright with his position. He states his thesis clearly and quickly. His use of rhetorical questions is also effective.

Northern Americans chose not to live together. Again, the operative word is *chose*. They chose to fight a war. The North and the South were always two nations, and by 1860 it was difficult to live together in the same house. But not impossible. They had solved their problems before—in 1820 and 1850, for instances. But suddenly in 1860, the political system failed.

The Civil War was neither the fault of the North or the South. Or rather, it was the fault of both! The combination of an expanding economy, a flood of immigrants, the Second Great Awakening, Manifest Destiny, and the failure of the American political system brought the young republic to the brink of Civil War. Ultimately, though, the failure of nerve manifested by American political leaders thrust the nation into its bloodiest war in American history.

I agree with historians who in their assessment of the causes of the Civil War wrote:

When the Union was originally formed, the United States embraced too many degrees of latitude and longitude, and too many varieties of climate and production, to make it practicable to establish and administer justly one common government which should take charge of all the interests of society. To the wise men who were entrusted with the formation of that union and common government, it was obvious enough that each separate society should be entrusted with the management of its own peculiar interests, and that the united government should take charge only of those interests which were common and general. (Hunter 1, 7-8)

What is ironic is that, in a way, the North and the South were fighting for the same thing. Both saw themselves preserving what was vitally important to America. The Confederacy was really fighting for the American dream as much as the Union! They saw themselves as the new patriots. The South had some justification; many Founding Fathers owned slaves (Hunter 1, 9-10).

Having a long quote in an Introduction can be a tactical error: long quotes quickly bore readers. However, it works for this author because the long quote is both interesting and controversial.

In summary, the Civil War was a struggle between conflicting worldviews. Each section held to a belief system that increasingly felt alienated from the other. They disagreed over the power of the federal government; they disagreed over tariffs; and they especially disagreed over slavery and its expansion westward (Williams 203). These disagreements were nothing new and did not bring a civil war. The War was avoidable. However, by the middle of the nineteenth century, these differing viewpoints—coupled with the almost violent change inflicted on America, and the collapse of compromise as a viable option in the political arena—brought the young Republic into a horrendous Civil War. Americans chose to fight because they were unwilling to choose an alternative.

The first American to observe that the Civil War was avoidable, not inevitable, was former President Buchanan. He argued that the cause of the Civil War was to be found in "the long, active, and persistent hostility of the Northern Abolitionists, both in and out of Congress, against Southern slavery, until the final triumph of President Lincoln; and on the other hand, the corresponding antagonism and violence with which the advocates of slavery resisted efforts, and vindicated its preservation and extension up till the period of secession." Buchanan's assumption that the war need not have taken place had it not been for Northern fanatics and, to a lesser extent, Southern extremists, was a correct one. To put it another way, there was no substantive issue important enough in 1861 to necessitate a resort to arms; the war had been brought on by extremists on both sides. The moderate political center refused to solve the problem and left the solution to extremists. The extremists brought on a civil war.

The remainder of this paper will examine several issues whose accumulated effect made the Civil War seem necessary to a generation of Americans. (Jessica Stobaugh)

In the introduction you must make no presumptions about the reader. You need to notify the reader about what your arguments will be. You don't have to explain everything, but after the introduction, the reader must know where you are going with your paper. Once the introduction is completed there can be no more surprises in the paper.

The introduction accomplishes six purposes. It piques the reader's interest. It presents contextual material. It defines any necessary terms. It focuses the paper and reveals the plan of attack. The student should never surprise the reader. Most of all, the thesis must be stated in the introduction.

STYLE (WRITING AND SPEAKING): INTRODUCTORY WORDS AND PHRASES

The introduction in a research paper may be 1-5 paragraphs. You need to give careful attention to the way you begin these critical paragraphs which will make or break your paper.

The first sentence of an introductory paragraph (s) must make clear the purpose of the research paper. Using a rhetorical question or a quote from a well-known, respected authority is one way to clarify the purpose. The second paragraph of the introduction, of course, must include a transition. It too, pulls the reader into the story that you are telling. An effective way to begin introduction paragraphs is to repeat a key word from the previous paragraphs. One final word: avoid the overused expression, "Webster's Dictionary defines . . ."

PUBLIC SPEAKING: ARGUING A POINT

As we discovered in a previous lesson, a persuasive speech is effective when it causes the listener to accept a viewpoint or course of action that he does not presently hold. The following is the famous eulogy of Julius Caesar by Mark Antony (http://www.classicreader.com/read.php/sid.1/bookid.155/sec.10/):

Friends, Romans, countrymen, lend me your ears!
I come to bury Caesar, not to praise him.
The evil that men do lives after them,
The good is oft interred with their bones;
So let it be with Caesar. The noble Brutus
Hath told you Caesar was ambitious;
If it were so, it was a grievous fault,
And grievously hath Caesar answer'd it.
Here, under leave of Brutus and the rest-
For Brutus is an honorable man;
So are they all, all honorable men-
Come I to speak in Caesar's funeral.
He was my friend, faithful and just to me;
But Brutus says he was ambitious,
And Brutus is an honorable man.
He hath brought many captives home to Rome,
Whose ransoms did the general coffers fill.
Did this in Caesar seem ambitious?
When that the poor have cried, Caesar hath wept;
Ambition should be made of sterner stuff:
Yet Brutus says he was ambitious,
And Brutus is an honorable man.
You all did see that on the Lupercal
I thrice presented him a kingly crown,

Which he did thrice refuse. Was this ambition?
Yet Brutus says he was ambitious,
And sure he is an honorable man.
I speak not to disprove what Brutus spoke,
But here I am to speak what I do know.
You all did love him once, not without cause;
What cause withholds you then to mourn for him?
O judgement, thou art fled to brutish beasts,
And men have lost their reason. Bear with me;
My heart is in the coffin there with Caesar,
And I must pause till it come back to me.
   (Act III, Scene ii)

SPEECH ASSIGNMENT

Write and then present a persuasive speech pro or con on this resolution: *Resolved: home-schoolers should be allowed to participate in local school athletic events.*

WRITING ASSIGNMENTS

1. Write the introduction to your research paper.

2. Read 150 to 200 pages this week and create vocabulary cards.

3. Complete the speech assignment and have a teacher complete a speech evaluation of your speech (Appendix).

4. While preparing the warm-ups, pay particular attention to your writing style this week.

5. Meditate on 2 Kings 2, the story of Elijah and Elisha.

6. Write a warm-up essay every day. Over the next few weeks, you will gradually be developing a "practice"

paper on each topic. Add to the same topic each week as you build the paper. For instance: On Day 1, Lesson 28, you will compare a research paper with a cold shower. On Day 1, Lesson 29, you will continue writing on the same topic but will add more information. On Day 1, Lesson 30, you will add even more information to the same topic, etc.

RESEARCH PAPER BENCHMARK

You should have your topic, thesis statement, preliminary bibliography, a preliminary outline to guide you in your note-taking, many notes, and an outline. During this lesson, you will begin the introduction to your research paper.

WARM-UP ESSAYS:

	DAY 1	DAY 2	DAY 3	DAY 4	DAY 5
Comparison/ Contrast	Compare a research paper with a cold shower.	Compare a research paper with your favorite CD.	Compare a foot-note and an end-note. Which do you prefer? Why?	Compare a question mark with a colon.	Compare active voice with pas-sive voice writing.

SUGGESTED
Weekly *Implementation*

DAY 1	DAY 2	DAY 3	DAY 4	DAY 5
Write a Warm-up Essay.	Write a Warm-up Essay.	Write a Warm-up Essay.	Write a Warm-up Essay.	Write a Warm-up Essay.
Read 35-50 pages/day.	Read 35-50 pages/day.	Read 35-50 pages/day.	Read 35-50 pages/day.	Read 35-50 pages/day.
Find five new vocabulary words.	Find five new vocabulary words.	Find five new vocabulary words.	Find five new vocabulary words.	Find five new vocabulary words.
Reflect on the speech assignment for the week.	Compose a first draft of your speech.	Revise your speech and submit to your evaluator/ parent.	Prepare to present your speech tomor-row.	Present your speech to a live audience.
Start the introduc-tion of your research paper.	Start the introduc-tion of your research paper.	Start the introduc-tion of your research paper.	Start the introduc-tion of your research paper.	Submit your assign-ments to your eval-uator/ parent.
Make a journal entry.	Make a journal entry.	Make a journal entry.	Make a journal entry.	Take Lesson 29 Test
				Make a journal entry.

WHEN TO GIVE THE AUTHOR CREDIT?

Quotations must match the source document word-for-word and must be attributed to the original author.

Paraphrasing involves putting a passage from source material into the writer's own words. A paraphrase must also be attributed to the original source.

Summarizing involves putting the main idea(s) into the writer's own words, including only the main point(s). Once again, it is necessary to attribute summarized ideas to the original source.

If in doubt, always give the author credit.

To give credit means that you mark with a footnote or endnote the passage/words/phrases that are quoted directly, paraphrased, or summarized. The number that marks the passage must correspond with a note at the end of the page or at the end of the chapter or paper, verifying the exact source of the material. Consult a grammar text for further information on when and how to provide notation. Not giving credit to the author of an original source is the same as stealing the author's information and claiming it as your own—plagiarism.

LESSON 30

BACKGROUND

Evaluate the effectiveness of the following introduction and determine where the author should have placed footnotes in order to cite sources of the information given:

The year 1989 marked the 200th anniversary of the French Revolution. To celebrate, the French government threw its biggest party in at least 100 years, scheduled to last all year. In the United States, an American Committee on the French Revolution was set up to coordinate programs on this side of the Atlantic, emphasizing the theme "France and America: Partners in Liberty." The French should be uneasy about their Revolution, for whereas the American Revolution brought forth a relatively free economy and limited government, the French Revolution brought forth anarchy, then dictatorship. The French Revolution brought forth Napoléon Bonaparte.

However, were the French and American Revolutions really similar? On the surface, there were parallels. Yet over the past two centuries, many observers have likened the American Revolution to the bloodless Glorious Revolution of 1688 while the French Revolution has been considered the forerunner of many modern violent revolutions that have ended in totalitarianism. Because the French Revolution ended so violently, many Frenchmen were troubled about celebrating its 200th anniversary. An Anti-89 Movement actually sold mementos including Royalist black arm bands and calendars that mocked the sacred dates of the French Revolution, reminding today's Frenchmen of the excesses of the Revolution.

July 14, 1789, marked a day that France will not soon forget. The mobs flocked to the Bastille Prison to free their friends and neighbors. Screaming, threatening, they did whatever they could to inflict fear on the

> Within three minutes the reader will decide whether to read or just to skim your paper. The introduction helps him decide.

Writing Skill: Research Paper: The Introduction (B)
Style (Writing and Speaking): Using the Right Word: Being Specific
Public Speaking Skill: Impromptu Speech
Looking Ahead: Body (A)

poor soldiers guarding this prison. At first, the officer in charge, Monsieur de Launay, refused to negotiate, refused to surrender. Soon, though, Luanay saw he had no choice but to surrender. He did so but only after the mob promised to let his troops go free.

However, the mob could not be stopped, could not be controlled, could not be satisfied until they had their revenge on the nobility. They stormed the Bastille, killing, looting, and destroying. Launay and his troops were slaughtered. Their heads were carried on pikes in the streets of Paris.

The French Revolution had begun. It began as an aristocratic revolution—a revolt of the nobility against the king when he was forced to call a meeting of the Estates-General in 1789. In 1789–91, a comparatively peaceful period, the National Assembly did much to modernize France. Despite the Declaration of Rights, the reformed franchise which promoted free trade still excluded the poor; but the public maintained its faith in freedom and unity, as shown in the first Festival of Federation, a celebration of national unity on July 14, 1790. However, the groundwork was laid for the secularization and tragedy that was to fall on France in later years. Power and special interests had joined together in the bloodbath called the French Revolution, and they were not going to step apart easily. Already French leadership was turning its back on centuries of Judeo-Christian morality and tradition.

By 1791 radical Jacobins had taken over the government. Louis XVI was beheaded because he had escaped and invited foreign intervention. A few years later his wife, the infamous Marie Antoinette, joined him at the guillotine. In the bloodbath that was called

The Reign of Terror, forty thousand Frenchman lost their lives. The young thirty-year-old Napoléon was a member of the Jacobins. It is at this point that the young soon-to-be dictator enters the story.

Napoléon Bonaparte, who is also known as the "little Corsican," was born on August 15, 1769 in Ajaccio, Corsica. His original name was Napoléon. He had seven brothers and sisters. His original nationality was Corsican-Italian, and he despised the French. He thought they were oppressors of his native land. His father was a lawyer and was also anti-French. One reason Napoléon may have been such a conqueror was that he was reared in a family of radicals. When Napoléon was nine, his father sent him to a French military government school. He attended Brienne in Paris. While there, he was constantly teased by the French students. Because of this, Napoléon started having dreams of personal glory and triumph.

In 1784 to 1785 Napoléon attended the E'cole Militaire in Paris. That was the place where he received his military training. He studied to be an artillery man and an officer. He finished his training and joined the French army when he was sixteen years old. Soon after that, his father died, and he was left with the responsibility of taking care of the huge Bonaparte family. Napoléon was stationed in Paris in 1792. After the French monarchy was overthrown on August 10, 1792, Napoléon decided to make his move up in the ranks. After this, Napoléon started becoming a recognized officer. Through hard work, bravery, political connections, and being born in a turbulent age, Napoléon rose to the rank of general. In 1799 Bonaparte was elected First Consul of France and Her Dependencies for Life and began his astonishing political career. Later he proclaimed himself France's emperor.

Among Napoléon's enduring legacies to France were his innovations in government. Napoléon drew up a new constitution and submitted it to the people in a plebiscite. Of course the people accepted it. The constitution established a phony parliamentary system, but everyone knew that the real power lay with the Council of State, whose leader was Napoléon. From the beginning then, the so-called "Republic" was really a paper government whose real leadership lay in one man: Napoléon Bonaparte. Napoléon was in control and meant to stay there.

Napoléon's views of religion were even more radical. It appeared that Napoléon was trying to work with the Church. In fact, Napoléon intended—and succeeded to a certain degree—to control the Church. To Napoléon religion was a tool. It was his practice to claim to be a follower of the religion of whomever he was dealing with at a given time. Gone were the days where a leader like Robiesperre in the Festival of the Supreme Being, June 8, 1794, held a ceremony where he set fire to a statue of Atheism, and it burned down to reveal an incorruptible statue of wisdom. Napoléon's religion was not open atheism; in some ways it was more dangerous to Christianity. His view of atheism, as his views of government, was manipulative and cynical. He used the Church and religion to gain whatever ends he could. In that sense, Napoléon Bonaparte was truly a Modern European. He represents what all European secular leaders will one day be.

Napoléon had it all—fame, money, authority, and respect, but there was one very important element he left out: God. His government brought order and peace and his religion brought control, but at what cost?

Napoléon saw no one but himself as the ultimate ruler and so his dictatorship was brought to an unhappy closure in 1815. Hitler, Stalin, King Saul, and Napoléon left God out of their decisions; their rules, leadership, and dictatorships did not prevail. (Jessica Stobaugh)

STYLE (WRITING AND SPEAKING): USING THE RIGHT WORD: BEING SPECIFIC

You should be as specific as possible in your writing. Metaphors should be concrete and drawn from ordinary experience. Adjectives should be specific in type and description. Technically correct, *The ocean is pretty* is too general. *The emerald-green ocean with its frothy waves and shimmering tide is breathtakingly beautiful* is more descriptive and specific.

PUBLIC SPEAKING: SHARING YOUR FAITH

The most frightening speech to many believers is the *witness*, which is a version of the impromptu speech. Like all speeches, the witness requires speakers to know their material, to know their audience, and to present the material in an organized and respectful way. The impromptu speech is the same as the extemporaneous speech. In both speeches, the speaker is presented a topic and given three to five minutes to prepare a speech in response to the topic. The following are strategies for presenting the impromptu speech:

*While it is impossible to anticipate all possible impromptu speech topics, it is helpful if the presenter invests some time reflecting upon what is occurring in current events. For instance, if one is presenting an impromptu speech on September 18, 2001, it is obvious that one topic could be on the World Trade Center catastrophe.

*The presenter should not try to write an entire speech. An outline is all that will be possible. The presenter should only make one or two good points.

*The introduction is critical in an impromptu speech. It basically should include the thesis statement and a rhetorical question and almost nothing else.

*Though time is an issue, the presenter should be careful to have an effective conclusion.

SPEECH ASSIGNMENT

Deliver a 2-3 minute impromptu speech on the following topic: In a three-point argumentative speech, persuade a friend of yours that he/she should not date but should practice *courtship*.

WRITING ASSIGNMENTS

1. Finish your introduction.

2. Read 200-250 pages this week and create vocabulary cards.

3. Complete the speech assignment and have a teacher complete a speech evaluation of your speech (Appendix).

4. While preparing the warm-ups, pay particular attention to your writing style this week.

5. Meditate on 2 Kings 2:23-25. What are the consequences for a person who mocks God's authority?

6. Write a warm-up essay every day. Over the next few weeks, you will gradually be developing a "practice" paper on each topic. Add to the same topic each week as you build the paper. For instance: On Day 1, Lesson 28, you will compare a research paper with a cold shower. On Day 1, Lesson 29, you will continue writing on the same topic but will add more information. On Day 1, Lesson 30, you will add even more information to the same topic, etc.

RESEARCH PAPER BENCHMARK

You should have your topic, thesis statement, preliminary bibliography, a preliminary outline to guide you in your note-taking, many notes, and an outline. During this lesson you will finish the introduction to your research paper.

WARM-UP ESSAYS:

	DAY 1	DAY 2	DAY 3	DAY 4	DAY 5
Comparison/ Contrast	Compare a research paper with a cold shower.	Compare a research paper with your favorite CD.	Compare a footnote and an endnote. Which do you prefer? Why?	Compare a question mark with a colon.	Compare active voice with passive voice writing.

SUGGESTED
Weekly *Implementation*

DAY 1	DAY 2	DAY 3	DAY 4	DAY 5
Write a Warm-up Essay.	Write a Warm-up Essay.	Write a Warm-up Essay.	Write a Warm-up Essay.	Write a Warm-up Essay.
Read 35-50 pages/day.	Read 35-50 pages/day.	Read 35-50 pages/day.	Read 35-50 pages/day.	Read 35-50 pages/day.
Find five new vocabulary words.	Find five new vocabulary words.	Find five new vocabulary words.	Find five new vocabulary words.	Find five new vocabulary words.
Reflect on the speech assignment for the week.	Compose a first draft of your speech.	Revise your speech and submit to your evaluator/ parent.	Prepare to present your speech tomorrow.	Present your speech to a live audience.
Finish the introduction of your research paper.	Finish the introduction of your research paper.	Finish the introduction of your research paper.	Finish the introduction of your research paper.	Submit your assignments to your evaluator/ parent.
Make a journal entry.	Make a journal entry.	Make a journal entry.	Make a journal entry.	Take Lesson 30 Test
				Make a journal entry.

LESSON 31

BACKGROUND

Finally! The day has arrived that you write the major part of your research paper. Gather your notes, preliminary bibliography, and, most importantly, your outline. Write from your outline, not your notes, not your memory. Write from the roadmap of your paper—the outline. You already have your introduction; now let's begin the main part of your paper.

If you have created computer files, insert or cut-and-place them into your document. If you have hard-copy file cards, you will need to type your notes in your paper. Add transitions between paragraphs to pull the paper together. Be careful to reference every thought or quote from a source. Typically, 80% of a research paper is footnoted and/or endnoted.

Once the reader is invited into the paper via the introduction, it is time to defend your thesis. In other words, restate your arguments and defend them. Evidence your arguments—with much evidence. The more controversial your argument, the more evidence you will need. Again, don't worry if you have a lot of endnotes/footnotes. Most valid research uses multiple footnotes. It demonstrates a well-researched topic.

Move the reader slowly, but methodically, through your arguments. Use transitions and constantly restate

Writing Skill: Research Paper: The Body (A)
Style (Writing and Speaking): Avoid Sexist Language
Public Speaking Skill: Didactic Speech
Looking Ahead: Body (B)

the thesis. Keep your readers focused. Remind them often about where they are going, how they will get there, and what they will find when they get there. Tell them what they are learning and why it is important. Don't patronize them. Don't say, "Any educated person knows my argument is correct." Instead, say: "The evidence clearly proves that my arguments are correct." It also helps to remind readers why they are investing so much time reading your paper. Say something like "The reader now understands why my topic is so important to so and so."

The following example represents a pretty good main body of a research paper. Notice that the writer closely follows her outline. In fact, this writer had all the paragraphs organized in computer files and was able to import them into the final document. In other words, by the time she reached this point, most of her work had been completed.

Does she effectively argue her points? Remember: a research paper is all about what *other scholars* know. It is not about what you know! Caution: Don't have one quote immediately after another—paraphrase your sources. Remember, you must reference paraphrases just like you reference quotes. Your job is to locate, to analyze, and then to offer the best information you can find to the reader.

One final point. Keep the thesis in front of you and your reader. As I write my research paper, I like to put the thesis on large bold letters and tape it on the edge of my computer screen. At least every other paragraph, refer the paper to your thesis. The thesis runs like a thread through the main body. Never let the reader forget why he is reading this paper and what he should learn from it. Make your case time and time again. Build your case on one evidence argument after another.

The use of a quote is a great way to pull the reader into a discussion. We all like to eavesdrop (so to speak) on a historical discussion.

The following is the body of a paper on the origins of the American Civil War.

II. TWO NATIONS, TWO ECONOMIES

"I heard much of the extreme difficulty of ginning cotton, that is, separating it from its seeds. . . . I involuntarily happened to be thinking on the subject and struck out a plan of a machine in my mind" (Van Doren, Charles, and Robert McHenry. *Webster's Guide to American History.* Springfield, MS: G. & C. Merriam Co., 1971, 89.) The machine was the cotton gin, and the author of this letter was Eli Whitney. More than anything else, the cotton gin made cotton a profitable business and assured its future in southern economy.

Originally, cotton had been a minor crop because of the difficulty of separating the fiber from the seeds. In 1793 Eli Whitney's cotton gin solved this problem. In 1800 only about 70,000 bales of cotton were produced in the South. By 1825 cotton production increased 700 percent. Demand for cotton of all sorts was growing, especially in England, where new textile factories, with their weaving and spinning machines, created an insatiable appetite. Demand and supply came together when Eli Whitney set his mind to the problem of short-staple cotton and its seeds (Nash, Gary B., et al., editor. *The American People: Creating a Nation and a Society.* New York: Harper Collins, 1990, 309). Eli Whitney supplied the technology for cotton to be king, and the industrial revolution supplied the market. By the early nineteenth century, British and American factories demanded more cotton. The expanding Southern plantation system was ready to meet that demand.

In 1813 Boston Manufacturing Company opened the first textile factory to perform all cloth-making operations by power in Waltham, Massachusetts. Financed with large capital, the company recruited New England farm girls as operatives, boarded them in dormitories, and produced a standard coarse cotton cloth requiring minimum labor skill. By 1826, in Lowell, Massachusetts, one plant turned out two million yards of cloth annually (Van Doren and McHenry, 128). Their production grew more and more over the next few years.

In 1828 a new sore spot appeared in North-South relations. That year Congress raised the tariff on imports in order to protect native industry struggling to compete with European manufacturers. On the grounds that it favored the North at her expense, the South protested loudly over the tariff. She was dependant almost wholly on the North and on Europe for manufactured goods. While an increase in prices would enrich the North, it would mean a rise in the cost of living for the Southerners, with no compensating increase in wealth. In their view, all the benefits of protection were going to Northern manufacturers. Though the country as a whole grew richer, South Carolina grew poorer, with its planters bearing the burden of higher prices. South Carolina planters, and Southern planters in general, sold their products to British industrials, who sold manufactured good to Southerners. When Northern tariffs raised the price of industrial goods, the price of cotton consequently fell. If one British table was worth 30 pounds of cotton, after tariffs increased British prices, the same table would then be worth 50 pounds of cotton.

Ironically, it was the Southern planter President Andrew Jackson who insisted that tariffs be increased. The protective tariff passed by Congress and signed into law by Jackson in 1832 was milder than that of 1828, but it further embittered many in the state of South Carolina. In response, a number of South Carolina citizens endorsed the states'-rights principle of "nullification," which was enunciated by John C. Calhoun, Jackson's vice president until 1832 in his *South Carolina Exposition and Protest,* 1828 (http://www.fact-index.com/s/so/southcarolina_exposition_and_protest.html).

South Carolina dealt with the tariff by adopting the Ordinance of Nullification, which declared both the tariffs of 1828 and 1832 null and void within state borders. The legislature also passed laws to enforce the ordinance, including authorization for raising a military force and appropriations for arms.

Resentment reached its highest pitch in South Carolina, which at this time was experiencing a depression because of the drop in cotton prices. The state legislative body met and threatened to nullify the act of Congress because it favored one section of the country at the expense of another. If carried out, this proposal would have placed the authority of a state over that of the federal government and would have made the Constitution useless.

The Nullification proceeding threw the country into turmoil. Abuse was heaped on South Carolina, which, as a result, threatened to withdraw from the Union (Barnes, Barnes, Eric Wollencott. *The War between the States.* New York: Whittlesey House, 1959.13). "We, therefore, the people of the state of South Carolina, in Convention assembled, do declare . . . that several acts of the Congress . . . are null, void, and no law, nor binding upon this state, its officers, or citizens" (Van Doren, 146). This was not the first attempt at secession. New England states first suggested it as a possibility with the Hartford Convention Resolutions of 1815. However, this attempt was more serious, and only the vigorous intervention of President Andrew Jackson stopped civil war from occurring.

Until the invention of the cotton gin, the North and the South were primarily farming communities, but the cotton gin put new value on slaves, profit, and demand in the South. The industrial revolution demanded workers and economic growth.

By the time of the Civil War, America was two nations. Eli Whitney's inspiring ingenuity gave a tragic guarantee that the North would welcome the industrial revolution, and the South would reject it. The North would go one way, and the South another; sooner or later they would collide.

III. A NATION OF IMMIGRANTS

Immigrants furnished much of the labor that made the productive explosion possible and many of the consumers who made it profitable. The industrializing processes that were at work opened job opportunities and uprooted millions in Europe whose occupations became unneeded or whose land was confiscated by the more "efficient." The immigrants moved the United States population up from four to thirty-two million in just ninety years. American culture simply molded itself around their presence (Weisberger, Bernard A. "A Nation of Immigrants." *American Heritage,* vol. 45 Feb./Mar. 1994, 75–91; also in *A Sense of History.* Washington, D.C.: American Heritage Foundation, 1995, 783).

Population growth can weaken the economy of a country that is limited in its natural and capital resources. The United States was not so limited, and therefore the economy soared (Cooke, Allistair. *America.* New York: Alfred A. Knopf, 1974, 273). This was good. What was bad was that bad feelings grew among some Americans toward immigrants. That was

PRE-CIVIL WAR TARIFFS

(Ed Fenton, *New American History*); the following chart was created by the author of this curriculum.

Name of Tariff	Provisions	Public Reaction
1789	Placed duties on 30 items such as molasses, nails, hemp, steel. Average, 8.5%. All other imported items, 5%.	Widely popular. Needed to raise federal revenue.
1792	Increased 5% duty to 7.5%	Farmers and New England shippers vigorously opposed these duties.
1816	25% protective tariff on most woolen, cotton, and iron manufactures.	General support.
1828	Duty of 50% on raw wool.	South strongly opposes.
1832	Increased duty on woolens; placed cheap raw wool and flax on duty-free list; reduced average duties to 35%.	South Carolina adopted Ordinance of Nullification and threatened secession.
1833	Provided for gradual reduction of tariffs.	Supported by South; opposed by Northeast.
1842	Returned tariff to 1832 levels.	Supported by Northeast; opposed by South.
1846	Reduced tariffs.	South supported and Northeast opposed.
1857	Increased duty-free list.	Northeast opposed and South supported.

called *nativism*. At the same time, while millions of Americans flooded into Northern cities, few came to the South, which only served to accentuate the growing differences between these two American sections. Foreign immigrants damaged an already enfeebled Whig party and created concern among many native-born Americans.

To the average hard-working Protestant American, foreigners pouring into the cities and following the railroads westward spoke unfamiliar languages, wore funny clothes, drank alcohol freely in the grogshops, and increased crime and pauperism. Worst of all, they attended Catholic churches, where the Latin mass and Eucharistic rituals offended those familiar to Protestant worship. Furthermore, they sent their children to their own schools. They also seemed content with lower standards of living and would work for lower pay in worse conditions than any American laborers, thus endangering American jobs.

Massive immigration, then, like economic differences, was one of the causes of the Civil War. It brought instability to the North. At the same time, immigrants were flooding into western territories. These new western immigrants had no wish to compete with black slaves.

III. Slavery Expansion as a Cause but not the Cause . . .

Rev. Abraham Essick, pastor of Chambersburg Lutheran Church, a moderate unionist, well-educated pastor, and a reliable witness, wrote a friend and admitted that slavery was an issue but was not the most important issue of the coming crisis. "Conservative men, who did all in their power to avert the collision before our flag was dishonored [the fall of Fort Sumter], are now burning with indignation. . . . The government must be sustained, rebellion suppressed and the honor of the nation vindicated. May God defend the right!" (Essick, Abraham. *The Diary of Reverend Abraham Essick, 1849–1880*. Charlottesville, VA: University of Virginia Online Collection). He expresses no outrage at slavery and is more concerned about the honor and dignity of his nation and the breaking away of the South from that nation than any other issue (Abraham Essick, May 8, 1861).

Other diarists concurred with Abraham Essick. James Lemuel Clark, a member of the Southern army, discussed the reasons he went to war with "Yankees" but never mentioned slavery as a cause (Fletcher. Essick, Abraham. *The Diary of Reverend Abraham Essick,*

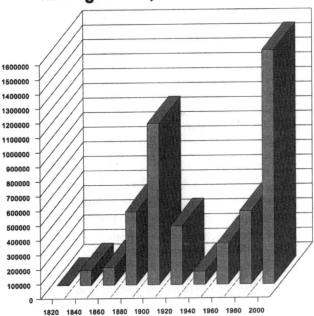

Immigration, 1820-2000

1849–1880. Charlottesville, VA: University of Virginia Online Collection). In 1860, Cooke County Texas, where James Lemuel Clark lived, had a population of nearly 4,000 white people and only 65 slave owners! There were only 300 to 400 slaves, and they were held by 10 slaveholders (Clark, 20). Another Texan, William A. Fletcher, was delighted when he heard he could fight the Yankees. He even entertained a thought of arming the slaves to fight Yankees, too! (Fletcher, William A. *Rebel Private, Front and Rear*. New York: Dutton, 1995, 2).

Fletcher and Clark did not fight on the Southern side for slavery.

As one of the earliest attempts to make sense of this tragedy, the Southern Historical Society concluded in 1876:

The late civil war which raged in the United States has been very generally attributed to the abolition of slavery as its cause. When we consider how deeply the institutions of southern society and the operations of southern industry were founded in slavery, we must admit that this was cause enough to have produced such a result. But great and wide as was that cause in its far-reaching effects, a close study of the history of the times will bring us to the conclusion that it was the fear of a mischief far more extensive and deeper even than this which drove cool and reflecting minds in the South to believe that it was better to make the death struggle at once than submit tamely to what was inevitable, unless its coming could be averted by force. Men, too old to be driven blindly by passion, women, whose gentle and kindly instincts were deeply impressed by the horrors of war, and young men, with fortune and position yet to be won in an open and inviting field, if peace could be maintained so as to secure the opportunities of liberty and fair treatment, united in the common cause and determined to make a holocaust of all that was dear to them on the altars of war sooner then submit without resistance to the loss of liberty, honor and property by a cruel abuse of power and a breach of plighted faith on the part of those who had professed to enter with them into a union of justice and fraternal affection. (Hunter, Taliaferro Robert Mercer. *Southern Historical Society Papers.* Vol. I, no. 1, Jan. 1876, 1).

Other evidence that slavery could not have been the cause of the Civil War was the issue of slavery in Brazil. Brazil and America were settled around the same time. Both had slavery. However, Brazil did not have a civil war in order to rid themselves of this injustice. Therefore, the presence of slavery, as controversial as it may be, as divisive as it may be, in no way assured that the United States would fight a civil war, just as it did not cause a civil war in Brazil.

What about slavery expansion? This issue is as heated as the issue of slavery. President Lincoln never intended to stop slavery; what he didn't want was slavery expansion. He stated this in his first Inaugural Address:

Apprehension seems to exist among the people of the Southern states that, by accession of a Republican Administration, their property and their peace and personal security are to be endangered. There has never been any reasonable cause for such apprehension. Indeed, the most ample evidence to the contrary has all the while existed and been open to their inspection. It is found in nearly all the published speeches of him who now addresses you. (Lincoln, Abraham. Lincoln Online. http://www.abrahamlincoln.com).

Lincoln said that there was no reason for the South to choose secession, for he by no means wanted the slaves free. We know that Lincoln changed later, but for now, this was his position. Lincoln, like the Republican Party, was opposed to slavery expansion, not to slavery itself (Republican National Platform, 1860, Louisiana State University Special Civil War Collection. Baton Rouge, LA, 1).

If slavery expansion threatened Northerners, the cessation of slavery expansion infuriated Southerners:

The gospel of prosperity and the defense of bondage were inseparable in the minds of most slave holders. But when they made explicit reference to slavery, masters drew also from an intellectual tradition that reaffirmed their faith in the destiny of the white man as the harbinger of global wealth. In the antebellum South, racism and the gospel of prosperity were joined in symbiotic relation, (Oakes, James. *The Ruling Race: A History of American Slaveholders.* New York: Vintage Books, 1983).

The end of no slavery expansion was tantamount to commercial poverty in the mind of most Southerners. The more slavery expansion, the more money for the slaveholders. Lincoln did not want slavery expansion because that meant less money for the paid workers; what the South wanted was inflated slavery prices. Southerners also needed the ability to expand westward with their slaves, to find rich farmland. The whole controversy about slavery was further exacerbated by Harriet Beecher Stowe's *Uncle Tom's Cabin* (1852). Moderate Northerners thought the novel was an exaggeration of slavery. Southerners thought it was downright libelous! They hated Mrs. Stowe (McCullough, David. "The Unexpected Mrs. Stowe." *American Heritage*, vol. 24, no. 5 Oct. 1973: 5–9, 76–80; also in *A Sense of History.* Washington, D.C.: American Heritage Foundation, 1995). Many Southerners, like my great-great-great uncle, Howard, fought for the South even though they had no or few slaves (Stobaugh, James P. "Racial Anger as an Obstacle to Racial Reconciliation." D.Min. dissertation, Gordon-Conwell Theological Seminary, South Hamilton, MS, 6).

Slavery, then, was an important cause of the Civil War. However, it was not the most important cause. In fact, there was no substantive issue important enough in 1861 to fight a civil war. The war was brought on by extremism and misunderstandings on both sides (Grob, Gerald N., and George Athan Billias. *Interpretations of*

American History, Vol. I: To 1877. New York: Macmillan, 1982, 392).

Another contributing factor was the Second Great Awakening that spread across antebellum America, creating instability and heightened expectations.

IV. FIRE ACROSS THE LAND: THE SECOND GREAT AWAKENING

While all this was occurring, the Second Great Awakening broke over the country. This awakening was preceded by what was called the Cane Ridge Revival, started in 1800 by a Presbyterian minister named James McGready, who preached against formality and the darkness of the churches. Many people were touched—even the "boldest most daring sinners in the county covered their faces and wept bitterly," and "many fell to the ground, and lay powerless, groaning, praying and crying for mercy." (Weisberger, Bernard A. *They Gathered at the River.* Boston: Little, Brown, & Co., 1958, 24). This was the beginning of a great change.

The Second Great Awakening represents the contradiction that was so much a part of American religious history. For one thing, the Awakening was a revival—a phenomenon that we will describe below. On the other hand, the Awakening grew in the fragile air of pluralism, which was both the greatest strength and greatest challenge of American religious life. For instance, the Second Great Awakening flourished in upstate New York, also the place where heretical Mormonism, the only indigenous American religion, originated.

In America, at least, from its beginning, religion has more or less embraced revivalism as a mode of church expansion, growth, and influence. According to historian D. E. Dieter, *revivalism*

> emphasizes the appeal of religion to the emotional and affectional nature of individuals . . . . It believes that vital Christianity begins with a response of the whole being to the gospel's call for repentance and spiritual rebirth by faith in Jesus Christ. . . . Modern revival movements have their historical roots in Puritan-pietistic reactions to the rationalism of the Enlightenment and the formalized creedal expression of the Reformation faith that characterized much of seventeenth century Protestantism.

Lutheran Pietist rejected the depersonalization of the Reformation and "discovered a more experiential personal commitment and obedience to Christ and a life regenerated by the indwelling Holy Spirit. [Revivalists] also emphasized witness and missions as a primary responsibility of the individual Christian and the church. Subjective religious experience and the importance of the individual became a new force in renewing and expanding the church." (http://www.inchristalone.org/RevivalismToPentecostalism.htm)

In the 1820s Charles Finney held a series of revivals in New York State. Finney was known as a *soul-winner* and a man who *made good* in his choice of work, which was to bring men to Christ (Weisberger, 95; Ahlstrom, 653; Ahlstrom, Sydney E. *A Religious History of the American People.* New Haven, CT: Yale University Press, 1972). All this change made Americans more willing to follow their own wishes and not follow the government or other authority. By 1860 more Americans than ever had personal relationships with their God and wished to make personal decisions about where they lived and what they owned. In a real sense, then, when the North tried to take away Southern slaves, or so they thought, the South saw it as a personal attack on their property and life. They were ready to do whatever was necessary to protect those rights—even if it was rebellion against the government. At the same time, Northern Christians were prepared to cause their southern brothers to stay in the Union no matter what the cost. The religious revivals of the early and middle nineteenth century prepared them for this decision.

V. MANIFEST DESTINY: WILL WESTERN STATES BE FREE OR SLAVE OWNERS?

In addition to the revivals, the issue of slavery expansion, and the tariffs, Americans also claimed a Manifest Destiny. The phrase *Manifest Destiny* was coined by John L. O'Sullivan, editor of the *Democratic Review.* It advanced the idea that America's superior culture and institutions gave us a God-given right to take over the entire continent (Nash, Gary B., et al., editor. *The American People: Creating a Nation and a Society.* New York: Harper Collins, 1990, 448). Manifest Destiny allowed the expansion westward but did not cause it to happen. Occurrences in Texas triggered the government's determination to take possession of the territories west of the Mississippi River (Nash et al., 448).

Many people in the North opposed the Mexican War. They thought it was a Southern plot to extend slavery. In 1846, David Wilmot, a U.S. congressman from Pennsylvania, introduced an amendment to a bill designed to appropriate $2 million for negotiating an agreement with Mexico. Part of his amendment suggested that slavery should be kept away from any territory acquired from Mexico. A bitter and prolonged debate broke out between those who were for slavery and those who were not. Finally, the Wilmot Proviso, as the amendment was called, was passed to the House of Representatives. However, it failed to pass the Senate. This debate showed how fragile the unity of North and South was. They had fought a war together because they had no idea about how to live together in peace.

The impulse to expand ran into problems when the nation discussed whether new states would be slave or free. Expansion, then, led to the failure of the American political system to keep as one these two nations, North and South. Nothing was working to unify the nations. They could not seem to agree on any ground. In every issue, situation, and problem, they were disagreeing. (Jessica Stobaugh)

WRITING STYLE: AVOID SEXIST LANGUAGE

When writing, use the plural form of pronouns. "They" refers to all genders. *They finished their assignment* is better than the exclusivist sexist language of *Everyone has finished his assignment*.

PUBLIC SPEAKING: DIDACTIC SPEECH

A didactic speech informs the audience about an issue with which they may be unfamiliar. Didactic speakers share revelation about a subject about which they know much and feel that what they know is important. The speaker must be almost dogmatic in his application of his new-found truth to a problem. Webster's Dictionary defines didactic as "Excessively prone to instruct, even those who do not wish to be instructed." Didactic speakers who are sensitive, enthusiastic, and informative can be effective teachers. However, their topic must have present and future implications, or it will not interest their audience.

SPEECH ASSIGNMENT

Write a 2-3 minute didactic speech highlighting the main points of your research paper. Typically, the didactic speech is greatly informed by the outline and thesis statement.

WRITING ASSIGNMENTS

1. Write the first-draft body of your research paper.

2. Read 200-250 pages this week and create vocabulary cards.

3. Complete the speech assignment and have a teacher complete a speech evaluation (Appendix).

4. While preparing the warm-ups, pay particular attention to your writing style this week.

5. Meditate on 2 Kings 3 (the Moabite revolt).

6. Write a warm-up essay every day. Over the next few weeks, you will gradually be developing a "practice" paper on each topic. Add to the same topic each week as you build the paper. For instance: On Day 1, Lesson 28, you will compare a research paper with a cold shower. On Day 1, Lesson 29, you will continue writing on the same topic but will add more information. On Day 1, Lesson 30, you will add even more information to the same topic. On Day 1, Lesson 31, you will add even more information to the same topic, etc.

RESEARCH PAPER BENCHMARK

You should have your topic, thesis statement, preliminary bibliography, a preliminary outline to guide you in your note-taking, many notes, the outline, and the introduction to your research paper. Congratulations! During this lesson you will begin the main body of your research paper.

WARM-UP ESSAYS:

	DAY 1	DAY 2	DAY 3	DAY 4	DAY 5
Comparison/ Contrast	Compare a research paper with a cold shower.	Compare a research paper with your favorite CD.	Compare a foot-note and an end-note. Which do you prefer? Why?	Compare a ques-tion mark with a colon.	Compare active voice with pas-sive voice writ-ing.

SUGGESTED
Weekly *Implementation*

DAY 1	DAY 2	DAY 3	DAY 4	DAY 5
Write a Warm-up Essay.	Write a Warm-up Essay.	Write a Warm-up Essay.	Write a Warm-up Essay.	Write a Warm-up Essay.
Read 35-50 pages/day.	Read 35-50 pages/day.	Read 35-50 pages/day.	Read 35-50 pages/day.	Read 35-50 pages/day.
Find five new vocabulary words.	Find five new vocabulary words.	Find five new vocabulary words.	Find five new vocabulary words.	Find five new vocabulary words.
Reflect on your speech assignment for the week.	Compose a first draft of your speech.	Revise your speech and submit to your evaluator/ parent.	Prepare to present your speech tomor-row.	Present your speech to a live audience.
Begin the main body of your research paper.	Begin the main body of your research paper.	Begin the main body of your research paper.	Begin the main body of your research paper.	Submit your rough draft to your instructor/ guardian/ parent.
Make a journal entry.	Make a journal entry.	Make a journal entry.	Make a journal entry.	Take Lesson 31 Test
				Make a journal entry.

LESSON 32

BACKGROUND

You are now ready to finish the core, the body, of your paper. Again, remember: the thesis is the controlling idea of your research paper. It should appear in one form or another in almost every section, if not paragraph, of the research paper. The paper should include both supportive and opposing arguments. By presenting both sides of the issue, the paper will reflect a much clearer perspective of the research topic. Notes gathered in files and organized in the outline become the skeleton of the paper. By using your notes to provide good quotes, paraphrases, and summaries, you are well on your way to writing an effective research paper.

The following sample is part of a chapter of a doctoral dissertation that is much like a research paper topic. The Turabian-style (*Chicago Manual of Style*) for footnotes has been used. The student should observe several things about this paper:

Text boxes are an effective way to highlight important points.

Topic headings are a helpful way to direct the reader in the right direction but are not typically used in the high school research paper.

Copious footnotes make the paper more effective.

SAMPLE FROM CHAPTER III: THE PROMISED LAND OR BABYLON REVISITED? SLAVERY TO THE END OF THE GREAT MIGRATION

A. INTRODUCTION

The most grievous historical metaphor for the African-American community is chattel slavery. It is the quin-

> **Writing Skill:** Research Paper: The Body (B)
>
> **Style (Writing and Speaking):** Avoid Pretentious Language, Evasive Language, and Euphemisms; Footnotes or Endnotes
>
> **Public Speaking Skill:** Summary
>
> **Looking Ahead:** Research Paper: Conclusion

tessential image of the apparent triumph of white racism in American civilization. This unhappy time captures the African-American heart as strongly as the Egyptian bondage motif captures the Old Testament community. Slavery presented African-American Americans with a disconcerting contradiction: legally, they were defined as property; but at the same time, they were called upon to act in sentient, articulate, and human ways.[1]

Within the context of chattel slavery, the African American community created patterns of resistance that remain today. Resistance—not accommodation, not abdication—was the behavioral outcome of three hundred years of white American prejudice. This resistance was usually passive but occasionally violent.[2] This pattern was repeated in one form or another throughout American history.[3]

The dominant white community did not allow the

> Within the context of chattel slavery, the African American community created patterns of resistance that remain today. Resistance—not accommodation, not abdication—was the behavioral outcome of three hundred years of white American prejudice.

---

1. Sidney W. Mintz and Richard Price, *The Birth of African American Culture* (Boston: Beacon Press, 1992), 25.

2. William L. O'Neill, *Coming Apart: An Informal History of America in the 1960's* (Chicago: Quadrangle Books, 1971; reprint, Times Books, 1974), chap. 3: "Slave Resistance, Slave Rebellion," 118–57.

3. Ibid., 25. Connected to anger and resistance was shame. Racism causes anger and resistance (or retaliation), and what sociologists call a "master emotion": shame. Shame produced aggression when it was repressed and disguised. Richard Felson, "Shame, Anger, Aggression," *Social Psychology Quarterly*, 1992 Symposium, 305.

African-American community overtly to express their frustration. Therefore, the African-American slave community used the folktale to express hostility toward their masters, impart wisdom to the young, and teach survival skills.[4] In the folktale "The Tar Baby Tricks Br'er Rabbit," Br'er Rabbit slyly convinced his arch enemies, Fox and Bear, to throw him into the brier patch rather than into the well.[5] Of course, that was exactly what Bear and Fox did and exactly what Br'er Rabbit wanted them to do. For, now, Br'er Rabbit escaped through the brier patch! The African-American slave community resisted slavery in every possible way. From the beginning the African community saw itself in an adversarial role to the white community and has sought to escape into its own culture as a way to defend itself against white domination.

Angry resistance was not inherent to most West African experiences.[6] The ultimate goal of many African peoples was preservation and promotion of community not retribution and revenge.[7] This community spirit of beneficence, forbearance, practical wisdom, improvisation, forgiveness, and justice was nurtured, preserved, and celebrated in the African-American community—but only at great personal sacrifice.[8] Therefore, African-American resistance was a uniquely American phenomenon. This resulted from three hundred years of historical oppression.

B. SLAVE RESISTANCE PATTERNS

> There are two of them, . . . Uncle Buck and Uncle Buddy. . . . They lived in a two-room log

house with about a dozen dogs, and they kept the niggers in the manor house. It don't have any windows now and a child with a hairpin could unlock any lock in it, but every night when the niggers come up from the fields Uncle Buck or Uncle Buddy would drive them into the house and lock the door with a key almost as big as a horse pistol; probably they would still be locking the front door long after the last nigger has escaped out the back. And folks said that Uncle Buck and Uncle Buddy knew this and that the niggers knew that they knew it.[9]

Most white masters—like William Faulkner's Uncle Buck and Uncle Buddy—knew that slaves were resisting their enslavement. Therefore, slaves had to be controlled, to be managed. White masters created slave dependence upon their owners.[10] The demon of white privilege lodged itself well into the institution of slavery.[11]

A basic step toward successful slave management was to implant in the slaves an identity of personal inferiority. They had to keep their places, to understand that bondage was their natural status.[12] Thus, from the beginning, African Americans understood that their resistance to white domination was a question of identity survival.[13] Indeed, resistance seemed to be the only way to survive in the face of profound white systemic racism. It was from this root that later separatism ideology sprang.

4. Gary Nash, Julie Roy Jeffrey, John Howe, Peter Frederick, Allen Davis, and Allan Winkler, *The American People: Creating a Nation and a Society* (New York: Harper & Row, 1990), 1:402–3. Theologian Cheryl A. Kirk-Dugan argued that African-American spirituals delineated an Afrocentric concept of theodicy, and ultimately a Christian response to the evil that was being perpetrated on them. Susan Brooks Thistlethwaite, "Virtual Reality Christianity," *Theology Today*, July 1995, 227. Thus, to Kirk-Dugan, African-American spirituals were a nonviolent, morally appropriate, Christian form of resistance to white domination.

5. This folktale is from William J. Faulkner, *The Days When the Animals Talked* (New York: Modern Curriculum Press, 1977). Also, see Roger D. Abrahams, ed., *Afro-American Folktales* (New York: Pantheon Books, 1985), Part IV, 177ff.

6. Don Nardo, *Braving the New World, 1619–1784: From the Arrival of the Enslaved Africans to the End of the American Revolution* (New York: Chelsea House Publishers, 1995), 82.

7. Peter J. Paris, *The Spirituality of African Peoples: The Search for a Common Moral Discourse* (Minneapolis: Fortress, 1995).

8. Dwight N. Hopkins, "Book Review of Peter J. Paris, *The Spirituality of African Peoples: The Search for a Common Moral Discourse*," in *The Princeton Seminary Bulletin*, vol. 16, no. 2, New Series (1995).

9. William Faulkner, *The Unvanquished* (New York: Vintage Books, 1965), 53.

10. Kenneth M. Stampp, *The Peculiar Institution: Slavery in the Ante-Bellum South* (New York: Vintage Books, 1956), 147.

11. "Wheel about, turn about, / Do jis so, / An' every time I wheel about / I jump Jim Crow." A song by Thomas D. Rice, 1830, in Wilber E. Garrett, ed., et al., *Historical Atlas of the United States* (Washington, D.C.: National Geographic, 1988).

12. Stampp, *The Peculiar Institution*, 145; cf. Charles Fager, *White Reflections on Black Power* (Grand Rapids, 1967), 27–28.

13. James A. Geschwender, "Explorations in the Theory of Social Movements and Revolutions," in James A. Geschwender, ed., *The Black Revolt: The Civil Rights Movement, Ghetto Uprisings, and Separatism* (Englewood Cliffs, N.J.: Prentice-Hall, 1971), 1.

STYLE (WRITING AND SPEAKING): AVOID PRETENTIOUS LANGUAGE, EVASIVE LANGUAGE, AND EUPHEMISMS

Do not show off in your speech and writing. Speak clearly and precisely what you mean to say. *The perfunctory reply caused the fecund friend to flinch* is ostentatious; *The dispassionate reply hurt the loyal friend* is better. Avoid pretentious language. Do not use evasive language. *The soldier experienced an awful dose of reality* should be *The soldier was shocked by all the violence around him.* Say what you mean clearly. Finally, euphemisms are words that camouflage harsh expressions. It is permissible to use a few euphemisms—*The man passed away*—is certainly a proper way to talk about death. If you do this too often, however, it makes your essay and speech trite.

PUBLIC SPEAKING: SUMMARY (A)

The basic speech outline includes:
Introduction: memorize the introduction
Exciting beginning
Importance of topic
Summary of argument
Thesis
Body
First point: evidence
Second point: evidence
Conclusion
Review
Restatement of argument
Final statement

SPEECH ASSIGNMENT

Present a 2-3 minute speech on your research paper topic. Memorize the introduction and give particular attention to your main body.

WRITING ASSIGNMENTS

1. Write the first draft body of your research paper.

2. Read 200-250 pages this week and create vocabulary cards.

3. Complete the speech assignment and have a teacher complete a speech evaluation (Appendix).

4. While preparing the warm-ups, pay particular attention to your writing style this week.

5. Meditate on 2 Kings 4 (the Shunammite's son).

6. Write a warm-up essay every day. Over the next few weeks, you have been gradually developing a "practice" paper on each topic. Add to the same topic each week as you build the paper. For instance: On Day 1, Lesson 28, you compared a research paper with a cold shower. On Day 1, Lesson 29, you continued writing on the same topic but will add more information. On Day 1, Lesson 30, you added even more information to the same topic. On Day 1, Lesson 31, you added even more information to the same topic. On Day 1, Lesson 32, you continued adding information to the growing paper, etc.

WRITING STYLE: FOOTNOTES OR ENDNOTES

Unless the instructor says otherwise, you should use endnotes or footnotes. The student paper in Lesson 34 shows a Modern Language Association (MLA) format—parentheses around short references to "Works Cited": (Crum, 93) or (Crum 1994, 93). Social science papers are typically in APA format.

RESEARCH PAPER BENCHMARK

You should have your topic, thesis statement, preliminary bibliography, a preliminary outline to guide you in your note-taking, many notes, the outline, the introduction, and you have begun the main body of your research paper. During this lesson you will finish the main body to your research paper.

WARM-UP ESSAYS:

	DAY 1	DAY 2	DAY 3	DAY 4	DAY 5
Comparison/ Contrast	Compare a research paper with a cold shower.	Compare a research paper with your favorite CD.	Compare a foot-note and an end-note. Which do you prefer? Why?	Compare a question mark with a colon.	Compare active voice with pas-sive voice writ-ing.

FOOTNOTING/ENDNOTING TIPS

Consistency is required. Examine the notes for "Chapter III: The Promised Land?" (above). This is a style expected in some college/university departments that require the use of *Chicago Manual of Style*.

Incomplete bibliographical data may be reestablished online from the Library of Congress at http://catalog.loc.gov/ or from www.amazon.com/exec/obidos/ats-query-page/.

Notes referring to books: Author, *Title*, vol. # [if any] (Place of Publication: Publisher, year of publication), page number(s). For example: William Faulkner, *The Unvanquished* (New York: Vintage Books, 1965), 53.

Notes referring to popular magazines: Author, "Title of Article," *Magazine Title*, date, page numbers. For example: Susan Brooks Thistlethwaite, "Virtual Reality Christianity," *Theology Today*, July 1995, 227.

Notes referring to scholarly journals: Author, "Title of Article," *Journal Title* volume # (year): page number(s). For example: Franklin B. Dexter, "Connecticut Ministers and Slavery, 1790–1795," *Journal of American Studies* 15/1 (1981): 27–44. The issue number (1) is not needed if the journal is paginated straight through volume 15.

Before page numbers, *p.* or *pp.* may be omitted unless ambiguity would result.

Try to use an en dash between inclusive numbers (22–34) rather than a hyphen or em dash.

The first reference to a source should present full data. Later references should be in a shortened form. If in the next note: Ibid, page number. If later: Author, *Short Title*, page number.

Examine long discursive material proposed to be in notes and consider whether some of that discussion should be transferred to the body, the text.

SUGGESTED
Weekly *Implementation*

DAY 1	DAY 2	DAY 3	DAY 4	DAY 5
Write a Warm-up Essay.	Write a Warm-up Essay.	Write a Warm-up Essay.	Write a Warm-up Essay.	Write a Warm-up Essay.
Read 35-50 pages/day.	Read 35-50 pages/day.	Read 35-50 pages/day.	Read 35-50 pages/day.	Read 35-50 pages/day.
Find five new vocabulary words.	Find five new vocabulary words.	Find five new vocabulary words.	Find five new vocabulary words.	Find five new vocabulary words.
Reflect on your speech assignment for the week.	Compose a first draft of your speech.	Revise your speech and submit to your evaluator/ parent.	Prepare to present your speech tomorrow.	Present your speech to a live audience.
Finish the main body of your research paper.	Finish the main body of your research paper.	Finish the main body of your research paper.	Finish the main body of your research paper.	Submit your rough draft to your instructor/ guardian/ parent.
Make a journal entry.	Make a journal entry.	Make a journal entry.	Make a journal entry.	Take Lesson 32 Test
				Make a journal entry.

LESSON 33

BACKGROUND

The conclusion of a research paper can be a summary of one's argument or a concluding exposition of the thesis statement.

SAMPLE CONCLUSION

CONCLUSION: NO WAY TO COMPROMISE

So what caused the Civil War? Why did Americans fight one another for four long years at the cost of 600,000 lives? The American Civil War occurred because Americans allowed it. They let their differences be more important than their similarities. The government was no help.

Before the Civil War, Americans had done a lot of compromising. In 1820, there was the Missouri Compromise, when Congress took charge of the question of slavery in the territories by declaring it illegal in the huge region acquired by the Louisiana Purchase.

When Andrew Jackson was president (1829–37), a sharp division arose between Northerners and Southerners over the tariff issue. The South favored free trade; the industrial North needed protection. Jackson confronted South Carolina, and it backed down.

Next, President Polk's war with Mexico opened the slavery issue again. Should slavery be allowed in the new territories? The Wilmot Proviso (1846), which was supposed to have excluded slavery, became an irritating subject for both the North and the South. It was also being voted on again and again in Congress and successfully held off by Southerners. Abolitionists led by William Lloyd Garrison and others became strong in many Northern circles and called for the immediate emancipation of slaves, with no compensation to slave owners. However, the majority of Northern whites disliked blacks and refused to support abolition; they did not want to allow slavery in the territories so that they would be preserved for white settlement based on Northern expectations: free labor, dignity of work, and economic progress.

Writing Skill: Research Paper: Writing the Conclusion

Style (Writing and Speaking): Mixed Metaphors

Public Speaking Skill: Enunciation

Looking Ahead: Research Paper: Rewriting and Submission

In 1848 Northern impatience with the existing parties helped form the Free-Soil party. By polling 300,000 votes for their candidate, Martin Van Buren, victory was denied to the Democrats, and the Whig Zachary Taylor was put in the White House. No one was happy, and the nation was ill-suited to handle the next crisis.

The Compromise of 1850 appeared to have settled the issue of slavery expansion by the principle of popular sovereignty, which said that the people who lived in the Mexican secession territories were to decide for themselves. A new Fugitive Slave Law, passed in 1850, enraged Northerners because it let slave owners cross into Northern states to claim their runaway slaves.

As the 1850s began, it seemed for a time that the issue of slavery and other sectional differences between North and South might eventually be reconciled. However, with the westward expansion of the American nation, all attempts to compromise disappeared, and contrasting economic, political, and philosophical endeavors became more evident. The resulting Civil War altered the American nation.

In 1860 the political system became dysfunctional. All consensus was lost. The American political system no longer functioned.

Southerners considered the rise of the Yankee-dominated Republican Party with great apprehension. They were convinced that the party was secretly controlled by abolitionists (although most Northerners loathed the abolitionists) and that Yankees believed in using government to administer their moralistic campaigns. Their fears were confirmed in 1859 when John Brown led a raid on the federal arsenal at Harpers

Ferry, Virginia, hoping to encourage a slave uprising. His action—and his subsequent adoration by some Northerners—helped convince Southerners that if Northerners attained authority in the country, the emancipation of the slaves was inevitable, sooner or later. They then fought a war to protect their rights and property.

Again, all the different causes that led up to the American Civil War—the expanding of the economy, a flood of immigrants, the Second Great Awakening, Manifest Destiny, and the rise of nativism—all these doomed the Republic to a Civil War. The war was essentially fought because the American political system failed to present a compromise that suited the North's demands as well as the South's. At the same time, massive immigration and Western expansion conspired to bring division in the nation. With no political consensus and cultural unanimity, the nation crumbled. The 1850s generation blundered into a needless war because they played on emotions to gain votes rather than facing the issues. Agitation over slavery led to mistaken and false sectional images and fanaticism (Crum, 93). Therefore, they fought it out in the great and awful Civil War. (Jessica Stobaugh)

STYLE (WRITING AND SPEAKING): MIXED METAPHORS

From previous lessons you know that preciseness is much desired in writing and speaking. Avoid mixed metaphors that combine two or more incompatible objects. *He runs like a deer but stops like a bad dream* is mixing metaphors. *He runs like a deer but stops like an elephant* is much better.

PUBLIC SPEAKING: ENUNCIATION

No matter how well organized or written a speech may be, it will not be effective if it is not presented well. It is beyond the scope of this introductory course to mention every speech challenge. However, know that in most speeches the pronunciation of *ng* causes problems. In general, all words ending in *ng* are pronounced like the final sound in *ring*. A combination like *nge* at the end of a word is pronounced *nj*, as in *mange* or *range*. In all other words, *ng* is pronounced as in *zinger* or *ringer*.

SPEECH ASSIGNMENT

Compose a speech with the following words: *tongue, fang, harangue, prong, anger, hunger, bungle,* and *jungle*. Then present it to an audience.

WRITING ASSIGNMENTS

1. Finish your paper with an inspiring conclusion. You are now ready to correct your paper, wait a few days, and then rewrite the paper.

2. Read 200-250 pages this week and create vocabulary cards.

3. Complete the speech assignment and have a teacher complete a speech evaluation (Appendix).

4. While preparing the warm-ups, pay particular attention to your writing style this week.

5. Meditate on 2 Kings 5: Naaman is healed of leprosy.

6. Write a warm-up essay every day. Over the past few weeks, you gradually developed a "practice" paper on each topic, adding to the same topic each week as you built the paper. For instance: On Day 1, Lesson 28, you compared a research paper with a cold shower. On Day 1, Lesson 29, you continued writing on the same topic but added more information. On Day 1, Lesson 30, you added even more information to the same topic. On Day 1, Lesson 31, you added even more information to the same topic. On Day 1, Lesson 32, you continued adding information to the growing paper. On Day 1, Lesson 33, you are concluding the information for this particular topic. You have now completed five "practice" papers on five topics.

RESEARCH PAPER BENCHMARK

You should have your topic, thesis statement, preliminary bibliography, a preliminary outline to guide you in your note-taking, many notes, the outline, the introduction, and now you have even finished the main body of your research paper. During this lesson you will write a conclusion to your research paper.

WARM-UP ESSAYS:

	DAY 1	DAY 2	DAY 3	DAY 4	DAY 5
Comparison/ Contrast	Compare a research paper with a cold shower.	Compare a research paper with your favorite CD.	Compare a footnote and an endnote. Which do you prefer? Why?	Compare a question mark with a colon.	Compare active voice with passive voice writing.

SUGGESTED
Weekly *Implementation*

DAY 1	DAY 2	DAY 3	DAY 4	DAY 5
Write a Warm-up Essay.	Write a Warm-up Essay.	Write a Warm-up Essay.	Write a Warm-up Essay.	Write a Warm-up Essay.
Read 35-50 pages/day.	Read 35-50 pages/day.	Read 35-50 pages/day.	Read 35-50 pages/day.	Read 35-50 pages/day.
Find five new vocabulary words.	Find five new vocabulary words.	Find five new vocabulary words.	Find five new vocabulary words.	Find five new vocabulary words.
Reflect on your speech assignment for the week.	Compose a first draft of your speech.	Revise your speech and submit to your evaluator/ parent.	Prepare to present your speech tomorrow.	Present your speech to a live audience.
Finish the conclusion of your research paper.	Finish the conclusion of your research paper.	Finish the conclusion of your research paper.	Finish the conclusion of your research paper.	Submit your rough draft to your instructor/ guardian/ parent.
Make a journal entry.	Make a journal entry.	Make a journal entry.	Make a journal entry.	Take Lesson 33 Test
				Make a journal entry.

LESSON 34

BACKGROUND

You are almost finished with your research paper! You have finished the first draft. Now, you will need to write one to three more drafts. Examine the following complete rough draft and compare it to the final copy. Caution: this rough draft is a *rough* draft!

SAMPLE ROUGH DRAFT

CAUSES OF THE CIVIL WAR

Jessica Stobaugh

I. INTRODUCTION: A TRAGEDY THAT COULD HAVE BEEN AVOIDED

For years the question, "What caused The Civil war?" has puzzled historians. There are many reasons they have suggested but what is the real cause? Slavery was the chief irritant but did not cause the conflict. Both Rachel and Samuel Cormany, Civil War contemporaries, supported their government's efforts to quell the southern rebellion. But neither of them were irritated by slavery. Rachel blamed the war on the "hotheadness

Writing Skill: Research Paper: Rewriting and Submission
Style (Writing and Speaking): Summary
Public Speaking Skill: Summary
Looking Ahead: Research Paper is due

of the South, and the invisibleness of the North (Mohr 132)." In fact, there were many things that contributed to the Civil War—some more than others. Certainly slavery was *a* cause but not *the* cause.

The Civil War was caused because Southern and Northern Americans could no longer live together. The North and the South were always two nations and by 1860 it was no longer possible to live together in the same house. The Civil war was neither the fault of the North or the South. The combination of an expanding economy, a flood of immigrants, the second Great Awakening, Manifest Destiny, and the failure of the American political system doomed the young republic to enduring the civil war.

I agree with historians who in their assessment of the causes of the Civil War wrote:

> When the Union was originally formed, the United States embraced too many degrees of latitude and longitude, and too many varieties of climate and production, to make it practicable to establish and administer justly one common government which should take charge of all the interests of society. To the wise men who were entrusted with the formation of that union and common government, it was obvious enough that each separate society should be entrusted with the management of its own peculiar interests, and that the united government should take charge only of those interests which were common and general (Hunter, 1).

What is ironic, is that in a way the North and the South were fighting for the same thing. They both saw

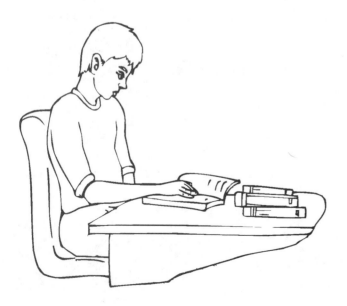

themselves preserving what was vitally important to America. The Confederacy was really fighting for the American dream as much as the Union! They saw themselves as the new patriots. The South had some justification. Many of the Founding fathers owned slaves (Hunter 1, 9-10).

In summary, the Civil War was a struggle between conflicting world views. Each section held to a belief system that increasingly felt alienated from the other. They disagreed over the power of the federal government; they disagreed over tariffs; they especially disagreed over slavery and its expansion westward (Williams 203).

For the remainder of this paper I will examine several issues whose accumulated effect caused the Civil War.

II. Two Nation, Two Economies

" . . . I heard much of the extreme difficulty of ginning cotton, that is separating it from its seeds . . . I involuntarily happened to be thinking on the subject and struck out a plan of a machine in my mind . . . " (Van Doren and McHenry, 89) The machine was the cotton gin, and the author of this letter was Eli Whitney. The cotton gin more than anything else made cotton a profitable business and assured its future in the southern economy.

Originally cotton had been a minor crop because of the difficulty separating the fiber from the seeds. But in 1793 Eli Whitney's cotton gin solved this problem. In 1800 only about 70,000 bales of cotton were produced in the South. By 1825 cotton production increased 700% (Fenton 185) Demands for cotton of all sort was growing, especially in England, where new textile factories, with their weaving and spinning machines, created an insatiable appetite for crop. Demand and supply came together when Eli Whitney set his mind to the problem of short-staple cotton and its seeds.(Nash, et al. 309). Eli Whitney supplied the technology for cotton to be king, but the Industrial Revolution supplied the market.

By the early nineteenth century, British and American factories demanded more cotton. The expanding Southern plantation system was ready to supply that cotton.

In 1813 Boston Manufacturing Company opened the first textile factory to perform all clothmaking operations by power in Waltham, Massachusetts. Financed with large capital, the company recruited New England farm girls as operatives, boards them in dormitories,

and produces a standard coarse cotton cloth requiring minimum labor skill. Cotton Mills began production in Massachusetts, with water powered machinery ; by 1826, in Lowell, one plant turned out 2,000,000 yards of cloth annually (Van Doren and McHenry, 128). Both American and British factories demanded more and more cotton.

A new sore spot appeared in North-South relations. That year Congress raised the tariff on the Imports, in order to protect native industry struggling to compete with European manufacturers. South protested loudly over the tariff on the grounds that it favored the North at her expense. She was dependant almost wholly on the North and on Europe for manufactured goods, and while an increase in prices would enrich the North, it would mean a rise in the cost of living for the Southerners with no compensating increase in wealth. Resentment reached its highest pitch in South-Carolina, which at this particular time was experimenting a depression because of a drop in cotton prices. The state legislative met and threatened to nullify the act of Congress because it favored one section of the country at the expense of another. If carried out, this proposal would have placed the authority of a state over that of the Federal government and would have made the Constitution useless. The Nullification proceeding threw the country into turmoil. Abuse was heaped on South-Carolina which, as a result, threatened to withdraw from the Union (Barnes Pg. 13). "We, therefore, the people of the state of South Carolina, in Convention assembled, do declare . . . that several acts of the Congress. . . are null, void, and no law, nor binding upon this state, its officers, or citizens." (Van Doren 146). This was not the first attempt at secession. New England states first suggested it as a possibility with the Hartford Convention Resolutions of 1815. But this was a more serious attempt and only the vigorous intervention of President Andrew Jackson stopped civil war from occurring.

Up until the invention of the cotton gin the north and the south were primarily farming communities. But the cotton gin brought new value on slaves, profit and demand in the south. As industrial revolution grow in the north demanding worker and economic growth. So going into the Civil war America was two nations. Eli Whitney nagging ingenuity gave a tragic guarantee that the North would welcome the Industrial and the South would reject it that the North would go one way and the South another—and that sooner or later they would collide.

III. A Nation of Immigrants

Another change was the mass of immigration. Immigrants furnished much of the labor that made the productive explosion possible and many of the consumers who made it profitable. The industrializing processes that was at work and it open job opportunity and uprooted millions in Europe whose occupations became unneeded or whose land was confiscated by the more "efficient". The immigrants moved the United States population up from 4,000,000 to 32,000,000 in just 90 years. American culture simply molded itself around their presence.(Weisberger, 783)

Population growth can weaken the economy of a country that is limited in its natural and capital resources. The United States was not limited, therefore the economy soared.(Fenton 280: Cooke 273). This was good. What was bad was that bad feelings grew among some Americans toward immigrants. That was called nativism. At the same time, while millions of Americans flooded into Northern cities, very few came South. This only served to accentuate the growing differences between these two American sections. Foreign immigrants damaged an already enfeebled Whig party and created concern among many native-born Americans. To the average, hard-working Protestant American, the foreigners pouring into the cities and following the railroads west-ward spoke unfamiliar languages , and wore funny clothes, drank alcohol freely in the grogshops increased crime and pauperism. Worst of all they attended Catholic churches, were the Latin mass and Eucharistic rituals offended those used to the Protestant worship, furthermore they sent their children to their own schools. They also seem content with lower standards of living and would work for lower pay and worse conditions than any American laborers, thus endangering their jobs.

Massive immigration then, like economic differences, was one of the causes of the Civil War. It helped bring the Civil War in general it brought instability to the North. At the same time, immigrants were flooding into the western territories. These new western immigrants had no wise to compete with black slaves.

III. Slavery Expansion as a Cause but Not the Cause . . .

Rev. Abraham Essick, pastor of Chambersburg Lutheran Church, a moderate unionist, well educated pastor, and a reliable witness, wrote a friend and admitted that slavery was an issue but not the most important issue. "Conservative men, who did all in their power to avert the collision before our flag was dishonoured [the fall of Ft. Sumter], are now burning with indignation. . . the government must be sustained, rebellion suppressed and the honor of the nation vindicated. May God defend the right!" He expresses no outrage at slavery and is more concerned about the honor and dignity of his nation and the breaking away of the South from that nation than any other issue (Abraham Essick, May 8, 1861). Other diarists concurred with Abraham Essick. James Lemuel Clark, a member of the Southern army, when he discussed the reasons he went to war with "yankees" never mentioned slavery as a cause. In 1860, in Cooke County, where James Lemuel Clark lived, had a population of nearly four thousand white people and only 65 slaveowners! There were only 300 to 400 slaves and they were held by 10 slaveholders (Clark 20). Another Texan, William A. Fletcher, was delighted when he heard he could fight the Yankees. He even entertained a thought of arming the slaves to fight Yankees too (Fletcher 2)! Fletcher and Clark did not fight on the Southern side for slavery!

As one of the earliest attempts to make sense of this tragedy, the Southern Historical Society concluded in 1876:

> The late civil war which raged in the United States has been very generally attributed to the abolition of slavery as its cause. When we consider how deeply the institutions of southern society and the operations of southern industry were founded in slavery, we must admit that this was cause enough to have produced such a result. But great and wide as was that cause in its far reaching effects, a close study of the history of the times will bring us to the conclusion that it was the fear of a mischief far more extensive and deeper even than this which drove cool and reflecting minds in the South to believe that it was better to make the death struggle at once than submit tamely to what was inevitable, unless its coming could be averted by force. Men, too old to be driven blindly by passion, women, whose gentle and kindly instincts were deeply impressed by the horrors of war, and young men, with fortune and position yet to be won in an open and inviting field, if peace could be maintained so as to secure the opportunities of liberty and fair treatment, united in the common cause and determined to make a holocaust of all that was

dear to them on the altars of war sooner then submit without resistance to the loss of liberty, honor and property by a cruel abuse of power and a breach of plighted faith on the part of those who had professed to enter with them into a union of justice and fraternal affection (Hunter 1).

Other evidence the slavery could not have been the cause of the Civil war is the issue of slavery in Brazil. Brazil and America were settled around the same time. Both had slavery. However Brazil did not have a Civil war in order to rid themselves of this injustice (Degler, xviii). Therefore the presence of slavery, as controversial as it might be, as divisive as it may be, in no way assured that the United States would fight a civil war.

What about slavery expansion? This issue is as heated as the issue of slavery. President Lincoln never intended to stop slavery, what he didn't was slavery expansion. He stated this in his 1st Inaugural Address, "Apprehension seems to exist among the people of the Southern states that by accession of a republic administration , their property and their peace and personal security are to be endangered . There has never been any reasonable cause for such apprehension. Indeed, the most ample evidence to the contrary has all the while existed and been open to their inspection. It is found in nearly all the published speeches of him who now address you . . ." (Lincoln 1). What Lincoln says is there is no reason for the South to choose secession for he by no means wanted the slaves free. Of course Lincoln changed later, but for now, this was his position. Lincoln, like the Republican Party, was opposed to slavery expansion, not to slavery (1860 Republican National Platform 1).

If slavery expansion threatened northerners, the possibility of no slavery expansion infuriated southerners. "The Gospel of prosperity and the defense of bondage were inseparable in the minds of most slave holders. But when they made explicit reference to slavery, masters drew also from an intellectual tradition that reaffirmed their faith in the destiny of the white man as the harbinger of global wealth. In the antebellum South, racism and the gospel of prosperity were joined in symbiotic relation (Oakes 130)." The possibility of no slavery expansion was tantamount to commercial poverty in the mind of most southerners. The more slave expansion the more money for the slave holders. So Lincoln didn't want slavery expansion because that meant less money for the paid workers; and the south wanted is for more money for them. Of course the

whole controversy about slavery was further exacerbated by Harriet Beecher Stowe's *Uncle Tom's Cabin*. Moderate northerners thought that it was an exaggeration of slavery. Southerners thought that it was downright libelous! They hated Mrs. Stowe (McCullough 337). Many southerners, like my great-great-great uncle, Uncle Howard, fought for the south even though they had no or very few slaves (Stobaugh 6).

Slavery, then, was an important cause of the Civil War. But it was not the most important cause. In fact, there was no substantive issue important enough in 1861 to fight a civil war. The war was brought on by extremism and misunderstandings on both sides (Grob and Billias 392).

Another contributing factor was the Second Great Awakening that spread across antebellum America creating instability and heightened expectations.

IV. FIRE ACROSS THE LAND: THE SECOND GREAT AWAKENING

While all this mixup was occurring the Second Great Awakening began. This was precluded by what was called the Cane Ridge Revival in 1800. The Cane Ridge Revival was started by a Presbyterian minister named James McGready. McGready preached against formality, and the darkness of the churches. Many people were touched—even the " boldest most daring sinners in the county covered their faces and wept bitterly," and " many fell to the ground, and lay powerless, groaning, praying and crying for mercy." This was the beginning of a great change. (Weisberger 24). Then, in the 1820's Charles Finney held a series of revivals in New York State. Finney was known as a " soul winner " and a man who" made good" in he choice of work, which was bring men to Christ. (Weisberger 95; Ahlstrom 653). All this change made Americans more willing to follow their own wishes and not follow the government or other authority. By 1860 more Americans than ever had personal relationships with their God and wished to make personal decisions about where they lived and what they owned. In a real sense then when the North tried to take away the southern slaves, or so they thought, they saw it as a personal attack on their property and life. They were ready to do whatever was necessary to protect those rights—even if it was rebellion against the government. At the same time, northern Christians were prepared to cause their southern brothers to stay in the union no matter what the cost. The religious revivals of the early and middle nineteenth century prepared them for this decision.

V. MANIFEST DESTINY: WILL WESTERN STATES BE FREE OR SLAVE?

On top of all the revivals, the issue of slavery, and the tariffs there was also Manifest destiny. The phrase "Manifest Destiny" was coined by John L. O'Sullivan, editor of the *Democratic Review*. It advanced the idea that America's superior culture and institutions gave us a God-given right to take over the entire continent (Nash, pp. 448). Manifest Destiny allowed the expansion west but did not cause it to happen. Occurrences in Texas triggered the government's determination to get possession the territories west of the Mississippi River (Nash et al. 448).

Many people in the North opposed the Mexican War. They thought that it was a southern plot to extend slavery. In 1846, David Wilmot, a congressman from PA, introduced an amendment to a bill designed to appropriate $2 million for negotiating an agreement with Mexico. Part of his amendment suggested that slavery should be kept away from any territory acquired from Mexico. A bitter and prolonged debate between those who were for slavery and those who were not broke out. Finally, the Wilmot Proviso, as the amendment was called, was passed to the House of Representatives. However it failed to pass the Senate.. Ed Fenton, pp. 282-283. This debate showed how fragile the unity of North and South was. They had fought a war together but had no idea how to live together in peace.

The impulse to expand ran into problems when the nation discussed whether new states would be slave or free. This then led to the failure of the American political system to keep these two nations—North and South—one. Now nothing was working to unify the nations. There was no ground it seemed that they could agree on. In every issue, situation, and problem they were disagreeing.

V. CONCLUSION: NO WAY TO COMPROMISE

So what caused the civil war? Why did Americans fight one another for four long years, at the cost of 600,000 lives? What did it all mean? The American Civil War occurred because Americans allowed it to happen. They let their differences be more important than their similarities. The government was no help.

Perier to the Civil War Americans had done a lot of compromising. In 1820, there was the Missouri Compromise, when Congress took charge of the question of slavery in the territories by declaring it illegal in the huge region acquired by the Louisiana Purchase.

When Andrew Jackson was President (1829-37) a sharp division was made again in the nation's politics. He asserted to the superior state's rights, and attempted to declare null and void within its borders the tariff of 1828. Needless to say he was not a favorite.

Now president Polk's war with Mexico opened the slavery issue again. Should it to be allowed in the new territories? The Wilmot Proviso (1846), which was supposed to have excluded slavery, became a irritating subject for both the North and the South. It was also being voted on again and again in Congress and successfully held off by southerners. Abolitionist led by William Lloyd Garrison and others became strong in many northern circles, it called for the immediate emancipation of slaves with no compensation to slave owners. The majority of northern whites disliked blacks and refused to support abolition; they did not want to allow slavery in the territories so that they would be preserved for white settlement based on northern expectation: free labor, dignity of work, and economic progress (Multimedia Encyclopedia Online).

In 1848 northerner's lack of patient with the existing parties formed and the Free-Soil party became intolerable. By polling 300,000 votes for their candidate, Martin Van Buren, victory was denied to the Democrats and the Whig Zachary Taylor was put in the White House. The Compromise of 1850 appeared to have settled the issue of slavery expansion by the principle of popular sovereignty, which said that the people who lived in the Mexican cession territories were to decide for themselves. A new Fugitive Slave Law was passed in 1850, giving powers to slave owners to steal back from the northern states the slave that had happily runaway.

As the 1850s began, it seemed for a time that the issue of slavery and other sectional differences between North and South might eventually be reconciled. But with the westward expansion of the American nation, all attempts to compromise to became nonresistant and contrasting economic, political, and philosophical endeavor became more evident. The resulting civil war altered the American nation.

In 1860 the political system became completely shattered. The American political system no longer functioned. The Democrats disjoined into northern and southern wings, broaching two different candidates for the presidency; the bantam Constitutional Union party aspired to rally the former Whigs behind a third. The Republicans, however, were able to assure the election of Abraham Lincoln to the White House.

Southerners had considered the rise of the Yankee-dominated Republican party with great apprehension. They were converted that the party was secretly controlled by abolitionists (although most northerners loathed the abolitionists) and that Yankees believed in using government to administer their moralistic campaigns. In 1859, John Brown led a raid on the federal arsenal at Harpers Ferry, Va., hoping to encourage a slave uprose. His action—and his subsequent adoration by some northerners—helped coax southerners that emancipation of the slaves, if northerners attained authority of the country, was sooner or later inevitable. They then fought a war to protect their rights and property.

I have laid before you all the different causes that led up to the American Civil war, the expanding of the economy, a flood of immigrants, the Second Great Awakening, Manifest Destiny, and the rise of nativism, all these doomed the Republic to a Civil war. Because of slavery and constitutional compromises America was never a real nation until after the civil war. The war was essentially fought because the American political system failed to present a compromise that suited the North's demands as well as the South's. The 1850s generation blundered into a needless war because they played on emotions to gain votes rather than face the issues. Agitation over slavery led to mistaken and false sectional images and fanaticism (Crum 93). Therefore they fought it out in a great and awful civil war.

SAMPLE FINAL COPY

Identify changes.

CAUSES OF THE CIVIL WAR

Jessica Stobaugh

I. INTRODUCTION: A TRAGEDY THAT COULD HAVE BEEN AVOIDED

As the Civil War was beginning to unfold, the Southerner Mary Chestnut wrote, "We [the North and the South] are divorced because we have hated each other so!" This hatred lead to a bloody and horrible civil war.

For years the question "What caused the Civil War?" has puzzled historians. They have suggested many reasons, but what is the real cause? Slavery was the chief irritant but did not cause the conflict. Both Rachel and Samuel Cormany, typical Civil War con-

temporaries, supported their government's efforts to quell the southern rebellion. But neither of them was irritated by slavery. Rachel blamed the war on the "hotheadedness of the South, and the invisibleness of the North" (Mohr, 132). In fact, there were many things that contributed to the Civil War—some more than others. Certainly slavery was *a* cause but not *the* cause.

The Civil War was caused because Southern and Northern Americans chose not to live together. Again, the operative word is *chose*. They chose to fight a war. The North and the South were always two nations, and by 1860 it was difficult to live together in the same house. It was not impossible, though. They chose to live apart. They had solved their problems before—in 1820 and 1850, for instances. But suddenly in 1860, the political system failed.

The Civil War was neither the fault of the North or the South. Or rather, it was the fault of both! An expanding economy, a flood of immigrants, the Second Great Awakening, Manifest Destiny, and the failure of the American political system—the combination of these events brought the young republic to brink of the Civil War. Ultimately, though, the failure of nerve manifested by American political leaders thrust the nation into its bloodiest war in American history.

I agree with a historian's assessment of the causes of the Civil War:

> When the Union was originally formed, the United States embraced too many degrees of latitude and longitude, and too many varieties of climate and production, to make it practicable to establish and administer justly one common government which should take charge of all the interests of society. To the wise men who were entrusted with the formation of that union and common government, it was obvious enough that each separate society should be entrusted with the management of its own peculiar interests, and that the united government should take charge only of those interests which were common and general. (Hunter, 1)

What is ironic is that, in a way, the North and the South were fighting for the same thing. They both saw themselves preserving what was vitally important to America. The Confederacy was really fighting for the American dream as much as the Union! They saw themselves as the new patriots. The South had some justification. Many of the Founding Fathers owned slaves (Hunter 1, 9-10). George Washington, Thomas

Jefferson, and James Madison were all slaveholding presidents.

In summary, the Civil War was a struggle between conflicting worldviews. Each section held to a belief system that increasingly felt alienated from the other. They disagreed over the power of the federal government; they disagreed over tariffs; and they especially disagreed over slavery and its expansion westward (Williams, 203). However, these disagreements were nothing new and did not bring a civil war. The War was not inevitable. By the middle of the nineteenth century, these differing viewpoints—coupled with the almost violent change inflicted on America, and the collapse of compromise as a viable option in the political arena—brought the young Republic into a horrendous civil war. Americans chose to fight because they were unwilling to choose an alternative.

The first American to observe that the Civil War was avoidable, not inevitable, was former President Buchanan. He argued that the cause of the Civil War was to be found in

the long, active, and persistent hostility of the Northern Abolitionists, both in and out of Congress, against Southern slavery, until the final triumph of President Lincoln; and on the other hand, the corresponding antagonism and violence with which the advocates of slavery resisted efforts, and vindicated its preservation and extension up till the period of secession.

Buchanan's assumption that the war need not have taken place had it not been for Northern fanatics and, to a lesser extent, Southern extremists, was essentially correct. To put it another way, there was no substantive issue important enough in 1861 to necessitate a resort to arms; the war had been brought on by extremists on both sides. The moderate political center refused to solve the problem and left the solution to extremists. The extremists brought on a civil war.

The remainder of this paper will examine several issues whose accumulated effect made the Civil War seem necessary to a generation of Americans.

II. TWO NATIONS, TWO ECONOMIES

"I heard much of the extreme difficulty of ginning cotton, that is separating it from its seeds . . . I involuntarily happened to be thinking on the subject and struck out a plan of a machine in my mind" (Van Doren and McHenry, 89). The machine was the cotton gin, and the author of this letter was Eli Whitney. More than anything else, the cotton gin made cotton a profitable business and assured its future in the Southern economy.

Originally cotton had been a minor crop because of the difficulty of separating the fiber from the seeds. In 1793 Eli Whitney's cotton gin solved this problem. In 1800 only about 70,000 bales of cotton were produced in the South. By 1825 cotton production increased 700 percent (Fenton, 185) Demand for cotton of all sorts was growing, especially in England, where new textile factories, with their weaving and spinning machines, created an insatiable appetite. Demand and supply came together when Eli Whitney set his mind to the problem of short-staple cotton and its seeds (Nash, et al., 309). Eli Whitney supplied the technology for cotton to be king, and the industrial revolution supplied the market. By the early nineteenth century, British and American factories demanded more cotton. The expanding Southern plantation system was ready to meet that demand.

In 1813 Boston Manufacturing Company opened the first textile factory to perform all cloth-making operations by power in Waltham, Massachusetts. Financed with large capital, the company recruited New England farm girls as operatives, boarded them in dormitories, and produced a standard coarse cotton cloth requiring minimum labor skill. By 1826, in Lowell, Massachusetts, one plant turned out two million yards of cloth annually (Van Doren and McHenry, 128). Their production grew more and more over the next few years.

In 1828 a new sore spot appeared in North-South relations. That year Congress raised the tariff on imports, in order to protect native industry struggling to compete with European manufacturers. The South protested loudly over the tariff on the grounds that it favored the North at her expense. She was dependant almost wholly on the North and on Europe for manufactured goods. While an increase in prices would enrich the North, it would mean a rise in the cost of living for the Southerners, with no compensating increase in wealth. In their view, all the benefits of protection were going to Northern manufacturers. Though the country as a whole grew richer, South Carolina grew poorer, with its planters bearing the burden of higher prices. South Carolina planters, and Southern planters in general, sold their products to British industrials, who sold manufactured good to Southerners. When Northern tariffs raised the price of industrial goods, the price of cotton consequently fell. If one British table was worth 30 pounds of cotton, the same table would be worth 50 pounds of cotton after tariffs increased British prices.

Ironically it was the Southern planter president Andrew Jackson who insisted that tariffs be increased. The protective tariff passed by Congress and signed into law by Jackson in 1832 was milder than that of 1828, but it further embittered many in the state of South Carolina. In response, a number of South Carolina citizens endorsed the states'-rights principle of "nullification," which was enunciated by John C. Calhoun, Jackson's vice president until 1832, in his *South Carolina Exposition and Protest* (1828). South Carolina dealt with the tariff by adopting the Ordinance of Nullification, which declared both the tariffs of 1828 and 1832 null and void within state borders. The legislature also passed laws to enforce the ordinance, including authorization for raising a military force and appropriations for arms.

Resentment reached its highest pitch in South Carolina, which at this time was experiencing a depression because of a drop in cotton prices. The state legislative body both met and threatened to nullify the act of Congress because it favored one section of the country at the expense of another. If carried out, this proposal would have placed the authority of a state over that of the federal government and would have made the Constitution useless.

The Nullification proceeding threw the country into turmoil. Abuse was heaped on South Carolina which, as a result, threatened to withdraw from the Union (Barnes 13). "We, therefore, the people of the state of South Carolina, in Convention assembled, do declare . . . that several acts of the Congress . . . are null, void, and no law, nor binding upon this state, its officers, or citizens" (Van Doren, 146). This was not the first attempt at secession. New England states first suggested it as a possibility with the Hartford Convention Resolutions of 1815. But this was a more serious attempt, and only the vigorous intervention of President Andrew Jackson stopped civil war from occurring.

PRE-CIVIL WAR TARIFFS

(Ed Fenton, *New American History*); the following chart was created by the author of this curriculum.

Name of Tariff	Provisions	Public Reaction
1789	Placed duties on 30 items such as molasses, nails, hemp, steel. Average, 8.5%. All other imported items, 5%.	Widely popular. Needed to raise federal revenue.
1792	Increased 5% duty to 7.5%	Farmers and New England shippers vigorously opposed these duties.
1816	25% protective tariff on most woolen, cotton, and iron manufactures.	General support.
1828	Duty of 50% on raw wool.	South strongly opposes.
1832	Increased duty on woolens; placed cheap raw wool and flax on duty-free list; reduced average duties to 35%.	South Carolina adopted Ordinance of Nullification and threatened secession.
1833	Provided for gradual reduction of tariffs.	Supported by South; opposed by Northeast.
1842	Returned tariff to 1832 levels.	Supported by Northeast; opposed by South.
1846	Reduced tariffs.	South supported and Northeast opposed.
1857	Increased duty-free list.	Northeast opposed and South supported.

Until the invention of the cotton gin, the North and the South were primarily farming communities. But the cotton gin brought new value on slaves, profit, and demand in the South. The industrial revolution demanded workers and economic growth.

By the time of the Civil War, America was two nations. Eli Whitney's inspiring ingenuity gave a tragic guarantee that the North would welcome the industrial revolution and the South would reject it. The North would go one way and the South another, and sooner or later they would collide.

III. A NATION OF IMMIGRANTS

Immigrants furnished much of the labor that made the productive explosion possible and many of the consumers who made it profitable. The industrializing processes that were at work opened job opportunity and uprooted millions in Europe whose occupations became unneeded or whose land was confiscated by the more "efficient." The immigrants moved the United States population up from four million to 32 million in just 90 years. American culture simply molded itself around their presence (Weisberger, 783).

Population growth can weaken the economy of a country that is limited in its natural and capital resources. The United States was not so limited and therefore the economy soared (Fenton, 280; Cooke, 273). This was good. What was bad was that bad feelings grew among some Americans toward immigrants. That was called nativism. At the same time, while millions of Americans flooded into Northern cities, very few came South. This only served to accentuate the growing differences between these two American sections. Foreign immigrants damaged an already enfeebled Whig party and created concern among many native-born Americans. To the average hard-working Protestant American, the foreigners pouring into the cities and following the railroads westward spoke unfamiliar languages, wore funny clothes, drank alcohol freely in the grogshops, and increased crime and pauperism. Worst of all, they attended Catholic churches, where the Latin mass and Eucharistic rituals offended those used to the Protestant worship. Furthermore, they sent their children to their own schools. They also seemed content with lower standards of living and would work for lower pay and worse conditions than any American laborers, thus endangering American jobs.

Massive immigration, then, like economic differences, was one of the causes of the Civil War. It brought

instability to the North. At the same time, immigrants were flooding into the western territories. These new western immigrants had no wish to compete with black slaves.

IV. SLAVERY EXPANSION AS A CAUSE BUT NOT THE CAUSE . . .

Rev. Abraham Essick, pastor of Chambersburg Lutheran Church, a moderate unionist, well-educated pastor, and a reliable witness, wrote a friend and admitted that slavery was an issue but not the most important issue of the coming crisis. "Conservative men, who did all in their power to avert the collision before our flag was dishonored [the fall of Fort Sumter], are now burning with indignation. . . . The government must be sustained, rebellion suppressed and the honor of the nation vindicated. May God defend the right!" He expresses no outrage at slavery and is more concerned about the honor and dignity of his nation and the breaking away of the South from that nation than any other issue (Abraham Essick, May 8, 1861).

Other diarists concurred with Abraham Essick. James Lemuel Clark, a member of the Southern army, discussed the reasons he went to war with "Yankees" but never mentioned slavery as a cause. In 1860, Cooke County, Texas, where James Lemuel Clark lived, had a population of nearly 4,000 white people and only 65 slave owners! There were only 300 to 400 slaves and they were held by 10 slaveholders (Clark, 20). Another Texan, William A. Fletcher, was delighted when he heard he could fight the Yankees. He even entertained a thought of arming the slaves to fight Yankees, too! (Fletcher, 2). Fletcher and Clark did not fight on the Southern side for slavery!

As one of the earliest attempts to make sense of this tragedy, the Southern Historical Society concluded in 1876:

The late civil war which raged in the United States has been very generally attributed to the abolition of slavery as its cause. When we consider how deeply the institutions of southern society and the operations of southern industry were founded in slavery, we must admit that this was cause enough to have produced such a result. But great and wide as was that cause in its far reaching effects, a close study of the history of the times will bring us to the conclusion that it was the fear of a mischief far more extensive and deeper even than this which drove cool and reflecting minds in the South to believe that it was better to make the death struggle at once than submit tamely to what was inevitable, unless its coming could be averted by force. Men, too old to be driven blindly by passion, women, whose gentle and kindly instincts were deeply impressed by the horrors of war, and young men, with fortune and position yet to be won in an open and inviting field, if peace could be maintained so as to secure the opportunities of liberty and fair treatment, united in the common cause and determined to make a holocaust of all that was dear to them on the altars of war sooner then submit without resistance to the loss of liberty, honor and property by a cruel abuse of power and a breach of plighted faith on the part of those who had professed to enter with them into a union of justice and fraternal affection. (Hunter, 1)

Other evidence that slavery could not have been the cause of the Civil War was the issue of slavery in Brazil. Brazil and America were settled around the same time. Both had slavery. However, Brazil did not have a civil war in order to rid themselves of this injustice (Degler, xviii). Therefore, the presence of slavery, as controversial as it might be, as divisive as it may be, in no way assured that the United States would fight a civil war, just as it did not cause a civil war in Brazil.

Immigration, 1820-2000

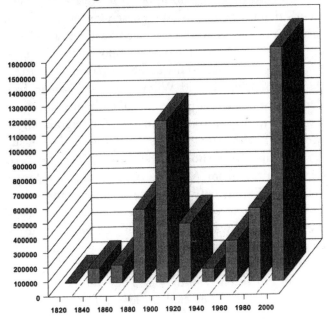

What about slavery expansion? This issue is as heated as the issue of slavery. President Lincoln never intended to stop slavery; what he didn't want was slavery expansion. He stated this in his first Inaugural Address:

> Apprehension seems to exist among the people of the Southern states that, by accession of a Republican Administration, their property and their peace and personal security are to be endangered. There has never been any reasonable cause for such apprehension. Indeed, the most ample evidence to the contrary has all the while existed and been open to their inspection. It is found in nearly all the published speeches of him who now address you. (Lincoln, 1).

Lincoln said that there was no reason for the South to choose secession, for he by no means wanted the slaves free. We know that Lincoln changed later, but for now, this was his position. Lincoln, like the Republican Party, was opposed to slavery expansion, not to slavery (1860 Republican National Platform, 1).

If slavery expansion threatened Northerners, the cessation of slavery expansion infuriated Southerners.

> The gospel of prosperity and the defense of bondage were inseparable in the minds of most slave holders. But when they made explicit reference to slavery, masters drew also from an intellectual tradition that reaffirmed their faith in the destiny of the white man as the harbinger of global wealth. In the antebellum South, racism and the gospel of prosperity were joined in symbiotic relation. (Oakes, 130).

The end of no slavery expansion was tantamount to commercial poverty in the mind of most Southerners. The more slavery expansion, the more money for the slaveholders. Lincoln did not want slavery expansion because that meant less money for the paid workers; and what the South wanted was inflated slavery prices. Southerners also needed the ability to expand westward with their slaves, to find rich farmland. The whole controversy about slavery was further exacerbated by Harriet Beecher Stowe's *Uncle Tom's Cabin* (1852). Moderate Northerners thought that it was an exaggeration of slavery. Southerners thought that it was downright libelous! They hated Mrs. Stowe (McCullough, 337). Many Southerners, like my great-great-great uncle, Howard, fought for the South even though they had no or few slaves (Stobaugh, 6).

Slavery, then, was an important cause of the Civil War. But it was not the most important cause. In fact, there was no substantive issue important enough in 1861 to fight a civil war. The war was brought on by extremism and misunderstandings on both sides (Grob and Billias, 392).

Another contributing factor was the Second Great Awakening that spread across antebellum America, creating instability and heightened expectations.

V. FIRE ACROSS THE LAND: THE SECOND GREAT AWAKENING

While all this was occurring , the Second Great Awakening broke over the country. This was preceded by what was called the Cane Ridge Revival, started in 1800 by a Presbyterian minister named James McGready, who preached against formality and the darkness of the churches. Many people were touched— even the "boldest most daring sinners in the county covered their faces and wept bitterly," and "many fell to the ground, and lay powerless, groaning, praying and crying for mercy." This was the beginning of a great change (Weisberger, 24).

The Second Great Awakening represents the contradiction that was so much a part of American religious history. For one thing, the Awakening was a revival—a phenomenon which we will describe below. On the other hand, the Awakening grew in the fragile air of pluralism, which was both the greatest strength and greatest challenge of American religious life. For instance, the Second Great Awakening flourished in upstate New York, also the place where heretical Mormonism, the only indigenous American religion, originated.

In America, at least, from its beginning, religion has more or less embraced revivalism as a mode of church expansion, growth, and influence. We must be careful to define all our terms. "Revivalism," according to historian D. E. Dieter, is

> the movement within the Christian tradition which emphasizes the appeal of religion to the emotional and affectional nature of individuals as well as to their intellectual and rational nature. It believes that vital Christianity begins with a response of the whole being to the gospel's call for repentance and spiritual rebirth by faith in Jesus Christ. This experience results in a personal relationship with God. Some have sought to make revivalism a purely American and even a predominantly frontier phenomenon.

In the 1820s Charles Finney held a series of revivals in New York State. Finney was known as a "soul-winner" and a man who "made good" in his choice of work, which was to bring men to Christ. (Weisberger, 95; Ahlstrom, 653). All this change made Americans more willing to follow their own wishes and not follow the government or other authority. By 1860 more Americans than ever had personal relationships with their God and wished to make personal decisions about where they lived and what they owned. In a real sense, then, when the North tried to take away the Southern slaves, or so they thought, the South saw it as a personal attack on their property and life. They were ready to do whatever was necessary to protect those rights—even if it was rebellion against the government. At the same time, Northern Christians were prepared to cause their Southern brothers to stay in the Union no matter what the cost. The religious revivals of the early and middle nineteenth century prepared them for this decision.

VI. MANIFEST DESTINY: WILL WESTERN STATES BE FREE OR SLAVE?

On top of all the revivals, the issue of slavery expansion, and the tariffs, Americans also claimed a Manifest destiny. The phrase "Manifest Destiny" was coined by John L. O'Sullivan, editor of the *Democratic Review*. It advanced the idea that America's superior culture and institutions gave us a God-given right to take over the entire continent (Nash, pp. 448). Manifest Destiny allowed the expansion westward but did not cause it to happen. Occurrences in Texas triggered the government's determination to take possession of the territories west of the Mississippi River (Nash, et al. 448).

Many people in the North opposed the Mexican War. They thought that it was a Southern plot to extend slavery. In 1846, David Wilmot, a congressman from Pennsylvania, introduced an amendment to a bill designed to appropriate $2 million for negotiating an agreement with Mexico. Part of his amendment suggested that slavery should be kept away from any territory acquired from Mexico. A bitter and prolonged debate broke out between those who were for slavery and those who were not. Finally, the Wilmot Proviso, as the amendment was called, was passed to the House of Representatives. However, it failed to pass the Senate (Fenton, 282–83). This debate showed how fragile the unity of North and South was. They had fought a war together because they had no idea about how to live together in peace.

The impulse to expand ran into problems when the nation discussed whether new states would be slave or free. This then led to the failure of the American political system to keep as one these two nations, North and South. Now nothing was working to unify the nations. They could not seem to agree on any ground. In every issue, situation, and problem, they were disagreeing.

VII. CONCLUSION: NO WAY TO COMPROMISE

So what caused the Civil War? Why did Americans fight one another for four long years, at the cost of 600,000 lives? What did it all mean? The American Civil War occurred because Americans allowed it to happen. They let their differences be more important than their similarities. The government was no help.

Before the Civil War, Americans had done a lot of compromising. In 1820, there was the Missouri Compromise, when Congress took charge of the question of slavery in the territories by declaring it illegal in the huge region acquired by the Louisiana Purchase.

When Andrew Jackson was president (1829–37), a sharp division arose between Northerners and Southerners over the tariff issue. The South favored free trade; the industrial North needed protection. South Carolina asserted superior state's rights and tried to declare the tariff of 1828 null and void within its borders. Jackson confronted South Carolina, and it back down. Needless to say, Jackson was not a favorite in that state.

Next, President Polk's war with Mexico opened the slavery issue again. Should slavery be allowed in the new territories? The Wilmot Proviso (1846), which was supposed to have excluded slavery, became an irritating subject for both the North and the South. It was also being voted on again and again in Congress and successfully held off by Southerners. Abolitionists led by William Lloyd Garrison and others became strong in many Northern circles and called for the immediate emancipation of slaves, with no compensation to slave owners. The majority of Northern whites disliked blacks and refused to support abolition; they did not want to allow slavery in the territories so that they would be preserved for white settlement based on Northern expectations: free labor, dignity of work, and economic progress (Multimedia Encyclopedia Online).

In 1848 Northern impatience with the existing parties helped form the Free-Soil party, which endorsed Martin Van Buren, nominated by the Barnburners, a group of Northern Democrats opposed to extending slavery. The polls gave Martin Van Buren 300,000 votes; he ran a poor third but denied victory to the Democrats. The Whig Zachary Taylor was put in the White House, no one was happy, and the nation was ill-suited to handle the next crisis.

The Compromise of 1850 appeared to have settled the issue of slavery expansion by the principle of popular sovereignty, which said that the people who lived in the Mexican cession territories were to decide for themselves. A new Fugitive Slave Law was passed in 1850. This enraged Northerners because it let slave owners cross into Northern states to claim their runaway slaves.

As the 1850s began, it seemed for a time that the issue of slavery and other sectional differences between North and South might eventually be reconciled. But with the westward expansion of the American nation, all attempts to compromise disappeared, and contrasting economic, political, and philosophical endeavors became more evident. The resulting Civil War altered the American nation.

In 1860 the American political system became completely dysfunctional and began to shatter. The Democrats fractured into Northern and Southern wings, broaching two different candidates for the presidency; the bantam Constitutional Union party aspired to rally former Whigs behind a third. The Republicans, however, were able to assure the election of Abraham Lincoln to the White House.

With great apprehension Southerners had watched the rise of the Yankee-dominated Republican Party, organized in 1856 to be against slavery. They were convinced that the Republican Party was secretly controlled by abolitionists (although most Northerners loathed the abolitionists) and that Yankees believed in using government to administer their moralistic campaigns. In 1859, John Brown led a raid on the federal arsenal at Harpers Ferry, Virginia, hoping to encourage a slave uprising. His action—and his subsequent adoration by some Northerners—helped convince Southerners that emancipation of the slaves, if Northerners attained authority of the country, was inevitable, sooner or later. They then fought a war to protect their rights and property.

Because of slavery and constitutional compromises, America was never a real nation until after the Civil War. That war was essentially fought because the American political system failed to present a compromise that suited the North's demands as well as the South's. The 1850s generation blundered into a needless war because they played on emotions to gain votes rather than face the issues. Agitation over slavery led to mistaken and false sectional images and fanaticism (Crum, 93). Therefore, they fought it out in the great and awful Civil War.

STYLE (WRITING AND SPEAKING): SUMMARY

Make every word count. Speak/write precisely and clearly. Use commas and pronouns to cut down on words. Repeat words and phrases for emphasis, but do so carefully. Avoid problems in parallelism. Choose your figurative language carefully. Make sure that it is appropriate to your task and to your audience.

PUBLIC SPEAKING: ENUNCIATE CLEARLY

You should not be guilty of lazy lips; you must speak clearly and slowly.

SPEECH ASSIGNMENT

Students should practice saying the following phrases aloud in a speech.

Loose lips sink ships.
The sixth soldier sold his soul to the shepherd.
The big black bug bit the bitter bright burglar.
Round and round the rugged rocks the ragged rascals ran.

WRITING ASSIGNMENTS

1. Rewrite your entire paper.

RESEARCH PAPER BENCHMARK

The first draft of your research paper is finished! Now, during this lesson, you will revise/rewrite your entire paper. Once the rewrite is complete, submit the entire project to your evaluator/parent/teacher. Your paper will include: a cover sheet (example below), outline, the paper itself, and a bibliography (see Lesson 25).

SUGGESTED
Weekly Implementation

DAY 1	DAY 2	DAY 3	DAY 4	DAY 5
Rewrite your paper and submit it to your teacher/ guardian/ parents. Make a journal entry.	Rewrite your paper and submit it to your teacher/ guardian/ parents. Make a journal entry.	Rewrite your paper and submit it to your teacher/ guardian/ parents. Make a journal entry.	Rewrite your paper and submit it to your teacher/ guardian/ parents. Make a journal entry.	Submit your final paper to your instructor/ guardian/ parent. Take Lesson 34 Test Make a journal entry.

SKILLS FOR RHETORIC

ENCOURAGING THOUGHTFUL CHRISTIANS
TO BE WORLD CHANGERS

APPENDICES

APPENDIX A

Writing Tips

How do students produce concise, well-written essays?

GENERAL STATEMENTS

• Essays should be written in the context of the other social sciences. This means that essays should be written on all topics: science topics, history topics, social science topics, etc.

• Some essays should be rewritten, depending on the assignment and the purpose of the writing; definitely those essays which are to be presented to various readers or a public audience should be rewritten for their best presentation. Parents and other educators should discuss with their students which and how many essays will be rewritten. Generally speaking, I suggest that students rewrite at least one essay per week.

• Students should write something every day and read something every day. Students will be prompted to read assigned whole books before they are due. It is imperative that students read ahead as they write present essays or they will not be able to read all the material. Remember this too: students tend to write what they read. Poor material—material that is too juvenile—will be echoed in the vocabulary and syntax of student essays.

• Students should begin writing assignments immediately after they are assigned. A suggested implementation schedule is provided. Generally speaking, students will write about one hour per day to accomplish the writing component of this course.

• Students should revise their papers as soon as they are evaluated. Follow the implementation schedule at the end of each course.

Every essay includes a *prewriting phase, an outlining phase, a writing phase, a revision phase,* and for the purposes of this course, *a publishing phase.*

PRE-WRITING THINKING CHALLENGE

ISSUE
State problem/issue in five sentences.

State problem/issue in two sentences.

State problem/issue in one sentence.

NAME THREE OR MORE SUBTOPICS OF PROBLEM.

NAME THREE OR MORE SUBTOPICS OF THE SUBTOPICS.

WHAT INFORMATION MUST BE KNOWN TO SOLVE THE PROBLEM OR TO ANSWER THE QUESTION?

STATE THE ANSWER TO THE QUESTION/PROBLEM
—In five sentences.

—In two sentences.

—In one sentence.

STATED IN TERMS OF OUTCOMES, WHAT EVIDENCES DO I SEE THAT CONFIRM THAT I HAVE MADE THE RIGHT DECISION?

ONCE THE PROBLEM/QUESTION IS ANSWERED/SOLVED, WHAT ONE OR TWO NEW PROBLEMS/ANSWERS MAY ARISE?

ABBREVIATED PRE-WRITING THINKING CHALLENGE

What is the issue?
State problem/issue in five sentences.
State problem/issue in two sentences.
State problem/issue in one sentence.
Name three or more subtopics of problem.
Name three or more subtopics of the subtopics.
What information must be known to solve the problem or to answer the question?
State the answer to the question/problem
—in five sentences —in two sentences —in one sentence.
Stated in terms of outcomes, what evidences do I see that confirm that I have made the right decision?

Once the problem or question is answered or solved, what are one or two new problems or answers that could arise?

PRE-WRITING PHASE

Often called the brainstorming phase, the pre-writing phase is the time you decide on exactly what your topic is. What questions must you answer? You should articulate a thesis (a one sentence statement of purpose for why you are writing about this topic. The thesis typically has two to four specific points contained within it). You should decide what sort of essay this is—for instance, a definition, an exposition, a persuasive argument—and then design a strategy. For example, a clearly persuasive essay will demand that you state the issue and give your opinion in the opening paragraph.

Next, after a thesis statement, you will write an outline. *No matter what length the essay may be, 20 pages or one paragraph, you should create an outline.*

Outline
Thesis: In his poem *The Raven*, Edgar Allan Poe uses literary devices to describe such weighty topics as *death* and *unrequited love*, which draw the reader to an insightful and many times emotional moment. (Note that this thesis informs the reader that the author will be exploring *death* and *unrequited love*.)

I. Introduction (Opens to the reader the exploration of the writing and tells the reader what to expect.)
II. Body (This particular essay will include two main points developed in two main paragraphs, one paragraph about death and one paragraph about emotions. The second paragraph will be introduced by means of a transition word or phrase or sentence.)
   A. Imagining Death
   B. Feeling Emotions
III. Conclusions (A paragraph which draws conclusions or solves the problem mentioned in the thesis statement.)

One of the best ways to organize your thoughts is to spend time in concentrated thinking, what some call brainstorming. Thinking through what you want to write is a way to narrow your topic.

Sample Outline:
Persuasive Paper with Three Major Points (Arguments)

I. Introduction: <u>Thesis statement</u> includes a listing or a summary of the three supportive arguments and introduces the paper.

II. Body
A. Argument 1
   Evidence
   (transition words or phrases or sentences to the next topic)
B. Argument 2
   Evidence
   (transition words or phrases or sentences to the next topic)
C. Argument 3
   Evidence
   (transition words or phrases or sentences to the conclusion)

III. Conclusion: Restatement of arguments and evidence used throughout the paper (do not use the words *in conclusion*—just conclude).

NOTE: For greater detail and explanation of outlining, refer to a composition handbook. Careful attention should be paid to parallel structure with words or phrases, to correct form with headings and subheadings, to punctuation, and to pairing of information. Correct outline structure will greatly enhance the writing of any paper.

Sample Outline:
Expository Essay with Four Major Points

I. Introduction: <u>Thesis statement</u> includes a listing or mention of four examples or supports and introduces the paper; use transitional words or phrases at the end of the paragraph.

II. Body
A. Example 1
   Application
   (transition words or phrases or sentences to the next topic)
B. Example 2
   Application
   (transition words or phrases or sentences to the next topic)
C. Example 3
   Application
   (transition words or phrases or sentences to the next topic)
D. Example 4
   Application
   (transition words or phrases or sentences to the conclusion)

III. Conclusion: Restatement of thesis, drawing from the evidence or applications used in the paper (do not use the words *in conclusion*—just conclude).

NOTE: For greater detail and explanation of outlining, refer to a composition handbook. Careful attention should be paid to parallel structure with words or phrases, to correct form with headings and subheadings, to punctuation, and to pairing of information. Correct outline structure will greatly enhance the writing of any paper.

The Thinking Challenge

The following is an example of a Thinking Challenge approach to Mark Twain's *The Adventures of Huckleberry Finn:*

The Problem or The Issue or The Question:

Should Huck turn in his escaped slave-friend Jim to the authorities?

State problem/issue in five sentences, then in two sentences, and, finally, in one sentence.

Five Sentences:

Huck runs away with Jim. He does so knowing that he is breaking the law. However, the lure of friendship overrides the perfidy he knows he is committing. As he floats down the Mississippi River, he finds it increasingly difficult to hide his friend from the authorities and to hide his feelings of ambivalence. Finally he manages to satisfy both ambiguities.

Two Sentences:

Huck intentionally helps his slave friend Jim escape from servitude. As Huck floats down the Mississippi River, he finds it increasingly difficult to hide his friend from the authorities and at the same time to hide his own feelings of ambivalence.

One Sentence:

After escaping with his slave-friend Jim and floating down the Mississippi River, Huck finds it increasingly difficult to hide his friend from the authorities and at the same time to hide his own feelings of ambivalence.

Name three or more subtopics of problem.
Are there times when we should disobey the law?
What responsibilities does Huck have to his family?
What should Huck do?

Name three or more subtopics of the subtopics.
Are there times when we should disobey the law?
Who determines what laws are unjust?
Should the law be disobeyed publicly?
Who is injured when we disobey the law?
What responsibilities does Huck have to his family?
Who is his family? Jim? His dad?
Is allegiance to them secondary to Jim's needs?
Should his family support his civil disobedience?

What should Huck do?
Turn in Jim?
Escape with Jim?
Both?

What information must be known?
Laws? Jim's character? If he is bad, then should Huck save him?

State the answer to the question/problem in five, two, and one sentence(s).

Five Sentences:

Huck can escape with Jim with profound feelings of guilt. After all, he is helping a slave escape. This is important because it shows that Huck is still a moral, if flawed, character. Jim's freedom does outweigh any other consideration—including the laws of the land and his family's wishes. As the story unfolds the reader sees that Huck is indeed a reluctant criminal, and the reader takes comfort in that fact.

Two Sentences:

Showing reluctance and ambivalence, Huck embarks on an arduous but moral adventure. Jim's freedom outweighs any other need or consideration.

One Sentence:

Putting Jim's freedom above all other considerations, Huck, the reluctant criminal, embarks on an arduous but moral adventure.

Once the Problem or Issue or Question is solved, what are one or two new problems that may arise? What if Huck is wrong? What consequences could Huck face?

Every essay has a beginning (introduction), a middle part (body), and an ending (conclusion). The introduction must draw the reader into the topic and usually presents the thesis to the reader. The body organizes the material and expounds on the thesis (a one sentence statement of purpose) in a cogent and inspiring way. The conclusion generally is a solution to the problem or issue or question or is sometimes a summary. Paragraphs in the body are connected with transitional words or phrases: *furthermore, therefore, in spite of*. Another effective transition technique is to mention in the first sentence of a new paragraph a thought or word that occurs in the last sentence of the previous paragraph. In any event, the body should be intentionally organized to advance the purposes of the paper. A disciplined writer *always* writes a rough draft. Using the well-thought-out outline composed during the pre-writing phase is an excellent way to begin the actual writing. The paper has already been processed mentally and only lacks the writing.

WRITING PHASE

The writer must make the first paragraph grab the reader's attention enough that the reader will want to continue reading.

The writer should write naturally, but not colloquially. In other words, the writer should not use clichés and everyday coded language. *The football players blew it* is too colloquial.

The writer should use as much visual imagery and precise detail as possible, should assume nothing, and should explain everything.

REWRITING PHASE

Despite however many rewrites are necessary, when the writer has effectively communicated the subject and corrected grammar and usage problems, she is ready to write the final copy.

Top Ten Most Frequent Essay Problems

Agreement between the Subject and Verb: Use singular forms of verbs with singular subjects and use plural forms of verbs with plural subjects.
WRONG: Everyone finished their homework.
RIGHT: Everyone finished his homework (*Everyone* is an indefinite singular pronoun.)

Using the Second Person Pronoun—"you," "your" should rarely, if ever, be used in a formal essay.
WRONG: You know what I mean (Too informal).

Redundancy: Never use "I think" or "It seems to me"
WRONG: I think that is true.
RIGHT: That is true (We know you think it, or you would not write it!)

Tense consistency: Use the same tense (usually present) throughout the paper.
WRONG: I was ready to go, but my friend is tired.
RIGHT: I am ready to go but my friend is tired.

Misplaced Modifiers: Place the phrase or clause close to its modifier.
WRONG: The man drove the car with a bright smile into the garage.
RIGHT: The man with a bright smile drove the car into the garage.

Antecedent Pronoun Problems: Make sure pronouns match (agree) in number and gender with their antecedents.
WRONG: Mary and Susan both enjoyed her dinner.
RIGHT: Mary and Susan both enjoyed their dinners.

Parallelism: Make certain that your list/sentence includes similar phrase types.
WRONG: I like to take a walk and swimming.
RIGHT: I like walking and swimming

<u>Affect vs. Effect:</u> Affect is a verb; Effect is a noun unless it means to achieve.
WRONG: His mood effects me negatively.
RIGHT: His mood affects me negatively.
RIGHT: The effects of his mood are devastating.

<u>Dangling Prepositions:</u> Rarely end a sentence with an unmodified preposition.
WRONG: Who were you speaking to?
RIGHT: To whom were you speaking?

<u>Transitions:</u> Make certain that paragraphs are connected with transitions (e.g., furthermore, therefore, in spite of).
RIGHT: Furthermore, Jack London loves to describe animal behavior.

APPENDIX B

COMPOSITION EVALUATION TECHNIQUE 1

Based on 100 points: _____

I. Grammar and Syntax: Is the composition grammatically correct?
(25 points) 15/25
      Comments: See Corrections. Look up Subject/Verb Agreement, Fragments, Verb Tense, Parallel Structure, and Use of the Possessive, etc. in a comprehensive grammar text; read about them, write the grammar rules on the back of your essay, and then correct these parts of your essay.

II. Organization: Does this composition exhibit well considered organization? Does it flow? Transitions? Introduction and a conclusion?
(25 points) 15/25
Comments: Good job with transitional phrases; introduction could be stronger. A clear thesis statement would provide the reader with a clear idea about the purpose of your paper. Your conclusion cold better summarize your thesis.

III. Content: Does this composition answer the question, argue the point well, and/or persuade the reader?
(50 points) 30/50
Comments: Nice insights. Using quotes from the novel to support your argument would enhance your writing. Also, support you specific position regarding male and female writers.

Please revise your paper and then come discuss your thoughts and revisions with me.

*To be duplicated and placed on each essay.

COMPOSITION EVALUATION TECHNIQUE 2

I. Organization
___ Is the writer's purpose stated clearly in the introduction? Is there a thesis sentence? What is it?
___ Does the writer answer the assignment?
___ Does the introduction grab the reader's attention?
___ Is the purpose advanced by each sentence and paragraph?
___ Does the body (middle) of the paper advance the purpose?
___ Does the conclusion accomplish its purpose?
Other helpful comments for the writer:

II. Mechanics
___ Does the writer use active voice?
___ Does the writer use the appropriate verb tense throughout the paper?
___ Is there agreement between all pronouns and antecedents?
___ Is there appropriately subject/verb agreement?
___ Are the transitions effective and appropriate?
Other mechanical trouble spots:

III. Argument
___ Are you persuaded by the arguments?
Other helpful comments for the writer:

COMPOSITION EVALUATION TECHNIQUE 3

Peer Checklist
(May Prefer to Use Evaluation Technique Forms One or Two)

I. Organization
___ Is the writer's purpose clearly introduced? What is it?
___ Does the organization of the paper coincide with the outline?
___ Does the writer answer the assignment?
___ Does the introduction grab the reader's attention?
___ Is the purpose advanced by each sentence and paragraph? (Are there sentences which don't seem to belong in the paragraphs?)
___ Does the body (middle) of the paper advance the purpose?
___ Does the conclusion solve the purpose of the paper?

Comments regarding organization:

II. Mechanics
___ Does the writer use active voice?
___ Does the writer use the appropriate verb tense throughout the paper?
___ Is there agreement between all pronouns and antecedents?
___ Are there effective and appropriately used transitions?

Comments regarding other mechanical problems:

III. Argument

___ Are you persuaded by the arguments?
___ Does the author need stronger arguments? More arguments?

Other helpful comments:

APPENDIX C

NOVEL REVIEW

BOOK _____ STUDENT _____

AUTHOR _____ DATE OF READING _____

I. BRIEFLY DESCRIBE:
PROTAGONIST—

ANTAGONIST—

OTHER CHARACTERS USED TO DEVELOP PROTAGONIST—

IF APPLICABLE, STATE WHY ANY OF THE BOOK'S CHARACTERS REMIND YOU OF SPECIFIC BIBLE CHARACTERS.

II. SETTING:

III. POINT OF VIEW: (CIRCLE ONE) FIRST PERSON, THIRD PERSON, THIRD PERSON OMNISCIENT

IV. BRIEF SUMMARY OF THE PLOT:

V. THEME (THE QUINTESSENTIAL MEANING/PURPOSE OF THE BOOK IN ONE OR TWO SENTENCES):

VI. AUTHOR'S WORLDVIEW: HOW DO YOU KNOW? WHAT BEHAVIORS DO(ES) THE CHARACTER(S) MANIFEST THAT LEAD YOU TO THIS CONCLUSION?

VII. WHY DID YOU LIKE/DISLIKE THIS BOOK?

VIII. THE NEXT LITERARY WORK I READ WILL BE . . .

SHORT STORY REVIEW

SHORT STORY _____ STUDENT _____

AUTHOR _____ DATE OF READING _____

I. BRIEFLY DESCRIBE
PROTAGONIST—

ANTAGONIST—

OTHER CHARACTERS USED TO DEVELOP PROTAGONIST—

IF APPLICABLE, STATE WHY ANY OF THE STORY'S CHARACTERS REMIND YOU OF SPECIFIC BIBLE CHARACTERS.

II. SETTING

III. POINT OF VIEW: (CIRCLE ONE) FIRST PERSON, THIRD PERSON, THIRD PERSON OMNISCIENT

IV. BRIEF SUMMARY OF THE PLOT

IDENTIFY THE CLIMAX OF THE SHORT STORY.

V. THEME (THE QUINTESSENTIAL MEANING/PURPOSE OF THE STORY IN ONE OR TWO SEN-
TENCES):

VI. AUTHOR'S WORLDVIEW:
HOW DO YOU KNOW THIS? WHAT BEHAVIORS DO(ES) THE CHARACTER(S) MANIFEST THAT LEAD YOU TO THIS CONCLUSION?

VII. WHY DID YOU LIKE/DISLIKE THIS SHORT STORY?

VIII. THE NEXT LITERARY WORK I READ WILL BE . . .

DRAMA REVIEW

PLAY _____ STUDENT _____

AUTHOR _____ DATE OF READING _____

I. BRIEFLY DESCRIBE
PROTAGONIST—

ANTAGONIST—

IF APPLICABLE, STATE WHY ANY OF THE PLAY'S CHARACTERS REMIND YOU OF SPECIFIC BIBLE CHARACTERS.

II. SETTING

III. POINT OF VIEW: (CIRCLE ONE) FIRST PERSON, THIRD PERSON, THIRD PERSON OMNISCIENT

IV. BRIEF SUMMARY OF THE PLOT

IDENTIFY THE CLIMAX OF THE PLAY.

V. THEME (THE QUINTESSENTIAL MEANING/PURPOSE OF THE PLAY IN ONE OR TWO SENTENCES)

VI. AUTHOR'S WORLDVIEW
HOW DO YOU KNOW THIS? WHAT BEHAVIORS DO(ES) THE CHARACTER(S) MANIFEST THAT LEAD YOU TO THIS CONCLUSION?

VII. WHY DID YOU LIKE/DISLIKE THIS PLAY?

VIII. THE NEXT LITERARY WORK I WILL READ WILL BE . . .

NON-FICTION REVIEW

LITERARY WORK _____ STUDENT _____

AUTHOR _____ DATE OF READING _____

I. WRITE A PRÉCIS OF THIS BOOK. IN YOUR PRÉCIS, CLEARLY STATE THE AUTHOR'S THESIS AND SUPPORTING ARGUMENTS.

II. ARE YOU PERSUADED? WHY OR WHY NOT?

III. WHY DID YOU LIKE/DISLIKE THIS BOOK?

IV. THE NEXT LITERARY WORK I READ WILL BE . . .

APPENDIX D

PRAYER JOURNAL GUIDE

Journal Guide Questions

Bible Passage(s): _____

_____

_____

1. Centering Time (a list of those things that I must do later):

2. Discipline of Silence (remain absolutely still and quiet).

3. Reading Scripture Passage (with notes on text):

4. Living in Scripture:

A. How does the passage affect the person mentioned in the passage? How does he/she feel?

B. How does the passage affect my life? What is the Lord saying to me through this passage?

5. Prayers of Adoration and Thanksgiving, Intercession, and Future Prayer Targets:

6. Discipline of Silence

APPENDIX E

Book List for Supplemental Reading

Note:
Not all literature is suitable for all students; educators and students should choose literature appropriate to students' age, maturity, interests, and abilities.

Jane Austen, EMMA

Charlotte Brontë, JANE EYRE

Thomas Bulfinch, THE AGE OF FABLE

Pearl S. Buck, THE GOOD EARTH

John Bunyan, PILGRIM'S PROGRESS

Agatha Christie, AND THEN THERE WERE NONE

Samuel T. Coleridge, RIME OF THE ANCIENT MARINER

Jospeh Conrad, HEART OF DARKNESS, LORD JIM

James F. Cooper, THE LAST OF THE MOHICANS, DEERSLAYER

Stephen Crane, THE RED BADGE OF COURAGE

Clarence Day, LIFE WITH FATHER

Daniel Defoe, ROBINSON CRUSOE

Charles Dickens, GREAT EXPECTATIONS, A CHRISTMAS CAROL, A TALE OF TWO CITIES, OLIVER TWIST, NICHOLAS NICKLEBY

Arthur C. Doyle, THE ADVENTURES OF SHERLOCK HOLMES

Alexander Dumas, THE THREE MUSKETEERS

George Eliot, SILAS MARNER

T.S. Eliot, MURDER IN THE CATHEDRAL, SILAS MARNER

Anne Frank, THE DIARY OF ANNE FRANK

Oliver Goldsmith, THE VICAR OF WAKEFIELD

Edith Hamilton, MYTHOLOGY

Nathaniel Hawthorne, THE SCARLET LETTER, THE HOUSE OF THE SEVEN GABLES

Thor Heyerdahl, KON-TIKI

J. Hilton, LOST HORIZON, GOODBYE, MR. CHIPS

Homer, THE ODYSSEY, THE ILIAD

W. H. Hudson, GREEN MANSIONS

Victor Hugo, LES MISERABLES, THE HUNCHBACK OF NOTRE DAME

Zora Neale Hurston, THEIR EYES WERE WATCHING GOD

Washington Irving, THE SKETCH BOOK

Rudyard Kipling, CAPTAINS COURAGEOUS

Harper Lee, TO KILL A MOCKINGBIRD

Madeline L'Engle, A CIRCLE OF QUIET, THE SUMMER OF THE GREAT GRANDMOTHER, A WRINKLE IN TIME

C.S. Lewis, THE SCREWTAPE LETTERS, MERE CHRISTIANITY, CHRONICLES OF NARNIA

Jack London, THE CALL OF THE WILD, WHITE FANG

George MacDonald, CURATE'S AWAKENING, ETC.

Sir Thomas Malory, LE MORTE D'ARTHUR

Guy de Maupassant, SHORT STORIES

Herman Melville, BILLY BUDD, MOBY DICK

Monsarrat, THE CRUEL SEA

C. Nordhoff & Hall, MUTINY ON THE BOUNTY

Edgar Allen Poe, POEMS & SHORT STORIES

E. M. Remarque, ALL QUIET ON THE WESTERN FRONT

Anne Rinaldi, A BREAK WITH CHARITY: STORY OF THE SALEM WITCH TRIALS

Carl Sanburg, ABRAHAM LINCOLN

William Saroyan, THE HUMAN COMEDY

Sir Walter Scott, IVANHOE

William Shakespeare, HAMLET, MACBETH, JULIUS CAESAR, AS YOU LIKE IT, ROMEO AND JULIET, A MIDSUMMER NIGHT'S DREAM, ETC.

George Bernard Shaw, PYGMALION

Sophocles, ANTIGONE

Harriet Beecher Stowe, UNCLE TOM'S CABIN

John Steinbeck, OF MICE AND MEN, GRAPES OF WRATH

R. L. Stevenson, DR. JEKYLL AND MR. HYDE, TREASURE ISLAND, KIDNAPPED

Irving Stone, LUST FOR LIFE

Jonathan Swift, GULLIVER'S TRAVELS
Booth Tarkington, PENROD
J.R.R. Tolkien, THE LORD OF THE RINGS
    TRILOGY
Mark Twain, ADVENTURES OF HUCKLEBERRY
    FINN, THE ADVENTURES OF TOM
    SAWYER
Jules Verne, MASTER OF THE WORLD
Booker T. Washington, UP FROM SLAVERY
H. G. Wells, COLLECTED WORKS
Tennessee Williams, THE GLASS MENAGERIE

FOR OLDER STUDENTS

Chinua Achebe, THINGS FALL APART
Aristotle, POETICUS
Edward Bellamy, LOOKING BACKWARD
Jorge Luis Borges, VARIOUS SHORT STORIES
Stephen V. Benet, JOHN BROWN'S BODY
Charlotte Brontë, WUTHERING HEIGHTS
Camus, THE STRANGER
Chaucer, THE CANTERBURY TALES, BEOWULF
Willa Cather, MY ANTONIA
Miguel de Cervantes, DON QUIXOTE
Fyodor Dostovesky, CRIME AND PUNISHMENT,
    THE IDIOT, THE BROTHERS KARAMAZOV
William Faulkner, THE HAMLET TRIOLOGY
F. Scott Fitzgerald, THE GREAT GATSBY
John Galsworthy, THE FORSYTHE SAGA
Lorraine Hansberry, RAISIN IN THE SUN
Thomas Hardy, THE RETURN OF THE NATIVE,
  , THE MAYOR OF CASTERBRIDGE

A. E. Housman, A SHROPSHIRE LAD
Henrik Ibsen, A DOLL'S HOUSE
Charles Lamb THE ESSAYS OF ELIA
Sinclair Lewis, BABBITT, ARROWSMITH
Kamala Markandaya, NECTAR IN A SIEVE
Gabriel Barcia Marquez, 100 YEARS OF SOLITUDE
John P. Marquand, THE LATE GEORGE APLEY
E. Lee Masters, A SPOON RIVER ANTHOLOGY
Somerset Maugham, OF HUMAN BONDAGE
Arthur Miller, THE CRUCIBLE, DEATH OF A
    SALESMAN
Eugene O'Neill, THE EMPEROR JONES
George Orwell, ANIMAL FARM, 1984
Thomas Paine, THE RIGHTS OF MAN
Alan Paton, CRY THE BELOVED COUNTRY
Plato, THE REPUBLIC
Plutarch, LIVES
O. E. Rolvaag, GIANTS IN THE EARTH
Edmund Rostand, CYRANO DE BERGERAC
Mary Shelley, FRANKENSTEIN
Sophocles, OEDIPUS REX
John Steinbeck, THE PEARL
Ivan Turgenev, FATHERS AND SONS
William Thackeray, VANITY FAIR
Leo Tolstoy, WAR AND PEACE
Edith Wharton, ETHAN FROME
Walt Whitman, LEAVES OF GRASS
Thornton Wilder, OUR TOWN
Thomas Wolfe, LOOK HOMEWARD ANGEL

APPENDIX F

GLOSSARY OF LITERARY TERMS

Allegory A story or tale with two or more levels of meaning—a literal level and one or more symbolic levels. The events, setting, and characters in an allegory are symbols for ideas or qualities.

Alliteration The repetition of initial consonant sounds. The repetition can be juxtaposed (side by side; e.g., simply sad). An example:

> I conceive therefore, as to the business of being profound, that it is with writers, as with wells; a person with good eyes may see to the bottom of the deepest, provided any water be there; and that often, when there is nothing in the world at the bottom, besides dryness and dirt, though it be but a yard and a half under ground, it shall pass, however, for wondrous deep, upon no wiser a reason than because it is wondrous dark. (Jonathan Swift)

Allusion A casual and brief reference to a famous historical or literary figure or event:

> You must borrow me Gargantua's mouth first. 'Tis a word too great for any mouth of this age's size. (Shakespeare)

Analogy The process by which new or less familiar words, constructions, or pronunciations conform to the pattern of older or more familiar (and often unrelated) ones; a comparison between two unlike things. The purpose of an analogy is to describe something unfamiliar by pointing out its similarities to something that is familiar.

Antagonist In a narrative, the character with whom the main character has the most conflict. In Jack London's "To Build a Fire" the antagonist is the extreme cold of the Yukon rather than a person or animal.

Archetype The original pattern or model from which all other things of the same kind are made; a perfect example of a type or group. (e.g. The biblical character Joseph is often considered an archetype of Jesus Christ.)

Argumentation The discourse in which the writer presents and logically supports a particular view or opinion; sometimes used interchangeably with *persuasion*.

Aside In a play an aside is a speech delivered by an actor in such a way that other characters on the stage are presumed not to hear it; an aside generally reveals a character's inner thoughts.

Autobiography A form of nonfiction in which a person tells his/her own life story. Notable examples of autobiography include those by Benjamin Franklin and Frederick Douglass.

Ballad A song or poem that tells a story in short stanzas and simple words with repetition, refrain, etc.

Biography A form of nonfiction in which a writer tells the life story of another person.

Character A person or an animal who takes part in the action of a literary work. The *main character* is the one on whom the work focuses. The person with whom the main character has the most conflict is the *antagonist*. He is the enemy of the main character (*protagonist*). For instance, in *The Scarlet Letter*, by Nathaniel Hawthorne, Chillingsworth is the antagonist. Hester is the protagonist. Characters who appear in the story may perform actions, speak to other characters, be described by the narrator, or be remembered. Characters introduced whose sole purpose is to develop the main character are called *foils*.

Classicism An approach to literature and the other arts that stresses reason, balance, clarity, ideal beauty, and orderly form in imitation of the arts of Greece and Rome.

Conflict A struggle between opposing forces; can be internal or external; when occurring within a character is called *internal conflict*. An example of this occurs in Mark Twain's *Adventures of Huckleberry Finn*. In this novel Huck is struggling in his mind about whether to return an escaped slave, his good friend Jim, to the authorities. An *external conflict* is normally an obvious conflict between the protagonist and antagonist(s). London's "To Build a Fire" illustrates conflict between a character and an outside force. Most plots develop from conflict, making conflict one of the primary elements of narrative literature.

Crisis or *Climax* The moment or event in the *plot* in which the conflict is most directly addressed: the main character "wins" or "loses"; the secret is revealed. After the climax, the *denouement* or falling action occurs.

Dialectic Examining opinions or ideas logically, often by the method of question and answer

Discourse, Forms of Various modes into which writing can be classified; traditionally, writing has been divided into the following modes:
Exposition Writing which presents information
Narration Writing which tells a story
Description Writing which portrays people, places, or things
Persuasion (sometimes also called *Argumentation*) Writing which attempts to convince people to think or act in a certain way

Drama A story written to be performed by actors; the playwright supplies dialogue for the characters to speak and stage directions that give information about costumes, lighting, scenery, properties, the setting, and the character's movements and ways of speaking.

Dramatic monologue A poem or speech in which an imaginary character speaks to a silent listener. Eliot's "The Love Song of J. Alfred Prufrock" is a dramatic monologue.

Elegy A solemn and formal lyric poem about death, often one that mourns the passing of some particular person; Whitman's "When Lilacs Last in the Dooryard Bloom'd" is an elegy lamenting the death of President Lincoln.

Essay A short, nonfiction work about a particular subject; *essay* comes from the Old French word *essai*, meaning "a trial or attempt"; meant to be explanatory, an essay is not meant to be an exhaustive treatment of a subject; can be classified as formal or informal, personal or impersonal; can also be classified according to purpose as either expository, argumentative, descriptive, persuasive, or narrative.

Figurative Language See *metaphor, simile, analogy*

Foil A character who provides a contrast to another character and whose purpose is to develop the main character.

Genre A division or type of literature; commonly divided into three major divisions, literature is either poetry, prose, or drama; each major genre can then be divided into smaller genres: poetry can be divided into lyric, concrete, dramatic, narrative, and epic poetry; prose can be divided into fiction (novels and short stories) and nonfiction (biography, autobiography, letters, essays, and reports); drama can be divided into serious drama, tragedy, comic drama, melodrama, and farce.

Gothic The use of primitive, medieval, wild, or mysterious elements in literature; Gothic elements offended 18th century classical writers but appealed to the Romantic writers who followed them. Gothic novels feature writers who use places like mysterious castles where horrifying supernatural events take place; Poe's "The Fall of the House of Usher" illustrates the influence of Gothic elements.

Harlem Renaissance Occurring during the 1920s, a time of African American artistic creativity centered in Harlem in New York City; Langston Hughes was a Harlem Renaissance writer.

Hyperbole A deliberate exaggeration or overstatement; in Mark Twain's "The Notorious Jumping From of Calaveras County," the claim that Jim Smiley would follow a bug as far as Mexico to win a bet is hyperbolic.

Idyll A poem or part of a poem that describes and idealizes country life; Whittier's "Snowbound" is an idyll.

Irony A method of humorous or subtly sarcastic expression in which the intended meanings of the words used is the direct opposite of their usual sense.

Journal A daily autobiographical account of events and personal reactions.

Kenning Indirect way of naming people or things; knowledge or recognition; in Old English poetry, a metaphorical name for something.

Literature All writings in prose or verse, especially those of an imaginative or critical character, without regard to their excellence and/or writings considered as having permanent value, excellence of form, great emotional effect, etc.

Metaphor (Figure of speech) A comparison which creatively identifies one thing with another dissimilar thing and transfers or ascribes to the first thing some of the qualities of the second. Unlike a *simile* or *analogy*, metaphor asserts that one thing is another thing—not just that one is like another. Very frequently a metaphor is invoked by the verb *to be*:

Affliction then is ours;
We are the trees whom shaking fastens more. (George Herbert)

Then Jesus declared, "I am the bread of life." (John 6:35)
Jesus answered, "I am the Way and the truth and the life." (John 14:6)

Meter A poem's rhythmical pattern, determined by the number and types of stresses, or beats, in each line; a certain number of *metrical feet* make up a *line* of verse; (pentameter denotes a line containing five metrical feet); the act of describing the meter of a poem is called *scanning* which involves marking the stressed and unstressed syllables, as follows:
   iamb A foot with one unstressed syllable followed by one stressed syllable, as in the word *abound*.
   trochee A foot with one stressed syllable followed by one unstressed syllable, as in the word *spoken*.
   anapest A foot with two unstressed syllables followed by one stressed syllable, as in the word *interrupt*.

   dactyl A foot with a stressed syllable followed by two unstressed syllables, as in the word *accident*.
   spondee Two stressed feet: *quicksand, heartbeat*; occurs only occasionally in English.

Motif A main idea element, feature; a main theme or subject to be elaborated on.

Narration The way the author chooses to tell the story.
   First Person Narration: A character and refers to himself or herself, using "I." Example: Huck Finn in *The Adventures of Huckleberry Finn* tells the story from his perspective. This is a creative way to bring humor into the plot.
   Second Person Narration: Addresses the reader and/or the main character as "you" (and may also use first person narration, but not necessarily). One example is the opening of each of Rudyard Kipling's *Just So Stories*, in which the narrator refers to the child listener as "O Best Beloved."
   Third Person Narration: Not a character in the story; refers to the story's characters as "he" and "she." This is probably the most common form of narration.
   Limited Narration: Only able to tell what one person is thinking or feeling. Example: in *A Separate Peace*, by John Knowles, we only see the story from Gene's perspective.
   Omniscient Narration: Charles Dickens employs this narration in most of his novels.
   Reliable Narration: Everything this Narration says is true, and the Narrator knows everything that is necessary to the story.
   Unreliable Narrator: May not know all the relevant information; may be intoxicated or mentally ill; may lie to the audience. Example: Edgar Allan Poe's narrators are frequently unreliable. Think of the delusions that the narrator of "The Tell-Tale Heart" has about the old man.

Narrative In story form.

Onomatopoeia. Use of words which, in their pronunciation, suggest their meaning. "Hiss," for example, when spoken is intended to resemble the sound of steam or of a snake. Other examples include these: *slam, buzz, screech, whirr, crush, sizzle, crunch, wring, wrench, gouge, grind, mangle, bang, blam, pow, zap, fizz, urp, roar, growl, blip, click, whimper*, and, of course, *snap, crackle, and pop*.

Parallelism Two or more balancing statements with phrases, clauses, or paragraphs of similar length and grammatical structure.

Plot Arrangement of the action in fiction or drama—events of the story in the order the story gives them. A typical plot has five parts: *Exposition, Rising Action, Crisis* or *Climax, Falling Action,* and *Resolution (*sometimes called *Denouement).*

Précis Summary of the plot of a literary piece.

Protagonist The enemy of the main character (*antagonist*).

Rhetoric Using words effectively in writing and speaking.

Setting The place(s) and time(s) of a story, including the historical period, social milieu of the characters, geographical location, descriptions of indoor and outdoor locales.

Scop An Old English poet or bard.

Simile A figure of speech in which one thing is likened to another dissimilar thing by the use of *like, as,* etc.

Sonnet A poem normally of fourteen lines in any of several fixed verse and rhyme schemes, typically in rhymed iambic pentameter; sonnets characteristically express a single theme or idea.

Structure The arrangement of details and scenes that make up a literary work.

Style An author's characteristic arrangement of words. A style may be colloquial, formal, terse, wordy, theoretical, subdued, colorful, poetic, or highly individual. Style is the arrangement of words in groups and sentences; *diction* on the other hand refers to the choice of individual words; the arrangement of details and scenes make up the *structure* of a literary work; all combine to influence the tone of the work; thus, diction, style, and structure make up the *form* of the literary work.

Theme The one-sentence, major meaning of a literary piece, rarely stated but implied. The theme is not a moral, which is a statement of the author's didactic purpose of his literary piece. A thesis statement is very similar to the theme.

Tone The attitude the author takes toward his subject; author's attitude is revealed through choice of details, through diction and style, and through the emphasis and comments that are made; like theme and style, tone is sometimes difficult to describe with a single word or phrase; often it varies in the same literary piece to suit the moods of the characters and the situations. For instance, the tone or mood of Poe's "Annabel Lee" is very somber.

Credits, Permissions, and Sources

Efforts have been made to conform to US Copyright Law. Any infringement is unintentional, and any file which infringes copyright, and about which the copyright claimant informs me, will be removed pending resolution.

All graphics are copyrighted by Clipart.com unless otherwise noted.

Most of the literature cited in this book is in the public domain. Much of it is available on the Internet through the following sites:

Bartleby.com, Great Books Online
Aeschylus, *Oresteia*
Budda, *The Bhagavad-Gîîtââ*
Confucius, *The Sayings of Confucius*
Epictetus, *The golden sayings of Epictetus*, with the Hymn of Cleanthes; translated and arranged by Hastings Crossley
Mohammed, *Koran*
Plato, *Apology*
Unknown, *The Song of Roland*

Susan Wise Bauer, *Writing The Short Story* (Charles City, VA)

Classical Short Stories: The Best of the Genre (http://www.geocities.com/short_stories_page/index.html)
Leo Tolstoy, The Death of Ivan Ilych, Translated by Louise and Aylmer Maude.

Early Christian Writings (http://www.earlychristianwritings.com/justin.html)
Writings, by Polycarp, Justin Martyr, and Clement

Enuma Elish translated by N. K. Sanders (http://www.piney.com/Enuma.html)

Everypoet.com
Dante, *Inferno*

Gilgamesh Epic, translated by E. A. Speiser, in *Ancient Near Eastern Texts* (Princeton, 1950), pp. 60-72, as reprinted in Isaac Mendelsohn (ed.), *Religions of the Ancient Near East*, Library of Religion paperbook series (New York, 1955). PP. 100-6; notes by Mendolenson (http://www-relg-studies.scu.edu/netcours/rs011/restrict/gilflood.htm).

Herodotus, *Histories*. Translated by Rawlinson. (http://www.concordance.com/)

Herodotus and the Bible, Wayne Jackson (http://www.christiancourier.com/archives/)

http://www.cyberhymnal.org/htm/m/i/mightyfo.htm
Martin Luther, *A Mighty Fortress is Our God*

Infomotions, Inc. The Alex Catalogue of Electronic Texts (http://www.infomotions.com/alex/).

Infoplease.com. 2002 Family Education Network. (http://aolsvc.aol.infoplease.com/ipa/A0874987.html)

The Internet Classics Archive (http://classics.mit.edu/Aristotle/poetics.1.1.html)

Aristotle, *Poetics*

Internet Applications Laboratory at the University of Evansville
Plato, *Symposium*

The Library of Congress Collection (http://www.loc.gov/exhibits/gadd/)

Lecture on Sor Juana Ines de la Cruz (http://www.latin_american.cam.ac.uk/SorJuana/)
Sor Juana Ines de la Cruz, "May Heaven Serve as Plate for the Engraving" and "Yet if, for Singing your Praise."

National Park Service (http://www.nps.gov/edal/index.htm)

The Pachomius Library (http://www.ocf.org/OrthodoxPage/reading/St.Pachomius/Liturgical/didache.html)
Unknown, *The Didache*, edited by Friar Martin Fontenot Gonzalez

Shinto Creation Stories (http://www.wsu.edu/~dee/ANCJAPAN/CREAT2.HTM)
The Creation of the gods (Translated by W.G. Aston, Nihongi (London: Kegan, Paul, Trench, Trüübner, 1896), 1-2

Stephane Theroux. Classic Reader (http://classicreader.com/)
Anton Chekov, *The Sea Gull*
Andrew Barton Paterson, The Man From Snowy River

University of Oregon. (http://www.uoregon.edu)
Iliad, Homer. Translated by Samuel Butler.

University of Pennsylvania (www.sas.upenn.edu/)
Author Unknown, *Ani Papyrus: Book of the Dead*

University of Virginia. Browse E-Books by Author (http://etext.lib.virginia.edu/ebooks/Wlist.html).

University of Wisconsin, Milwaukee. The Classic Text: Traditions and Interpretations (http://www.uwm.edu/Library/
special/exhibits/clastext/clshome.htm)

NOTES

NOTES

NOTES

NOTES

NOTES